ANCIENT JEWISH PHILOSOPHY

Tel-Aviv University ISRAEL I. EFROS

A STUDY IN METAPHYSICS AND ETHICS

1976 Bloch Publishing Co. Inc.

ancient jewish * philosophy *

ISBN-0-8197-0014-2

TO MILDRED

CONTENTS

INTRODUCTION

The idea which I try to present in this work has been shaping itself in my mind for many years. This idea is twofold. First, Jewish philosophy, as a statement of a unified world view, starts not with Rab Saadia Gaon, but with the Bible. The very first verse of Genesis contains a whole philosophy: there is a God and a world which He created, and the world is not God and God is not the world. There is here also a quivering glance into the mystery of beginning, into time at its detachment from nought. It presents a philosophy of conclusions and crystallizations, the result of long brooding and deliberation which, however, are kept under the surface.

That we must look to the Bible for the beginnings of Jewish philosophy has already been emphasized by David Neumark, but this thought needs new consideration and unfoldment because it involves basically the same set of problems which weaves in and out of the Bible and the Talmud and which receives syllogistic elaboration during the Middle Ages.

Second, there is in Jewish philosophy a struggle between two opposite tendencies. One tendency appeared on the historic stage in the form of a protest, the Hebraic protest against the materialistic monism of the pagan environment, and proclaimed the existence of another higher world. This was the tendency of Holiness. And the counter-tendency began at the same time to establish connecting channels, and these represent Glory.

1

The question is asked, why was it only among the Jews that prophecy attained such heights? The answer is because they proclaimed Holiness. The transcendence itself necessitated contacts, chief of which was prophecy. But as transcendence grew continuously more transcendent, it strained this chord until it snapped. Holiness gave birth to prophecy and then devoured it.

This is the tension which exists in Hebraic thought, and which exists in varying degrees in every religious thought. The flutter between the extremes of Holiness and Glory, between deism and pantheism, is what makes religion an experience, what gives religion its pangs and ecstasies. This dichotomy will also serve as a means of orientation in a vast, confusing field. Views which seemed haphazard and disconnected will surprisingly arrange themselves like iron filings around magnetic poles and acquire philosophical consistency.

As to the second part, my aim has not been to present the ethical material contained in the Bible, but to attempt a philosophy of this material, to seek the hidden principles and concepts that shaped it. Fundamental ideas, even before time gives them language, have a way of thinking themselves out in their submerged state, though appearing sporadically, fragmentarily, and stammeringly; and we must discover the links that join them, when the language already exists, or seems to exist.

This ethical system, then—what is its nature? How did it begin? What is its authority and sanction? And what is its goal?

It is all tied up with the biblical metaphysics presented in Part I. There we saw the negative, the Holyistic protest. Not this, but above this, above every this. And ladders were thrown upwards, different ladders in each period, but the heights receded continually, grew ever higher. Here, in this part, comes the affirmation. God is infinite morality, infinite because there are no other attributes to delimit it. But if so, it needs human history to realize its being. That is to say, the drama below, begun "in the beginning" and continuing until "the end of days," is essentially a drama above. And the static and peaceful concept of God, presented to us in the Middle Ages, is not at all the original Hebraic God.

The infinite morality then embodies itself in man. There it struggles and strains, so that the moral self—and there is no other self, all is *sub specie ethicae*—is an identification with the divine ethicalness. The transcendence is felt immanently, and the immanence is conceived transcendently, and religion and ethics become one in the prophetic view.

We may therefore define biblical ethics as infinite idealism, infinite in its metaphysical psychology, infinite in scope and passion, and infinite in its historiosophy. How different from the harmony and the golden mean and the deterministic intellectualism of Greek philosophy!

Here Glory and Holiness meet in a high tension. And perhaps it is for this reason that we have here the perfect expression of the Hebraic genius, an ever restless, ever striving genius.

And is not this the deep hunger of our times or, better, a hunger for a hunger—the infinite, something infinite?

The first part of this work first appeared in Hebrew (Jerusalem, 1959). Some revisions were made for this English edition. The first chapter, which I delivered at a public lecture at Hebrew University in 1950, was published in the *Jewish Quarterly Review* in 1951. I am grateful for permission to reprint this material. I also wish to thank the Jewish Theological Seminary of America for its permission to reprint Chapter 3, which first appeared under the title, "Prophecy, Wisdom and Apocalypse," in the Kaplan Jubilee Volume.

I. E.

part I

STRUGGLES WITH
TRANSCENDENCE

PROPHETIC PHILOSOPHY

Two opposing concepts have always operated in Jewish philosophy, and their very oppositeness has stimulated and steered their course. These concepts, which we may call Holiness (*kedushah*) and Glory (*kavod*), never existed separately because then Hebraic thought would have expired either in a deistic frost or in a pantheistic flame. They were always intermingled, and it was all a question of dominance and emphasis. Holiness tries to lift the God-idea ever above the expanding corporeal universe, and Glory tends to bring the Creator ever nearer to man. We have chosen these biblical terms because no philosophical term seems adequate for these concepts. The terms transcendence and immanence are static, and we deal here with tendencies, with dynamics. At any rate, the term Glory does not mean immanence because it does not identify God with the world. On the contrary, it posits transcendence, but nevertheless adds immanence—a contradiction which philosophy cannot resolve and therefore cannot name. Only religion can span the gap.

Let us begin with a clarification of these concepts, their implications, and the parts they played in prophetic literature during the First Commonwealth.

HOLINESS

The Bible emphasizes not just one God, but a unique God. "Thou shalt worship no other God" (Exod. 34:14) not even one.

Even in the Shema (Deut. 6:4) the word *ehad* probably does not mean "one" but "alone," "only," as already interpreted by Rashbam and Ibn Ezra. What this uniqueness is we may learn from the *halakic* passages in the Bible, which are clear and stern: "No graven image nor any likeness of anything in heaven above or in the earth beneath or in the water under the earth" (Exod. 20:4; Deut. 5:8). Nothing so kindles divine jealousy and anger and calls forth such threats of dire castastrophy as image-worship. Even some of the oldest passages, like Exod. 20:23 and 34:17, contain prohibitions against graven and molten images. This can mean only one thing, dimly perceived at first but bound to grow in clarity and import, that God is imageless and ultimately—words were then extremely inadequate—spiritual. For, repelled by crass Canaanitish idolatry, the more sensitive spirits of early Israel did not seek to modify or refine the image-system but offered a sweeping negative and posited at first a God who resides in heaven.[1] This negative—and all negatives are infinite in extent—started them on the road of transcendence until the heavens, too, could no longer contain the deity, and the whole course of Jewish thought became an incessant effort toward an evermore precise definition of God's spirituality, that is, toward an ever higher transcendence.

Here we have the Hebraic protest against paganism. For while all the pagan peoples lived together with their gods in one closed universe, Israel came forth with a discovery, which needed centuries for unfoldment, of another order of being, the realm of the spirit, metaphysics. Hence the Hebraic view is ontologically dualistic: two worlds, the physical and the metaphysical, and in the beginning there was the metaphysical world alone.

No other people knew such thoroughgoing dualism, for in the pagan theogony the gods come from elementary world-matter, from primeval Apsu and Chaos or from a "movement in the sea." [2] Neither, it should be added, did Greek philosophy produce such a dualism. Plato's world of Ideas was real at the expense of this world of reflections and copies, so that ontologically there was only one world; furthermore, his ideas were completely inert, like paintings in a dream. This was true also of Aristotle's pure Form, which performed no function except as a final cause and was entirely inactive—a pagan god contemplating eternally its own navel. The element of action and doing never entered the minds of these thinkers in their theological speculations; they were ashamed of "doing." But in the Bible we have the first proclamation of two active worlds, with the tension between them providing the backdrop for the whole religious drama of man.

Words were lacking to express this metaphysical concept, this sublimation and spiritualization of the deity; but the word "holy" *kadosh* is an attempt to express both ontological and moral transcendence. Three meanings are imbedded in this term which primarily denotes "set aside," or "separate." First, it suggests separate or unapproachable because of danger, as in the case of Mount Sinai (Exod. 19:12) or the Ark (I Sam. 6:29; II Sam. 6:5-7) and hence the prohibition of even looking at holy objects evolved (Num. 4:20). Second, and perhaps latest, the term means set aside for moral excellence and divine worship, as in the expression "a Kingdom of priests and a *holy* nation" (Exod. 19:6). And the third use, which alone concerns us here and which came between the other two strata of meaning, denotes unapproachable not because of danger but because of ontological and ethical excellence. It is this third sense of absoluteness that obtains in the Seraphic song of thrice *kadosh* (Isa. 6:3).

GLORY

Developing along with this process of sublimation, there was also the opposite tendency to bring the deity back into the world, a tendency born out of the longing for nearness and for a responsiveness to our cries of distress. Otherwise, what benefit is He to the world and what use to man? And here we note a strange and striking phenomenon. Not only does man crave for the nearness of God, but also God craves for the nearness of man. In no other religious work of antiquity does God call incessantly to man as He does in the Bible. How concerned He is to be known; how He pleads time and again, in varied phrases, that man should understand and know Him! And after the making of the golden calf, He changes His plan of complete destruction as soon as Moses advances the argument that the Egyptians will misunderstand. Why is He so concerned in man's knowledge? Why does He seem to be knocking on all the windows of the universe and the human soul in order to be admitted? The answer seems to be that, just because He is so transcendent, He longs for the concrete. The great Nought—to use the Neoplatonic-cabalistic term [3]—craves to be real, and the key to His reality lies in the soul, in man's understanding and moral behavior. One is tempted to say that God needs man even more—because He is so much more—than man needs God.

Thus the Hidden God becomes a Revealed God. The former concept is born out of the infinite negative, Holiness, out of an intellectual process always denying and transcending the Here; the latter grows out of the longing for contact and the faith that in some mystic way the Highest can also be the nearest and dwell among us. Thus the Revealed God comes out of the hidden man, and the Hidden God from the revealed man.

For this self-manifestation of divinity, we have the biblical term Glory (*kavod*), which medieval Jewish philosophy identifies with Kingdom (*malekut*) and the Divine Presence (*shekinah*).[4] Spinoza too recognizes the terminological character of the word *kavod* and remarks, "This love or blessedness is called Glory in the sacred writings, and not without reason." [5] Hence we can understand somewhat differently the anthropomorphic statements in the Bible. The Talmud and medieval Jewish philosophers apply to these statements the dictum "the Torah speaks in the language of man," and Bible-critics discern in them an earlier stratum. We may say that they represent the *kavod*-literature, just as the biblical *halakah* represents the *kedushah*-literature. And when Isaiah's Seraphim sing "holy holy holy" and add "the whole earth is full of His glory," we hear the whole song of Israel containing both transcendence and immanence.

In the earliest documents, the term *kavod* denotes: (1) an object in which divinity rests, like the Ark; (2) signs and miracles, like those shown in Egypt and in the wilderness; and (3) the ethical nature of God, His thirteen attributes.[6] The prophets, as we shall see, added (4) His self-manifestation in history,[7] and (5) a *nogah*,[8] or radiance, which was enlarged into (6) a variety of physical phenomena accompanying a theophany, such as fire and cloud.[9] This physical manifestation medieval Jewish philosophers sought to refine, to apply the process of *kedushah* to the notion of a physical *kavod*, so that Saadia produced his theory of a "created light" and a "second air." [10] The Psalms added still another meaning, namely, (7) His self-revelation in the beauty and harmony of the Cosmos: "The heavens declare the glory of God and the firmament showeth His handiwork." [11]

RELATED IDEAS

These two concepts, Holiness and Glory, constitute focal points, and around each concept attitudes cluster on such related problems as the chief attributes of God, the existence of angels, and the selection of Israel.

The first of these problems concerns the thirteen attributes [12] (Exod. 34:6-7) which really resolve themselves into two: mercy and justice. It is obvious, however, that justice emanates from *kedushah* and mercy from *kavod* because justice is objective. It is a law of moral causality: sin inevitably leads to suffering as any physical cause leads to a physical effect. It was on this law that the prophets based all their predictions concerning the destiny of nations. Later on, the prophets were sometimes shaken in their trust and cried out against the defying facts of life (see, for example, Jer. 12:1), and the whole Book of Job was devoted to this problem. Yet, they could not relinquish this law because all their faith and understanding of history depended on it. Justice then works automatically like any law in nature and needs no divine interference. Mercy, on the other hand, is subjective. Here the judge appears on the scene, momentarily halts the wheel of justice, and reveals himself in pity and atonement. This quality then is related to *kavod*, as Spinoza clearly saw when he said: "this *love* or blessedness is called Glory." It is God and man in miraculous nearness.

Concerning the existence of angels, that second problem which revolves about the concepts of Holiness and Glory, in the Glory-passage of Exod. 33:12-23, God yields to the plea of Moses: "My Face shall go with thee" (Exod. 33:14). Whatever is meant by "Face," it is undoubtedly a higher degree of divine intimacy than an angel and represents the deepest longing for *kavod*. This idea of the Face is echoed in Deutero-Isaiah 63:9, where the Septuagint may have the more correct reading: "No messenger nor angel, His Face saved them." [13] But angels too, though intermediaries, would be favored by *kavod* in the Bible as a form of divinity in self-manifestation. Indeed, medieval Jewish thinkers called them Glories (*kevodim*).[14] *Kedushah*, however, would object to angelic appearances as too anthropomorphic, even as the oldest documents objected to statements of God's personal appearance and substituted angels, though traces were left of the earlier texts. A distinction, however, must be made between angels and celestial beings like the Seraphim and the host of heaven. The former are sent down to earth and therefore are anthropomorphic, while the latter, the *kedoshim*, the transcendent one, even *kedushah* would accept.

As to the third problem related to the conflict between Holiness and Glory, universalism harmonizes more with the idea of Holiness, but the doctrine of the covenant and the selection of Israel are more in line with *kavod*, for it insists on the particular manifestation of God in Israel and interferes with the even and impartial law of moral causality.

TWO SCHOOLS

We are now ready to trace these two concepts in the thought of the great prophets, and we shall see how their world views arrange themselves like iron filings around positive and negative poles. Indeed, Holiness, with its denial of divine accessibility, may be called the negative pole; and Glory, with its quest of contact, may be called the positive pole.

It may be said that Amos started the school of thought called Holiness and Hosea started the school of Glory. Amos speaks of "My holiness" and "His holiness" (2:7; 4:2). Hosea too uses the term *kadosh*. But in the sense which converts it to the idea of *kavod*: "the Holy One in the midst of thee" (Hos. 11:9)—a watchword which, as we shall soon see, was taken up both by people and prophet and had varied implications. Amos speaks in the spirit of stern justice, Hosea in loving-kindness and mercy. Amos never refers to angels; Hosea does refer to them, calling them *elohim* (Hos. 12:4-5). Amos takes a universalistic attitude. "Are you not as children of the Ethiopians unto me, O children of Israel? saith the Lord" (Amos 9:7). He does not deny the election of Israel, but the election only means that the law of moral causality operates with greater force (Amos 3:2). The covenant between God and Israel he never mentions. Hosea on the other hand speaks of a covenant of complete security. Heaven and earth will combine for greater fertility, and there will be a personal, intimate relationship, a betrothal in loving-kindness and mercy, which to mankind is "Knowledge of God," (Hos. 4:1, 6; 6:6), not philosophical knowledge but, as a parallel to *hesed*, a love and union with God. Thus, Amos starts the school of Holiness, and Hosea, the school of Glory.

Following Amos, Isaiah gives fuller development to the thought of the Holiness school. His term for God is "Holy" and "the Holy One of Israel." In the Seraphic song (Isa. 6:3) the thrice-repeated word *kadosh* indicates absolute transcendence, and in the second distich the term *kavod* no longer means a physical manifestation but is sublimated to mean God's majesty and power unfolding themselves in history. This new meaning is echoed in Num. 14:21. But this is the only time Isaiah uses the concept *kavod*;[15] his message is transcendence, so that the word *kadosh* is synonymous with "high" and "exalted."[16]

In face of this divine holiness and majesty, man's stature shrinks in significance. "Cease ye from man, whose breath is in his nostrils, for what account is he?" (Isa. 2:22). Hence, Isaiah rebuked pride and haughtiness, and his cardinal virtue was humility. This virtue was included by Micah in his program for man (Mic. 6:8) in which he seems to summarize the ethical teachings of his three masters: "He hath shewed thee, O man, what is good and what doth the Lord require of thee, but to do justice [Amos], and to love mercy [Hosea] and to walk humbly [Isaiah] with thy God."

Isaiah consistently follows the concept of Holiness in its three related ideas. He never uses the word *hesed* (loving-kindness) or *rahamin* (mercy),[17] but rather *mishpat* (judgment). And he never refers to angels, as Isa. 37:36 is taken from the historical books of the Bible; but of course he speaks of the Seraphim, to which, as already stated, the concept of Holiness does not object so long as they are not sent down to earth to appear in human flesh. As for universalism, he envisions the universal recognition of God and a spiritual alliance among men, "whom the Lord shall bless, saying, Blessed be Egypt my people, and Assyria the work of my hands, and Israel mine inheritance" (Isa. 19:24-25). Perhaps no sharper recognition of the equality of all mankind can be found anywhere else. And he does not even mention the convenant, except in a general sense of law (Isa. 24:5; 33:8). Thus Isaiah may be taken as the great exponent of the *kedushah*-school.

Prima facie Jeremiah derives from Isaiah and Amos. He uses the term "The Holy One of Israel." There is also an opinion that he may have had a part in the "hiding" of the Ark of the Covenant,[18] which was called Glory.[19] Indeed, he does make some disparaging remarks about the Ark and the Temple.[20] But all this was an attempt to eliminate a false sense of security pinned to something which was in danger of becoming a fetish. The idea of *kavod* he does not deny. The whole of Jerusalem becomes the Throne of Glory.[21] And together with the Deuteronomic school he re-echoes Hosea's watchword in the outcry: "And Thou art in our midst. O Lord," that is, God is indwelling.[22]

It is important to compare Micah with Zephaniah in reference to this clause in order to understand the atmospheric change that occurs from the time of Isaiah to the time of Jeremiah. Micah (3:11) complains of the moral chaos of the people and their certainty that retribution will not come, and he refers probably to the Ark or to the Temple in the challenge "Is not the Lord among us? None evil can come upon us." In Zephaniah, after more than a century, we find the people in a different mood. The Ark is gone, and the people begin to think that God is too *kadosh*, too transcendent to care, that "the Lord will not do good, neither will he do evil" (Zeph. 1:12). This is not atheism, but too much transcendence. Similarly Jer. 5:12; Ezek. 8:12, 9:9; Mal. 2:17; and Ps. 10:4, 14:1 echo this mood. Therefore, Zephaniah (1:5) refers to the people as those "that swear by the Lord and swear by Malcham," that is, those who for their material benefits resort to the local deities as vice-regents or the Lord's representatives on earth. Now was the time for a new emphasis on the indwelling Lord, and this is what Zephaniah (3:5, 15, 17), Jeremiah, and the Deuteronomists effected, and this is *kavod*. It is noteworthy in this connection that Deuteronomy never speaks of God as holy but only of the people as holy to God.

Jeremiah never refers to angels; but in the light of Zephaniah's reference to those "that swear by the Lord and swear by Malcham," we may have an explanation for this too. Because these *be'alim*, these local deities, performed the functions of angels, a belief in angels would provide the ideological basis for faith in these deities. Thus Hugo Gressman [23] derives "the angel of *berit*," or "the messenger of the covenant" (Mal. 3:1) from the Ba'al-Berith of the Shechemites (Judg. 8:33; 9:4, 46). At any rate the elimination of angels only makes for that more intimate contact craved by Moses in Exod. 33:14-15. The clause "and he laid it upon my mouth" occurs in the inaugural visions of both Isaiah and Jeremiah, but in the latter it is a touch by the very hand of God.

Aside from eliminating angels, Jeremiah entirely follows Hosea. Tried as he was in the crucible of suffering at the hands of the aristocracy, it was not justice that he pursued, but mercy. In 3:12 Jeremiah's God Himself proclaims "for I am merciful" (*hasid*) and many are the passages that tenderly sing in the manner of Hosea. In addition, his breaking with the old belief that God visits the sins of fathers upon the children was inspired by loving-kindness (31:26-29). And he also follows Hosea when he promises that between Israel and God there will be a new, intimate and eternal covenant, as permanent as the laws of nature (31:30-33; 32:40; 33:20, 21, 25, 26; 50:5).

But the chief prophet of *kavod* and all its implications is Ezekiel. He uses *kadosh* but once in the *phrase* "the Holy One in Israel" (39:7) which echoes the above-mentioned Hoseanic watchword and which converts the term to mean immanence.[24] He also uses the expression "my holy name" [25] to indicate God's concern that His Holy Name be known and not profaned, but here too the word "name" gives the expression the sense of the manifestation of Holiness, that is, the sense of Glory. He never uses the term "the Lord of hosts," which is used by all the prophets except Hosea and which denotes sublimity. His favorite term is "the glory of God," and his main interest is God as revealed.

In the inaugural vision of Isaiah, the hems of His garment fill the Temple, meaning the manifestation of God in the universe. However, here in Ezekiel, the manifestation is more intimate, more personal. God Himself is halfway indwelling and halfway transcendent. This seems to be the meaning of Ezekiel's division of the Man on the Throne into *hashmal* (amber) from His loins upward and fire from His loins downward. And it is the *nogah* and the rainbow colors around the fire of the lower half, that is, of the immanent God, that constitute the Glory.[26] Therefore, this world shares, though in a fainter degree, the very essence of divinity, and the splendor of the indwelling God may be experienced by a prophet through a physical sensation. But the term Glory also denotes that all people can see God revealing Himself in the affairs of nations.[27] Hence the prophet's zeal that the above-mentioned Holy Name be not profaned, that is, misunderstood, and also his tirelessly repeated refrain "and they shall know that I am the Lord"; for without this knowledge the Glory is gone.

It is generally believed that Ezekiel admitted the existence of angels into his faith. Perhaps his Cherubim need not be classed together with Isaiah's Seraphim. Noteworthy in this connection is the fact that, the Cherubim, unlike the Seraphim, are placed *under* "the firmament" and that they seem to be composite beings. Therefore, they may be only symbols of the orders of life on earth, even as the wheels with their many-eyed rims were not meant to be the angels of a later age, but only symbolic of matter which supports life and is in itself also alive. The symbols of today, with all their compressed meaning, may always ignite and be the angels of tomorrow. But the six men with the tools of destruction, the man clothed in linen (chapter 9), and the man with the brass-like appearance who holds a line of flax in his hand and who speaks to the prophet (chapter 40)—all seem to be visions of angels sent down to earth, which, as said above, *kavod* would favor and *kedushah* would reject.

Ezekiel is an angry prophet, and many are the harsh words he expresses against "the house of rebellion." But the attributes of loving-kindness and mercy enter also into his philosophy, if not for the sake of Israel, then for the sake of the Holy Name that it be not profaned and that it be known in the world. It is this spirit which permeates particularly chapters 36 and 37, the latter with its vision of the dry bones. And like Jeremiah he speaks of the eternal covenant, borrowing words directly from Hosea to describe what he calls twice "the covenant of peace" (compare Ezek. 34:25; 37:24 with Hos. 2:20) and he also emphasizes the personal relationship between Israel and God (Ezek. 37:24-28). Thus Ezekiel on all these questions takes a stand opposite to that of Isaiah.

In Deutero-Isaiah, however, we find the refiner and harmonizer of the two schools. His favorite term, like Isaiah's, is "the Holy One of Israel," and he stresses the transcendence and incomparability of God. "To whom will ye liken Me or shall I be equal? Saith the Holy One" (Isa. 40:25). He also reverts to the term "the Lord of hosts." But he avails himself of Ezekiel's term "the glory of God," dwelling more than anyone has before on the Glory unfolding itself in history.[28] He does not refer to angels,[29] in the usual sense of the term, but elevates the prophets to angelhood.[30]

As to the divine attribute, this prophet is entirely on the side of consolation and mercy. He is the bearer of good tidings. But the term that he uses so frequently and which for him has a deeper meaning than usual is "righteousness" (*zedeq* or *zedaqah*), and his God is "righteous" (*zaddiq*),[31] whereas Jeremiah's God was "merciful" (*hasid*). The terms "judgment" (*mishpat*) and "loving-kindness" (*hesed*) of Amos and Hosea respectively carry a limited immediacy, and "loving-kindness" seems to interfere with the free course of moral causality—God, as it were, interfering with Himself. But the term "righteousness" commands a wider vista and denotes a *triumph* of God's plan in history, in international vicissitudes, in which the "God that hideth himself," as Deutero-Isaiah states, unveils Himself as a Savior.[32] In this term the dichotomy of judgment and loving-kindness is elevated and resolved. The word "righteous" means triumphant.

Similarly, in the question of universalism versus nationalism, there is an elevation and reconciliation. Surely all the chapters of this prophet are permeated with an ardent feeling for the "chosenness" of his people. He speaks of God's glory shining upon Israel (60:1-3), about Israel being called by His name and created for His glory (43:7), and about the regathering being an act of God's glory (58:8), though he sometimes reiterates Ezekiel's angry thought that salvation will come only for the sake of God's name (48:11). He speaks of the "eternal covenant" of Jeremiah-Ezekiel and of the "peace-covenant" of Ezekiel.[33] But he adds a new term, "a covenant of mankind," [34] so that the very term which has heretofore implied election now achieves the meaning of universalism. Israel is to be the bearer of the covenant of mankind, and "a light for Gentiles." [35] It is this combination of a belief in Israel's uniqueness and a concern for all mankind that inspired his theory of "the servant of God," [36] wherein the thought of Amos 3:2 that there is a special connection between the election of Israel and the punishment of its sins [37] develops into the doctrine that the Servant "shall be exalted and extolled and be very high" through vicarious suffering, through being the sacrifice for the world's iniquities. Here the Glory which is in Israel becomes reconciled with the Holiness which regards equally all mankind, and judgment itself becomes, in a divine mystery, loving-kindness.

Thus we see how the two schools of thought, started by Amos and Hosea, found their protagonists in Isaiah on the one hand and in Jeremiah and Ezekiel on the other, and how they were combined in a lofty harmony by Deutero-Isaiah. But the conflict between the two basic tendencies continues in the biblical literature of the Second Commonwealth, in the Apocrypha, in the Talmud, and in the mysticism of the cabala and Hasidism. Always the two poles exist, the beyond and the near, the mind and the heart. And between them is the human soul, whose vibrations constitute religious experience. Now it is filled with the joy and ecstasy of nearness and now it is caught in the anguish of distance and loneliness—all the gamut of emotions that permeate the Psalms and the poems of Yehudah Halevi.

And the deity too seems involved in this gamut, for the deity, as we have seen, in all its loftiness needs the world and seeks to pour itself over into man, though the receptacle is too frail and inadequate. So, God may be said to share in this religious experience, in a transabysmal love, which, like the love rising from man, is essentially tragic because it cannot be fulfilled until the end of days. This is the meaning of the rabbinic dictum that God too puts on phylacteries, but with their paean of praise directed toward Israel. Thus one unfulfilled love combines the upper and lower worlds, and both God and man are involved in the hope for redemption at the end of days.

THE CLOSE OF PROPHECY AND
THE HAGIOGRAPHA

We have called attention to two conflicting tendencies characterizing and stimulating Hebraic thought: one seeking to transcendentalize the God-idea (Holiness), and the other stressing divine nearness and manifestation (Glory). We have shown how problems, such as, the divine attribute of justice versus mercy, the existence versus the nonexistence of angels, and the election of Israel versus universalism, grouped themselves around the poles of those two basic tendencies and how pre-exilic and exilic prophecy constituted a march from Holiness to Glory.

In postexilic biblical literature the march is in reverse. The conflict between our two basic concepts now shifts, perhaps as an effect of the national collapse, from the life of the nation and from the theologico-ethical insistence to the life of the individual, to his condition and destiny. Hebraic thought becomes humanistic. Of importance now are intermediaries (in a new form), man and his suffering, and the Hereafter.

INTERMEDIARIES

In Israel, the conception of angels sprang from the doctrine of God's invisibility, which expresses the Hebraic protest against paganism. The need for Glory, for some visible divine manifestation, gave

them being, but Holiness, insisting upon the impassable border between the upper and lower worlds, kept a stern silence about them.
At first the term angel was used in the singular only, and in a manner
somewhat undistinguished from God Himself; then came the plural
usage. But throughout pre-exilic and exilic literature the angels among
themselves were undifferentiated. They were a temporary descent of
God into visibility for some special purpose.[1]

Under the influence of Persian angelology, a new view develops
according to which angels, now also called Holy Ones,[2] acquire differentiation, their own being, and proper names. Thus in Zechariah's
visions we have for the first time an angelic hierarchy with a variety
of functions. There is the Man in the Myrtles, the Horsemen, and
the Man with the measuring line, angels running in and out, speaking
to one another, reporting, conveying hurried messages—all like satraps
in the corridors of a Persian court. And there is, above all, the Interpreting Angel who relays the divine words to Zechariah. The philo-
sophic importance of this development is the growth of an intervening
realm between God and man, and hence on the one hand a new upward fling of the God-idea, a new triumph of transcendence, and on
the other a recession of the prophet, a greater humility, and a loss of
intimacy between the prophet and God. Formerly God was above
visibility only —"Ye heard the voice of words, but saw no similitude;
only a voice" (Deut. 4:12)—now His audibility too is questioned.
It is this overwhelming sense of God's loftiness, now even greater
than in Isaiah, this feeling of uncertainty about hearing God's direct
voice, that accounts for the speedy decline of prophecy. The new triumph of Holiness—we shall soon see other phases of it—blew out the
prophetic fire.

In Proverbs we meet another metaphysical being—Wisdom.
Zechariah's angels appear only to the prophet, and we are not told
whether they are eternal or temporal. The Book of Proverbs never
uses the Hebrew word malak in the sense of angel; instead we have
Wisdom, begotten before the beginnings of creation, the darling of
God then, taking delight in men after the world came into being,
singing, and calling upon all to follow in its ways.

What gave rise to this conception? It was not the cosmogonic
need to bridge the chasm between God and the world so as to account
for the imperfections of creation, because Wisdom was not conceived
here, no matter what the later development of this idea was, as a
Demiurgus. It was the need for knowledge that stimulated this conception, for with the disappearance of prophecy, angels, too, in this

enlightenment-literature ceased to visit the earth in order to convey divine guidance. Thus a new transcendental step was taken, by adding God's unknowability to His being beyond human eyes and ears. All the Hokmah literature emphasized it. God now transcends not only the senses but also the mind. What then can man know in order to regulate his life? The answer is: moral wisdom, the Law and the accumulated experience of the Sages, an intermediate being whom God loves and who in turn loves man. It was not a progressive notion, but, on the contrary, a notion of something complete and fixed from all eternity.

The third metaphysical being, a part of Persian angelology, is Satan. In pre-exilic times, the thought which leads man to disastrous action was ascribed to divine anger. Thus in II Sam. 24:1 we read: "And again the anger of the Lord was kindled against Israel, and he moved David against them to say, Go number Israel and Judah." Thus the disastrous thought of numbering the Jews was instigated, as a punishment, by divine anger. In I Kings 22:21, a similarly disastrous thought, occurring to King Ahab, that he go up and fall at Ramoth-Gilead, was ascribed to a spirit, which however was probably no more than a dramatic presentation of the will of the deity itself. But later such enticements to merited misfortune were blamed on Satan. Thus we read in I Chron. 21:1, "And Satan stood up against Israel, and provoked David to number Israel." Thus the very same divine anger has dissociated itself and become an entity of its own. In Zech. 3:1-2, Satan appears in the role of a prosecutor incurring the divine anger for his official zeal; and in the prose-narrative of the Book of Job he holds the same office and is granted in addition powers of destruction, disease, and death.

Therefore, this Being too sprang primarily not from a quest for the solution to the problem why the righteous suffer, but from a tendency of Holiness to purge the God-idea of responsibility for human suffering, merited and unmerited. God then becomes the source of all good, and good only. But this demonism impinged on God's sovereignty and also, in so far as it implied an occasional severance of the fortunes of life from ethical conduct, on the very foundation of all prophecy, moral causality.

WHAT IS MAN?

The new humanism is also apparent in the question, what is man, which occurs in Psalms in two places with different conclusions. In chapter 8:6, the question evokes the answer "And thou hast made him a little less than God and thou hast crowned him with glory and honor" but in 144:3, the answer is, "Man is like to vanity, his days are like a shadow that passeth away." These represent two different moods concerning the significance of man. According to the second, man is a weak and pitiful creature. His life is all too brief. His days are as a hand-breadth; his age is nothing before God (Ps. 39:6). He is conceived in sin—an idea which goes even further than Gen. 5:21—and needs divine cleansing and a spiritual rebirth granted from on high.[3] The spiritual distance between such a creature and the divine being is so unspeakably vast that humility is his fitting virtue and haughtiness is an abomination.[4] This Isaianic virtue pervades all postexilic thought. Already Zechariah conceives of Messiah as a poor man, riding on an ass. And the Hebrew terms for poverty (*'ani*) and humility (*'anav*) merge in meaning and become synonymous with the good, even as the term for rich (*'ashir*) acquires the sense of its anagram *rasha*; which means wicked. Through the constant championing of the qualities of pity and justice, the poor person, invested with warm ethical emotions, became a special concern, until he became a quality of the Messianic ideal. Hence already Zephaniah speaks longingly for "a people humble and poor." Similarly reads Ps. 18:28: "For thou wilt save the humble people and bring down high looks." Also the expression "fear of the Lord" [5] contains the idea of humility. All this circle of ideas starts from a consciousness of divine holiness and loftiness.

But in the first mood, which is more prevalent in the Psalms, there is a consciousness of divine nearness or Glory. All the teachings of the great prophets are embodied in this book. God manifests Himself in nature. "The heavens declare the Glory of God" (Ps. 19:2). "The voice of the Lord is upon the waters; the God of glory thundereth: the Lord is upon many waters . . . and in his temple all speaks of his glory" (Ps. 29:2-9). He reveals Himself in history: "Who is the King of glory? The Lord strong and mighty, the Lord mighty in battle" (Ps. 24:8) [6] And He reveals Himself in Zion. "Lord, I have loved the habitation of thy house, and the place where thy glory dwelleth" (Ps. 26:8; 63:3; 65:2; 68:17). "In Salem also is his tabernacle, and his dwelling place in Zion" (Ps. 76:3). "Surely his salvation is nigh them that fear him; that glory may dwell in our land (Ps. 85:10). Here also belongs the view concerning loving-kindness as the cosmic architecture. "Mercy shall be built up for ever" (Ps. 89:3) and "Both man and beast thou savest, O Lord" (Ps. 36:7)—which recalls the closing words of the Book of Jonah.

In this mood, man is a little less than angels (or, perhaps, God), crowned with glory and honor, ruler of all earthly life. The human soul too is regarded as a divine manifestation and is called glory (Ps. 7:6; 16:9; 30:13; 57:9; 108:2; and compare Gen. 49:6); and its highest felicity is divine nearness. "My soul thirsteth for thee, my flesh longeth for thee . . . for thy loving-kindness is better than life" (Ps. 63-24). It is the union of glory with Glory, of the spark with the flame. And here also the two virtues, humility and the fear of God, give way to trust and love of God. Hosea introduced God's love of man. The Deuteronomist introduced man's love of God. The Psalmist combines both loves.

Somewhat nearer than Psalms to the second mood is the Book of Proverbs. There is a consciousness here of human sinfulness. "Who can say I have made my heart clean, I am pure from my sin?" (Prov. 29:9). Hence, there are three cardinal virtues. First, humility. "Pride goeth before destruction, and an haughty spirit before a fall. Better it is to be an humble spirit with the lowly" (16:18-19; and see also 21:4; 22:4). Second, trust in God (as in 3:5; 20:22; 22:19). And third, fear of God, that is to say, obedience, which is the beginning of wisdom (1:7; 2:5; 3:7; et al.) These three virtues are not stated as intrinsically good, nor are they meant to be spontaneous reactions. They are utilitarian virtues, motivated by consequences of reward. "By humility and the fear of the Lord are riches, and honor, and life" (22:4). One automatically recalls the contrasting outcry of the Psalmist, "For thy loving-kindness is better than life" (Ps. 63:4). And there is no mention of a relation of love toward God. It is that intermediary being, Wisdom, which seeks love and speaks for her lovers (Prov. 4:6, 8, 17, 21).

And the soul in Proverbs is conscience. "The soul of man is the lamp of the Lord, searching all the inward parts" (Prov. 20:27). In the Psalms it is Glory, a longing for the great Glory; here it is a rigorous principle of conduct, the inner moral eye.

In the Book of Job, likewise, the question, what is man? is asked twice (Job 7:17; 15:14), and twice man's insignificance informs the answer. All three human limitations are here expounded: the physical limitation, for man is of few days, and full of trouble (14:1); the moral limitation, for "what is man that he should be clean? and he who is born of a woman, that he should be righteous? Behold, he putteth no trust in his saints, and the heavens are not clear in his sight. How much more abominable and filthy is man, who drinketh iniquity like water" (15:14-16); and the intellectual limitation, for man knows not the place of wisdom. Furthermore, man dies without wisdom (4:21;

15:7-8; and see chapters 38-41). What is the whole intention of God's speech out of the whirlwind, if not to show the littleness of human knowledge. Thus the stature of man shrinks in the face of the exaltedness of God and the greatness of the cosmos, the wonders of which the Wisdom literature has just discovered. How different is the feeling of the Psalmist in his song: "When I consider thy heavens, the work of thy fingers, the moon and the stars which thou hast ordained . . . and thou hast made him a little less than God!"

The philosophy of Ecclesiastes is dominated by a transcendence which leaves man and the universe naked, cold, and trembling. All human values are proven false. Wisdom is doomed to failure. The progress of knowledge is a progress in pain. The higher social levels are full of corruption. The pursuit of wealth is much toil for an inheritor who may be a fool. A good name is fleeting. Blind and weak, man knows not what is gone; he understands not what is present; he is frightened by what is to come. And he is always in the entrails of a fatalistic mill of circular periods. All that man can do is to try to satisfy his normal material needs. A mild hedonism is all the author can offer us in his despairing quest of free happiness.

What is man is a question, then, that finds in the Hagiographa two answers: Glory and Holiness. The Book of Psalms is pervaded by the first mood. The sadder one is found in various degrees in the other books. The same distribution will characterize the reactions to the next question.

WHY DO THE GOOD SUFFER?

Why do the good suffer—is a question, already asked by the prophets Habakkuk and Jeremiah (Hab. 1:13; Jer. 12:1), which stirred greatly the minds of the Hagiographic authors, who offered mainly three answers.

The characteristic attitude in the Book of Psalms is naive optimism, the utter denial of the existence of the question. "I have been young, and now am old; yet have I not seen the righteous forsaken, nor his seed begging bread." [7] This is a complete confirmation of the law of moral causality which was the firm rock upon which the prophets built all their forecasts for peoples and men. If the wicked do prosper, it is only temporary, leading to their everlasting destruction; whereas "the righteous shall flourish like the palm tree, he shall grow like a cedar in Lebanon." [8]

Less glowing, but still optimistic, is the attitude of the Book of

Proverbs. "My son, forget not my teaching; but let thy heart keep my commandments; for length of days, and years of life, and peace, will they add to thee" (Prov. 3:1-2; and see also 3:16-18 *et al.*) Optimism pervades this book, and it is rooted in utilitarian ethics. A frequent expression is "the lamp of the wicked shall be put out." [9]

On the other hand, Ecclesiastes represents the view of despair. The author sees wickedness and corruption and no retribution. Life does not seem responsive to the law of moral causality. "There is a just man that perisheth in his righteousness, and there is a wicked man that prolongeth his life in his wickedness" (Eccles. 7:15). "I have seen servants upon horses, and princes walking as servants upon the earth" (10:7). Chance reigns, and destiny carries no retribution to either virtue or vice. It is against such a deistic despair that the prophet Malachi cries out, when he quotes the people as saying: "It is useless to serve God. . . . What profit is it to do His bidding?" In Ps. 14:1, the deist is designated "villain" (*nabal*) because indifference leads to moral chaos. Divinity and indifference are, to the Hebraic mind, mutually exclusive.

But the book entirely devoted to the clarification of this problem is Job. Various thoughts are proposed as solutions: one, evil is due to the intervention of Satan (the prosaic parts); two, there is no problem, for there is the moral causality of crime and punishment (the three friends); and, three, suffering teaches, and therefore we must embrace it lovingly, because it comes from love (Job 5:17, and the same thought occurs in Ps. 94:12 and Prov. 3:12). As for Job himself, drunk with his suffering, reeling between triumphant faith and an awareness of divine indifference and arbitrariness, he sometimes admits a Persian idea that Satan is the cosmic ruler. Perhaps this is the meaning of the verse which enigmatically ends: "The earth is given into the hand of the wicked: he covereth the faces of the judges thereof; if not, where and who is he?" (Job 9:24). And then God Himself appears and unrolls before Job the cosmic grandeur and the divine wisdom. But to the question itself, God says only that man is insignificant compared to the totality of the universe and that God's moral administration of the world is, like His essence, a mystery. Job falls to his knees, overwhelmed by God's omnipotence, and Holiness celebrates another triumph. Hitherto one thought was clear and firm, the law of moral causality, which was the foundation of the prophets and the philosophy of human events in the historical books, especially in the Book of Judges. Now this law too is excluded from the realm of human knowledge. That is to say, the law exists. Divine justice demands its existence. But its application as a key to biography and history cannot be undertaken by the human mind.

These are the three answers: optimism, pessimism, and mystery; and only the first answer, that of the Psalms, fully belongs to the circle of ideas characterized by Glory.

ESCHATOLOGY

The problem of eschatology did not attain literary expression till the beginning of the Second Commonwealth—in the popular consciousness it must have awakened even before—when the individual inherited the place of the group in the meditation of sages and scribes. The crushing thought of death and decay, together with the search for the value of life in spite of its brevity and frailty and for the meaning of, and compensation for, suffering, created a restlessness which was the beginning of faith in the Hereafter. Why was this belief controversial? Why did the Pharisees accept it, while the Sadducees opposed it? The novelty of the idea (which is not explicitly stated in the Pentateuch) did not play a part in this clash of parties; it was something deeper, something rooted in their fundamental philosophies. Our general viewpoint in this work may explain this problem and the psychological motivations of these parties in Israel.

We saw that Glory is the mystical tendency to divine nearness, a longing for contacts; whereas Holiness, the original Hebraic protest against paganism, is the rationalistic insistence on divine transcendence and on an unbridgeable gulf between spirit and matter. These two tendencies need each other as the mind needs the heart, and the rhythm of their mutual succession has in it something of the systole and the diastole of the God-concept. Hence, all faith in the Hereafter, whether it is a union of the soul with God, called immortality, or the violation of natural law by the wonder of resurrection, fits into the tendency of Glory, but Holiness rejects such faith because it blurs the border line between the mortal and the immortal. Let us see now how the Hagiographic books arrange themselves around these two fundamental views on the question of eschatology.

In the Psalms, there are verses (6:6; 30:10; 115:17; and especially 35:6-13) that describe death as the end of being, as the land of forgetfulness, denying all eschatological hopes. These verses belong to the mood which opposes the heroic view and finds human life devoid of value. But, on the other hand, there are also clear expressions 16:9-11; 49:16; 73:23-26) of the mood of Glory that consider the human soul as glory, that is, a divine manifestation, and proclaim the soul's immortality and the fulness of joy it experiences in the future world at His right hand for ever. Moreover, the future world itself, as in many passages in the Apocrypha to be discussed at the end of chapter 3, is probably here too, in the Book of Psalms, called glory and wonder. "Thou shalt guide me with thy counsel, and afterward receive me to glory" (73:24). "Wilt thou do a *wonder* to the dead? Shall the dead arise and praise thee?" (88:11). Perhaps this is the "wonders" which Ben Sira cautions us not to seek to understand (Sira 3:21).[10] At any rate, in the Psalms, immortality seems to be granted only to the pious; the others perish.

In the book of Job, as we have seen, Holiness dominates. But in the speeches of Job himself there is occasionally a stir of Glory. See, for example, chapter 29:2-4, where he longs for a renewal of divine nearness experienced in his youth "when His lamp shone upon my head . . . when the secret of God was upon my tent." His outcry for a divine answer was a cry for such renewal. It was Eliphaz, penetrated with Holiness, who provoked him: "Call now, if there be any that will answer thee; and to which of the saints wilt thou turn?" (5:1). The tragedy of Job is that he longs for Glory, but when God at last answers him, he again receives Holiness. Hence, in spite of his doubts and charges, there sometimes awakens in him a triumphant faith in the Hereafter (14:13-15; 19:25-26; and therefore also 13:15).

In Isa. 26:19, which some scholars regard as postexilic, there is an affirmation of bodily resurrection, though limited to martyrs. But in Dan. 12:2, this limitation is removed: *many* will arise, the righteous to everlasting life and the wicked to everlasting shame.

On the other hand, the rationalistic, pragmatic Book of Proverbs, which emphasizes transcendence by positing Wisdom as an intermediary, is generally held to be silent on this belief in the Hereafter. Some even think that the injunction "Add thou not unto his words" cautions against this belief, which was regarded as an innovation.[11] But in light of the eschatological meaning of the term "hope" in apocryphal literature and in the Dead Sea Scrolls, as we shall prove later, this idea about immortality in Proverbs should now be revised. There is no longer any reason to ignore the eschatological value of chapter 11:7 particularly: "When a wicked man dies hope perisheth, and the expectation of the unjust perisheth," and therefore also "For surely there is a future, and thy hope shall not be cut off" (23:18) and "For there will be no future to the evil man, the lamp of the wicked shall be put out" (24:20). In all these places one cannot avoid finding eschatological hints in the terms "hope," "expectation," and "future." The more explicit, term, *'olam ha-ba,* or the world to come, has not yet been coined. It first appears in the apocalyptic book En. 71:15. For the time being less precise terms were current.

But the deistic book Ecclesiastes clearly doubts this belief in the Hereafter. "For there is no work, nor account, nor knowledge, nor wisdom in the grave, whither thou goest" (9:10; see also 3:19-20). And as for immortality, this author has only a Pyrrhonic answer: Who knows? (3:21; but compare 12:7).

And soon the sects appeared with this problem as one of their main issues. The Sadducees in their eschatological thinking were inclined to Holiness, and the Pharisees conversely followed Glory. But about the parties in Israel, more will be said later.

Thus biblical postexilic thought moved mainly from Glory to Holiness. This is seen in the appearance of intermediaries, in the three triumphs of transcendence which lifted the God-idea above prophetic hearing, above human knowledge, and also above an understanding of His moral administration of the universe; and, finally, this change is reflected in the sober outlook on human life and, in some sections, on the Beyond.

APOCRYPHAL THINKING

We are coming now to Hokmah, or Wisdom-literature, and apocalypse, and we must show what they did with the ideological heritage or prophecy when they came to take its place. Prophecy carried two main ideas: revelation and retribution. The first is metaphysical, maintaining that some chosen men have the power to receive the word of God so as to transmit it to others, for which reason they may be called angels of God.[1] The second idea we may describe as the law of moral causality: sin brings punishment. It was with a sharp sense for the operation of this law that the prophets predicted the destiny of nations with the certainty of any prediction based on natural law, and that the biblical histories were written, particularly the Book of Judges. The first idea is the authority, the second is the sanctions, for the prophetic message which was dominantly ethical. The reactions to these two ideas are of the essence of both Hokmah and apocalypse.

First we must determine why prophecy ceased after Haggai, Zechariah, and Malachi. The distinguished scholar, R. H. Charles,[2] maintains that after Ezra and Nehemiah the Torah was regarded as the full and final revelation, leaving no room for prophecy; and that the apocalypse, which was according to him a continuation of prophecy, therefore had to hide itself under a pseudonym. I cannot help seeing various difficulties in this explanation. First, there was always a Torah in Israel, just as every people has its laws; and every Torah, as long as it lasts, is by its nature final. Nevertheless, the prophets prophesied. Second, the prophets were not opposed to Torah. On the contrary, they urged its retention and warned against its violation.[3] Third, what is the evidence that the finality of the Torah included a finality of prophetic revelation? Lastly, apocalypse, as we shall try to show, was different from prophecy, and its pseudonymity is to be differently explained.

Recalling the distinction we are making between Holiness and Glory, between the rational tendency to transcendentalize the deity and the mystic tendency to bring God nearer to man, we can understand the cessation of prophecy and the two roads Hebraic thought subsequently took: Hokmah and apocalypse. The transcendental tendency became particularly strong in the Babylonian exile with the result that the prophet began to doubt his direct contact with God. Hence already in Zechariah we find that God speaks to an angel and the angel speaks to the prophet. An intermediary has to be admitted. Formerly it was emphasized, "Ye hear the voice of words but see no image, only a voice" (Deut. 4:12), and Holiness celebrated its triumph over divine visibility. Now comes the second triumph, that over God's audibility. It was Holiness then that blew out the flame of prophecy.

Soon prophecy became only a proud memory—"We are sons of the prophets," says Tobit to his son (Tob. 4:12)—and also a hope for a distant future when a prophet will come and settle questions of law, as in 1 Macc. 4:46; 14:41. Perhaps the prophet here is the Messiah himself as in Test. Benj. 9:2.

Hokmah was one stream of thought that entered into this spiritual vacancy. According to it, Wisdom, a spiritual essence emanated from God, sings from "the top of high places by the way" at all times and to each person, and anyone can through her acquire happiness. Hence no prophecy is needed. Indeed, she herself makes men prophets.[4] She is also the Demiurge, governor and judge of all creation.[5] She fulfills the functions of the biblical angel of God.[6] In Wisd. 1:3 she is called power ($\delta\acute{v}\nu\alpha\mu\iota\varsigma$).[7] This is really a name of God, as in the talmudic expression "from the mouth of the Power" (gevurah), and also, I think, in Sir. 48:24 "By the spirit of Power (gevurah) he saw the end"; however the Greek has $\pi\nu\epsilon\acute{v}\mu\alpha\tau\iota$ $\mu\epsilon\gamma\acute{\alpha}\lambda\omega$. Thus in Hokmah, Holiness elevates the deity beyond revelation and even beyond any immediate creative act. To be sure, Hokmah also speaks of God's creativeness and administration, but logically such passages must be taken in an indirect sense; otherwise the entire notion becomes super-fluous.

And what does Wisdom teach? Not only in Proverbs and in Sira, but also in the Hellenic Book of Wisdom, the teaching is to keep the Torah,[8] to have "soberness and understanding, righteousness and courage,[9] which conforms to prophetic ideals. And furthermore, it teaches that the observance of these ideals brings all good things and innumerable riches,[10] glory and honor,[11] and an immortality which is only subjective,[12] i.e., undying fame. In short, Wisdom provides mundane blessings. Thus Hokmah abandons revelation but keeps moral causality, and in general its tendency is to Holiness, transcendentalism.

Furthermore, it avoids speculations regarding angels and the Hereafter. Knowledge obtained through Wisdom is all of this world.[13] And according to Sir. 3:21-22, there are two areas: one a permissible area of investigation, namely this world, which is in itself more than the human mind can grasp; and, two, a prohibited, hidden realm, which is, of course, the angelic world, the ma'aseh merkabah, or the Chariot, as the Talmud in Hag. 13a explains it, and also no doubt the Hereafter.[14] This does not mean that Sira was a Sadducean[15] and disbelieved in these things; in fact, it proves the contrary. It means that one should not speculate about their form and nature: "Thou must have nothing to do with mysteries." It should be noted that the Sadducees not only denied resurrection but also looked upon this belief as heresy and sin, as is reflected in the Talmud: "Said that Sadducee to Gebiha ben Pesisa, woe to you, sinners, who maintain that the dead will come to life" (Sanhedrin 91a), whereas Sira only forbids speculation about these mysteries. It is a prohibition that may go back to Deut. 29:29[16] and it is incorporated in the Mishnah Hag. 11b. And into this forbidden area entered the apocalyptists, who constituted the other stream of thought. They knew the ban. They themselves spoke of the sin and the punishment of Azazel who revealed the eternal mysteries of heaven.[17] They therefore attached their words to revered names of former times and filled their writings with an atmosphere of secrecy.[18] Thus we have the answer to the question raised by Charles: Why were the apocalyptic writings pseudonymous until the advent of Christianity? The answer is not the finality of the Torah, but the prohibition on such speculations.

Now what was the attitude of apocalypse to the metaphysical element of prophecy, revelation? The starting point, as in Hokmah, seems to be transcendentalism. In the whole Book of Daniel, God speaks not once to the seer. And a similar tendency is noticeable in other apocalyptic works. A glimpse of Him is caught, but there is no direct communion. Instead, an elaborate angelology is developed with various hierarchies: national angels, angels of the presence, angels of the sanctification, angels of punishment, and angels in charge of natural phenomena. And God received the prayers of men through angels.[19] The Torah was given to Moses only through an angel.[20] God spoke to the patriarchs through angels.[21] All this is definitely along the line of Holiness. But one must differentiate between angels and Wisdom. Wisdom is really not an intermediator, but only an intermediate power. Messengership is not a part of the notion of Wisdom. Angels on the other hand are true intermediators [22] and messengers, so that God constantly manifests through them His will in the universe. Therefore, angels are a bridge of Glory over the infinite gulf of Holiness.

But one must note some new features about these angels. For one, the direction of the angels changes. Formerly their direction was from heaven to earth, from God to man. God spoke but the human ear was too weak, so angels were needed. One may say, God was near, but man—too far. Now, under the influence of Holiness, God too became remote, so that angels, as we have seen, had to take up man's prayers to God, and, according to another account, inferior angels had to transmit the prayers to the angels of the presence, and the latter relayed them to God.[23] And sometimes man had to appeal to angels to take his prayers to God.[24] The direction now became bilateral. Angels were not only the messengers of God but also became, as the sequel will further illustrate, the messengers and helpers of man.

And a process of humanizing the angels takes place. In Tob. 12:18-19, the angel still has no will of his own, but is only a power sent from on high, and too spiritual to partake of food. But in Dan. 4:14, angels already issue their own decrees, and in En. 17:1 they are endowed with a free will. Indeed, in Enoch we already have the whole elaborate account, based on Gen. 6:2, of how some angels lusted and sinned and how they prayed to the man Enoch that *he* should pray for *them* (13:4). In Test. Levi 5:5, reference is made to man's praying directly to angels. In Test. Dan 6:2, man is urged to draw nigh to God and angel. In Test. Asher 7:1, man is warned not to sin against angels (cf. Exod. 23:21).[25] Therefore, the Test. of XII seems to stress the distance between man and angel. But the various opinions regarding the day on which angels were created reflect a growing tendency to stress the distance between *God* and angels. Thus in Jubilees 2:2, angels are said to be created on the first day; in 11 En. 29:1—on the second, which is also the opinion of R. Yohanan in Gen. Rab. 1:3; however, R. Haninah maintains that they were created on the fifth day, so that no one should maintain that they shared in the act of creation.[26] And in Jubilees itself, they appear circumcized and keep the Sabbath and holidays, except, of course, those in charge of natural forces; and the righteous are regarded superior to this latter category and equal to the former.[27] Together with this process of making angels human, there is also the correlative effort to lift man until he feels at home in heaven. We sense this already in Dan. 7:16, in the words "I came near unto one of them that stood by," which characterizes the whole literature of ascension. Angels take man for sightseeing flights in heaven and reveal to him secrets without any particular command from God. Adam, Enoch, Abraham, Moses, Baruch, Ezra—all with the aid of angels ascend to heaven, discover secrets, and are brought back to earth. According to Charles,[28] such achievements were originally ascribed only to Enoch; but when Enoch was accepted by Christians, he was rejected by Jews, and his achievements were transferred to the others mentioned above. So whenever such a transference occurs, the date cannot be earlier than 50 c. e. It is difficult to accept this view because such a "transference" with reference to Moses occurs already in Bk. Jub. 1:4, 27 and in Ass. Mos. 12:6, and because, in its quest for Glory, for human nearness to God, the apocalyptic imagination reveled in the invention of ever new ascensions. The opposition of orthodox Judaism was directed not only against Enoch but also against all these names, and R. Jose (2nd century) denied that even Moses and Elijah ever ascended to heaven or that the Shekinah ever came down (Suk. 5a). And the reason for this opposition is that such stories of ascension, as well as speculation about the Chariot, or the *merkabah*, blur the sharpness of a dualistic upper and lower world. Formerly, man was only a recipient of revelation and God came down in fire or spoke to the prophet. When Holiness winced at the thought of God's coming down, Glory came and made man ascend. Classical Judaism also saw in man's ascension a removal of boundaries.

Thus apocalypse abandoned prophetic communion and offered a kind of revelation, not in which God is active and man passive but in which man rises and with the aid of angels unveils the tablets of heaven. It was not really divine revelation but a mystic human ascent and discovery.

What of the other idea, which we called the law of moral causality? This law, which Hokmah retained, constituted a philosophy of history, a philosophy which did not survey all the aeons in quest of historic development, because the law maintained its validity in every situation. Apocalypse, on the other hand, which was given a special impact during the trying days of Antioches' persecutions, was forced to abandon that approach [29]—first, because here Judaism itself sustained a defeat, an idol stood in the sanctuary; second, because that law was already questioned in various circles, and the Book of Job is the classical expression of that questioning; and third, because that law chastised and warned, and it was encouragement that was needed now. In this abandonment of moral causality and direct revelation and in the acknowledgment that moral preachment is not its main burden, we see that, far from being a continuation of prophecy, apocalypse is really a different approach in theme and in thought. It carved a new path which we may call historiosophy. In this system, all is already inscribed above in the "book of truth" as in Dan. 10:21 or in the "tablets of heaven," as they are called in other apocalyptic works. There are important differences between that philosophy of history which is embodied in the law of moral causality and this historiosophy. The former is based on free will; the latter is deterministic. Perhaps it is against such historiosophic determinism, rather than Stoic fatalism, that Sira speaks in 15:11-16. Second, both prophecy and Hokmah dealt with the present and the immediate future as flowing causally from the moral situation of the present; whereas apocalypse, with the bright light of moral causation extinguished, sees the whole *via dolorosa* of Israel as one enigma wrapped in dim twilight, and tries to find in the whole evolution of mankind a hidden meaning, something struggling to come forth as the sun from the clouds. Third, in this quest, it arrives at the idea of development, namely, that history is a long drama in which mankind involves itself ever deeper in sin and cruelty [30] until the crisis comes, the whole world explodes from excessive iniquity, and redemption comes.

Certainly, in that Messianic era, goodness will be rewarded and evil punished. Nevertheless, it is not the same as that prophetic law of moral causality. It is not retribution merely deferred to the next world because of despair in this world. For the coming of the Messianic era does not depend upon human action, but is a part of a predetermined historiosophic drama of empires, year-weeks, or aeons.[31] Apocalypse takes over the Hokmah-idea of the pre-existence of the Torah and extends it, as is seen particularly in Jubilees, to include human history. All is written in advance, including the time of the Messiah, on the tablets of heaven.

Furthermore, prophecy and Hokmah are essentially individualistic because ethical conduct, which is their main theme, is individualistic. We may read page after page in Isaiah and hear the same call to the individual to act justly toward the other individual, the poor, the orphaned, and widowed. Jeremiah and Ezekiel did not discover the individual; they only emphasized individual retribution.

Apocalypse, on the other hand, is entirely nationalistic in its concern and symbols. Its unit of thought is the nation. The four metals and four beasts in Daniel (chaps. 2, 7) are nations; the beasts and the birds of prey in Enoch (chaps. 85-90) are nations, and the sheep are Israel. The three-headed eagle and the lion in 4 Ezra (chaps. 11-12) are the fourth kingdom and Messiah respectively. Thus, even the interest in eschatology is nationalistically motivated. Oesterley,[32] I believe, stresses here unduly an individualistic element, seeing therein a Hellenic influence. It was the sorrows of Israel that gave impact to eschatology, and all the strivings of eschatology were directed to bringing hope to the people. The righteous who will rise to eternal life are the Jewish martyrs, and the wicked who are doomed to eternal shame are the enemies of Israel, within and without. In the Book of Enoch, no mention could be made of Israel, but the "plant of righteousness" in 10:16, 84:6 is Israel. The nationalistic character comes out clearly in other books, and with particular pathos in 4 Ezra. The belief in immortality and resurrection, frequently designated as "hope," [33] no matter how conceived, is a natural development of Messianic speculation in days of martyrdom.

Resurrected, the righteous will turn into angelic beings in heaven.[34] Thus the boundary line, so zealously guarded by Holiness, between the upper and the lower worlds, is dimmed, and the tendency to Glory triumphs. Indeed, in many places, the Hereafter, or the world above, is called Glory (δόξα, gloria),[35] which incidentally strengthens the view that the phrase, "and afterward thou wilt receive me to glory," in Ps. 73:24, refers to resurrection. In Vita Adae 12:1; 16:1-2, 17:2, the term denotes eternal life in heaven. Hence, such expressions as "crowns of glory," "garments of glory," "oil of glory," and "the temple of glory" [36] refer to the celestial world. The term also denotes angels [37] and the Shekinah,[38] and God Himself is called the Great Glory; [39] and "to be glorified" [40] is to be admitted into heaven, to become angelic, or to receive a portion of the Hereafter. Thus the dualism of the upper and the lower worlds is to be overcome in the End.

To sum up, prophecy was silenced by the growth of Holiness. As to its two tenets, revelation and moral causality, Hokmah dispensed with the former but retained the latter, and thus followed the tendency of Holiness; whereas apocalypse dispensed with both and therefore differed completely with prophecy, positing (1) revelation in the form of human ascent and discovery, and (2) historiosophy which culminates in resurrection, in both cases turning to the tendency of Glory.

ESSENE PHILOSOPHY

In the previous chapters, we endeavored to trace the development of Hebraic thought in the Bible and Apocrypha by showing two fundamentally opposite, but always jointly operating, tendencies. We called them Holiness and Glory, Holiness striving to lift the deity ever higher than man and the universe, and Glory trying to bring it ever nearer. We chose those biblical designations because of the lack of precise philosophical terms. The terms transcendence and immanence are static (God *is* above; God *is* indwelling), but we deal with *tendencies*, with ever progressive concepts. Glory, in particular, cannot be replaced by immanence, because Glory does not encase God in the world. Quite on the contrary, it posits transcendence, but adds, nevertheless, immanence—a contradiction which philosophy cannot resolve and so therefore cannot name. Only religion can leap over the gulf. From this standpoint we found that the Bible, during the First Commonwealth, moved from Holiness to Glory; and, during the Second Commonwealth, it turned from Glory to Holiness. Then came the Apocrypha, which split into two streams: Wisdom continued in the direction of the Second Commonwealth, to Holiness, and apocalypse returned to Glory.

Now about the time of the beginning of the Apocrypha, books were written and held sacred by a Jewish sect, and these books have now been excavated in the Qumran Caves on the Dead Sea. How do these books relate to the two apocryphal streams and to the history of this dialectic of Jewish thought? The answer will become clear when we examine these books for their views on three central problems: man, intermediaries, and the Hereafter.

WHAT IS MAN?

In the Psalms, we found two moods, the first lifted man almost to divinity: "What is man, that thou art mindful of him, and the son of man, that thou thinkest of him? Yet thou hast made him but little lower than the angels, and thou hast crowned him with glory and honor" (8:5-6). The second reduced man to nothingness: "Lord, what is man, that thou takest knowledge of him, or the son of man, that thou makest account of him? Man is like unto a breath, his days are as a shadow that passeth away" (144:3-4). The first is Glory, God and man in mutual nearness; the second is Holiness, infinite distance. It is this second mood that characterizes the Qumranis in their approach to man, an approach which is perhaps the key to their attitude on all the problems we shall here discuss.

Biblical pessimism rehearses man's physical frailty and his sinfulness, and so does the Qumran literature. "And what then is he, the son of man, among Thy marvelous works; what shall one born of woman be accounted before thee? He is kneaded from dust, and his dwelling is the food of worms. He is an emission of spittle, a cut-off bit of clay" (*Manual of Discipline* 11:20). "He is built of dust and kneaded in water . . . His element is nakedness of shame . . . and a perverted spirit rules over him" (*Thanksgiving Psalms* 13:15; see also 12:24-25). "And I am formed of clay and kneaded in water, an element of nakedness, a source of uncleanness, a furnace of iniquity and a frame of sin, a spirit of error and perversion" (*Thanksgiving Psalms* 1:21-23). All this surely is contained in one verse, Ps. 51:7: "Behold, I was brought forth in iniquity, and in sin did my mother conceive me." But here it seems like an endless self-flagellation. Socrates, before drinking his hemlock, consoled his friends that the body is only a bundle of disturbances to one who seeks knowledge (*Phaedo* 66); here body-negation becomes body-disgust.

Nor do we have here the platonic dualism of body versus soul, wherein the body is a grave, but the soul divine, longing for its origin —a view which, according to Josephus (*Wars* 2:8, 11), was also maintained by the Essenes. Such a dualism could indeed support a sense of human dignity, but it is nowhere even hinted at in these scrolls. We cannot therefore assume that the soul strives to do good, but is prevented by the body. There is no such inner struggle. The dualism here is rather of the Persian variety, and the struggle for man is entirely outside. There are forces of light and darkness fighting for soul and body together, without any sharp differentiation, and in this struggle the soul is passive. If there is any moral significance in the soul, it is only as an "inheritance and possession," a certain prenatal, predetermined proportion of the two forces that determines the whole moral road of man (see *Manual of Discipline* 4:15-26). Therefore, souls, upon entering the body, are already good or bad, according to their "inheritance and possession" of the struggling forces, a view like that found in the apocryphal books, the Wisdom of Solomon and IV Maccabees.

And here we come to the second characteristic of this psychology, to Essene determinism, rejected by the Sadducees, and accepted by apocalyptic literature, which speaks of events as inscribed from eternity on the "tablets of heaven." "From the God of Knowledge is all that is and that is to be; and before they come into being, he established all their designing . . . and nothing is to be changed" (*Manual of Discipline* 3:14-16). The day of judgment is decreed from of yore, together with all historical and eschatological eras. The priest appointed for the season of vengeance is the decreed priest. The men destined for the last war are called those decreed for war. The word *decreed* itself (*neherasah*) becomes a term for the day of judgment. And the word *goral*, which in Dan. 12:13 means the human lot at the end of days, is frequently used, especially in the *War of the Sons of Light*, in a deterministic sense, like the Greek term εἰμαρμένη.

Determinism permeates the language and even the moral thinking of the Essenes. God guides the steps of man to the paths of righteousness and determines not only his actions, but also what he speaks, thinks, and knows (*Thanksgiving Psalms* 7:14; 10:5-12). While the Pharisees introduced a compromise between the freewillist Sadducees and the deterministic Essenes by saying that all is in the hand of heaven except the fear of heaven, the Essenes admitted to no exception. "And what shall I speak unless thou hast opened my mouth, and how shall I understand unless thou hast given me intelligence, and . . . how shall I make my path straight unless . . ." (*Thanksgiving Psalms* 12:33-34). "Only through thy goodness is a man righteous . . . and I, thy servant, know by the spirit which thou hast given me" (*Thanksgiving Psalms* 13:18-19). "And I know by thy understanding . . . and I know that in thy hand is the thought of all spirit. Only thou hast created the righteous, and from the womb hast thou pre-

pared him for the era of good will . . . and the wicked hast thou
created . . . and from the womb hast thou prepared them for the
day of slaughter" (*Thanksgiving Psalms* 15:12-22). And again, from
another work, "For God hath not chosen them from the beginning of
the world" (*Damascus Document* 2b). And since there is prior judgment, there is also prior hate and an impulsion to sin. Consequently,
". . . he despised the generation from of yore . . . and those he hated
he caused to go astray" (*Damascus Document* 2:11). The Essenes
were not at all aware of the paradox involved, which always follows
religious determinism: compulsion and hate, misguidance and judgment.

Perhaps this is why God is called "Will" in the *Manual of Discipline* 5:6 ("chosen by the Will") [1] for in the eyes of these Qumranis,
human will exists only figuratively as a tendency inherited from the
two struggling demons, good and evil. Nevertheless, those authors had
so little faith in man that they regarded the human will as evil. Thus,
the generation of the Flood perished "because they did their own will,"
and Abraham was accounted as God's friend "because he did *not*
choose his own will," and the earlier members of the sect were killed
"because they chose their own will" (*Damascus Document* 3:7; 4:2).

Together with man's limited moral power, there is his limited intellectual powers. "What shall I say without being instructed, or declare
without being told (*Thanksgiving Psalms* 1:23). "It is thou who
teachest all knowledge, and all that happens comes by thy will" (*Manual of Discipline* 11:17). This is man according to the Scrolls of the
Dead Sea—a far cry from apocalyptic man who ascends to heaven and
wrests eternal secrets. This is the conclusion of Isaiah's "holyistic"
outcry: "Cease ye from man," a conclusion of deep despair, of absolute self-effacement before divine transcendence. With God so high
and man so worthless, the question then arises: what mediates between
them?

INTERMEDIARIES

We may say that the angels in apocryphal literature served four
mediating purposes: foretelling the future, providing religious guidance,
interceding in heaven, and providing an answer to the origin of sin.
The first two functions, prophecy and guidance, received a special
impetus after the last prophets, Haggai, Zechariah, and Malachi, because the progress of Holiness or divine transcendence had weakened
the faith in man's contact with God and extinguished the fire of

prophecy, so that there was a need of an angelic hierarchy to reveal man's future and develop his laws. That is why angelology thrived during the Second Commonwealth. The Qumran community, however, needed no such mediation because among them some prophetic power and authority continued. In this power to foretell the future and to develop the law—both on the basis of a symbolic study of the Bible called midrash—these sectarians are at one with the Essenes, who, according to Josephus, had among them seers who foretold the future by means of an esoteric biblical exegesis.[2] They were quite different both from the Wisdom-authors, according to whom Wisdom sings always and to all men, and from the apocalyptists, who maintained that all is engraved in the tablets of heaven and posited ascent and a union of earth and heaven, but not prophecy. But in this somewhat Montanistic belief in progressive revelation, they are even more sharply separated from the Pharisees. To be sure, the Pharisees also, in opposition to the Sadducees, directed themselves toward legalistic development, but they carried out this development, mainly on the basis of logical inference, in accordance with hermeneutic principles, but the Qumranis, who were skeptical, as we have seen, about the intellectual capacities of man, had to resort to mystery and revelation to the chosen few. This was not, of course, the direct prophecy of "Thus said the Lord"—over such a power transcendence had celebrated its victory already in Zechariah where God spoke to the angel, and the angel spoke to the prophet—but a secondary prophecy which was inspired by a prophetic text, and its authority was like the authority of the original prophecy, sometimes even exceeding it in its degree of the holy spirit (*Manual of Discipline* 8:15: *Habakkuk Commentary* 7:7-8).

Such a prophet appeared in this sect as a "teacher of righteousness," whom "God notified all the secrets of the ways of his servants, the prophets." He is also the priest in whose heart God gave wisdom "to interpret all the words of his servants, the prophets" with reference to the future of his people and his land and the events in the last generation.[3] He is strangely entitled "the glory of God." It is interesting that in Hebrew this title, *Kevod El*, is numerically—that is, counting the arithmetical value of each Hebrew letter—equal to the word *nabi*, prophet, thus hinting perhaps at his being the carrier of divine revelation. It seems that he is also "the legislator and expounder of the law," and the expression "until the teacher of righteousness will arise at the end of days" does not oppose this identification, for the term "teacher of righteousness" is not a particular name

—and here is where many scholars erred—but a general title, as will be shown later. Hence he is also "the star that expounds the law, that came to Damascus." Thus, he was both a seer of the future and a developer of the law through the use of a "midrash Torah" [4] or an "exposition of the Torah" (*Damascus Document* 8:9, 16; 9:13, 45, 64).

The terminology of this symbolic midrash is noteworthy. It is called "the revealed," "the found," *sekel* (understanding).[5] Perhaps in Neh. 8:8 the words "distinct and they gave the sense (*sekel*)" really refer to such a midrashic interpretation.

The sectarians believed that this type of prophecy occurred from time to time, in every generation, to the Messiah, or prophet, or teacher of righteousness (*Manual of Discipline* 8:15; 9:11-15; *Damascus Document* 2:10, 11). Therefore we will understand the exegetic verse in the *Damascus Document* 9:12 as referring to "the books of the prophets whose words Israel despised." Where do we find that Israel despised the words of the prophets? Charles thinks that this refers to the Pharisees' refusal to infer laws from the prophets.[6] But first one wonders whether that constitutes a slur. Secondly, some Pharisees did derive laws from the prophetical books.[7] Thirdly, the sectarians themselves differentiated between the law and the prophets. But the reference is not to the *biblical*, but to their own prophetical books, which the Pharisees refused to include in the prophetic canon.

Hence, the Qumran sect did not need the angels for foretellling and guidance because these functions were discharged through continued prophecy. There were left then for the angels the two other functions, one of which was mediation and intercession above for the righteous. It is noteworthy that within the Qumran sect there is no hint of such an angelological development, the beginnings of which were biblical but which received impetus in the Apocrypha, as in Baruch, chapters 11-17. In fact, angelological development seems to be explicitly repudiated.[8] This means that the angels are still only messengers of God, and not yet representatives of man. The second function, the role played by the satans and fallen angels, is the origin of sin. For this purpose Persian dualism was introduced. On the one hand there were the spirits of truth, the prince of light, the angels of the Presence, the spirits of knowledge, and "the knowers"—a gnostic term—which should perhaps be rendered "gnoses," meaning the spheres or the aeons; [9] and on the other there were the angel of darkness, Belial, the angel of hate, the spirits of destruction, and the fallen angels with their sons, the giants. Darkness dominates in this world, and hence corruption and wickedness exist. But in the Era of Visitation a final war will take place both in heaven and on earth, between the sons of darkness and the sons of light, the latter with their banners carrying the names of the four angels of the Presence: Michael, Gabriel, Sariel, and Raphael. But "where is an angel like unto the help of thine own presence?" (*War of the Sons of Light* 3:5-6). God Himself will appear on the arena. Evil will end; truth will prevail.

This is the only function of the angels in the scrolls; but nowhere is there a hint to the apotheosis of Wisdom or Logos as an intermediary or a participant in creation, as in the Wisdom literature; nor to the humanization of angels, who, for example, in the Book of Jubilees are circumcized and keep the Sabbath and the holidays; nor to the inverted direction of the angels in the apocalypse, the direction from earth to heaven, from man to God, the direction of angels who become *man's* messengers, carrying his prayers to the throne of Glory and interceding for him, carrying man himself heavenward in order to show him divine secrets and then bringing him back to the earth. The literature of apocalyptic ascent, like that of Adam, Enoch, Abraham, Moses, Baruch, and Ezra, does not seem to be acceptable here in Qumran. The distance of Holiness is zealously maintained not only between God and man, but also between *angels* and man. The entire angelology is cautiously restrained so that, outside of the *War of the Sons of Light*, no angel's name is even mentioned. It seems, therefore, that by employing this restraint the sectarians kept themselves apart from the Essenes, who had a secret and complicated angelology, and the Sadducees, who denied angels altogether, but rather approached the Pharisees. Both the admission and restraint of angels stemmed from the same root: strict Holiness. God is transcendent: hence there must be angels to serve as partial intermediaries. But, as the angels are to be regarded as pure spirits, they too must be kept away from that apocalyptic contact of man which was the fashion of the times.

ESCHATOLOGY

The Qumran authors frequently use the term borrowed from Daniel, *razim* (secrets), and forbid the divulgence of these secrets beyond their group.[10] The author of the *Thanksgiving Psalms* lyricizes his gratitude for the "secrets of wonders" God revealed to him, and also the author of the *Manual of Discipline* speaks of the light in his heart because of the "secrets of wonders." It should be observed that according to Josephus (*Wars* 2, 8, 7, 141) the Essenes too were pledged not to reveal the secrets of their party.

There are three kinds of secrets in these scrolls. First, there is the divine decree concerning future events. Thus human behavior, in so far as it is predetermined, is dependent upon "God's secrets." Secondly, there is revelation; hence the Qumram midrash is called secret.[13] It seems, however, that neither of these two secrets is the one about which the author of the *Thanksgiving Psalms* sings. But there is another kind. It is noteworthy that throughout this literature there is no interest in the origin of the world nor in speculation concerning the upper worlds, what the Talmud calls respectively "the work of the beginning" and "the work of the chariot," but there is a deep interest in the end of days, which was deemed to be imminent. And when the word *raz* (secret) occurs in a clear and definite context, it is eschatological.[14] This is the third secret, and it consists of controversial ideas not yet crystallized in terminology, and not explicitly authorized in the Bible. What are these new eschatological secrets?

First, there is the Messiah. In several places mention is made of the annointed of Aaron and Israel.[15] Charles saw in these expressions a rejection of a Davidic Messiah, who of course belongs to the tribe of Judah, not to Aaron and Israel, and he proposed that it refers to one of the two sons of Herod and Miriam who descended from Israel on his father's side and from Aaron the priest on his mother's side.[16] This view is untenable because throughout this literature the phrase "Aaron and Israel" is a synonym for the whole people, which, however, were mainly from Judah.[17] But in addition to a non-Davidic Messiah, recent scholars read into this and other phrases other beliefs, such as two Messiahs, or a heavenly Messiah who was killed and rose from his grave, a Christian prototype;[18] and they do not note that these scriptures nowhere speak about a personal, heavenly Messiah, but only about an earthly Messiah and mainly about the Messianic period.

Let us first clarify the numerical problem. The *Damascus Document* speaks of the Messiah, or the Annointed, as one. But in the *Manual of Discipline* 9:10 we read "until the coming of a prophet and the Messiahs of Aaron and Israel," that is, two, one from Aaron and one from Israel. But this contradiction disappears when it becomes clear, first, that the expression "Aaron and Israel" means, as we said, not certain tribes but the whole of Israel, and, secondly, that the term "Messiah" in this literature mainly means not an eschatological Messiah, but, as in the Bible, a priest, or a king, or a prophet. Indeed the *Damascus Document* (2:10) tells us that there were Messiahs in every generation. In some of these places the term "Messiah" is synonymous with the Teacher of Righteousness, as is proven by parallel passages. Thus the term "Messiah" does not denote one who will appear at the end of days, but a spiritual leader. There were such Messiahs in the past and there will be more in the future, and they will not be limited to two—one spiritual and one political—as in talmudic literature.

And just as "Messiah" is a general term for a leader, so the title "Teacher of Righteousness" is general, as evident from the various parallels. Therefore, the hint to the resurrection of the Teacher of Righteousness, which could have disturbed the uniqueness of Jesus of Nazareth, also disappears. This is not the same Teacher of Righteousness who lived at the beginning of the sect and who will lead his people at the end of days, but another leader who will likewise bear the title Teacher of Righteousness or Messiah. Nor can one prove from the *Habakkuk Commentary* 11:4 that the wicked priest who persecuted the Teacher of Righteousness actually killed him, and that he, the Teacher of Righteousness, revealed himself after his death on Atonement Day to wreak vengeance on his enemies, as A. Dupont-Sommer, in his *Jewish Sect of Qumran and the Essenes*, maintained.[19] Quite to the contrary. The fragments of the *Nahum Commentary* read:

> ... the wicked priest who was sent to the Teacher of Righteousness to slay him . . . and God will not leave him in his hand . . . the wicked ones of Ephraim and Manasseh who will seek to put their hand on the priest and on the men of his counsel in the Time of the crucible that will come upon them and God will redeem them from their hands.[20]

So they did *not* succeed in killing him, and we have here no parallel to the Christian faith, nor any account of the Christian drama itself. Consequently, many Gentile scholars were disturbed in vain.

But the important thing for understanding the spirit of this sect is not the fact that we have no Christian precedent here, but that it *could* not be here because it runs counter to the whole tendency of these Qumranis, the strictly "holyistic" tendency to widen the gulf between the above and the below, to guard most carefully the sharp dividing line between God and man. In fact, it seems that the enemies of Israel fight against the apocalyptic tendency to lift the Messianic figure to the level of divinity, against the *Testaments of the XII Patriarchs*, for example, which were known in Qumran and which taught that the Messiah will be the king of the whole world, will fight the enemies of Israel and the demonic powers, headed by Belial himself, and will open the gates of Eden for the righteous. There is here an effort to eclipse Messiah's personality, to preach a Messianic Kingdom without a Messiah, that is, to come nearer to the Book of Jubilees.

It is noteworthy that in the *War of the Sons of Light*, which would be the most fitting place for an account of Messiah's exploits, there is no mention of Messiah. In the *Damascus Document* he is only hinted at under the symbol of the scepter who "shall break down all the sons of Seth" (9:15). This description might indicate a militant Messiah, one who will deliver the wicked to the sword, but the author carefully attributes all destruction to Belial himself. Also, such messianic functions as atonement and punishment are taken away from Messiah and transferred to the group as a whole (*Manual of Discipline* 3:5-7). Thus Messiah himself is denied any part of the messianic drama. He is passive only, the emphasis being on the period, not on the man. Nor is there anything supernatural in his personality. He does not sit at the right of the deity, nor does he come down from heaven.[21] There is nothing to describe him as higher than man. The line of Holiness is tightly drawn between the above and the below. And if we add that in the public council the priest was to take his seat prior to the Messiah,[22] we have four features: his eclipse, his passivity, his naturalness, and his secondary rank, which together point clearly to a decrease in Messiah's stature under the impact of Holiness; and this is in spite of—perhaps really because of—the fact that the period generally tended to lift his stature to the highest heaven.

To complete the picture, let us add the earthliness of the Messianic period. The order of the eschatological eras, though never explicit, seems to be as follows. After "the period of the visitation," which denotes the time of the sword, when God Himself will move against Belial, there will come the "period of salvation," which will mark the end of the struggle between the two powers and the beginning of truth.[23] The description of this second period is occasioanlly gnostic, reminding us of Sophia held captive by the forces of darkness. At any rate, the Messianic period will begin, and, as noted, without Messiah taking an active part. There will be long life, but no immortality. From all corners of the world, the world's trade will flow into the gates of Zion. Michael, the archangel of Israel, will be highest among the national archangels, and Israel below will rule over all nations. This is earthly, political Messianism, but it is also moral-spiritual; and the sons of Truth will rejoice in eternal knowledge.[24]

So far there is no supernaturalism, no confusion of earth with heaven. Then, after the Messianic kingdom, there occurs the resurrection, which is the burden of many *Thanksgiving Psalms*. We have already shown [25] that the words "hope," "eternal secret," and "glory" are frequently used in an eschatological sense to mean the Hereafter or immortality, and they are so used in these scrolls. This is the meaning of phrases like "and I know that there is hope for those whom thou hast formed for an eternal hope" [26] (*Thanksgiving Psalms* 3:20), "and I know that there is hope for those who turn from iniquity" (*Thanksgiving Psalms* 6:6), "and I know that there is hope in thy loving-kindness" (*Thanksgiving Psalms* 9:14), "from the secret of flesh for those whom God hath chosen" [27] (*Manual of Discipline* 11:7), "and the children of the eternal secret" (*Manual of Discipline* 2:25). Similarly the term "glory" denotes here, as in the Apocrypha, the entrance into the world to come.[28] "For them hath God chosen for an eternal covenant and unto them is all the glory of man" (*Manual of Discipline* 4:22-23), "they who hold fast to Him are for the life of eternity, and all the glory of man is for them" (*Damascus Document* 5:9), "and to cause them to inherit all the glory of man (*Thanksgiving Psalms* 17:15). The precise term *'olam ha-ba* (the world to come) has not yet come into being; and this too, incidentally, may show an early date, for the earliest use of the term occurs in I Enoch 71:15 (see Charles *ad loc.*), that is, in the Parables written between 94-64 B.C.

But how is this resurrection to be conceived? Is it meant to be the revival of the body with the soul, or only of the soul in the manner of immortality in Plato and the Book of Jubilees? The answer is bodily resurrection, which is quite in accord with this sect's psychological rejection of platonic dualism, which posits body and soul as hostile to each other, and its conception of one miserable entity of body-soul. Consequently, resurrection too can be only of the entire entity. Some claim that there is no hint of physical resurrection in this literature, but there is no need to explain away such verses, full of eschatological terminology, as: "*And they that lie in the dust* [italics added] shall lift up the mast, and the human worm shall raise a banner for the [. . .] (eternal hope)" (*Thanksgiving Psalms* 6:34). "To lift up from dust the human worm *for an eternal secret*" (*Thanksgiving Psalms* 11:13). But man will undergo a transformation—and here the sect comes near to the Similes of I Enoch—and will enter a new creation in which there will be eternal life; and, crowned with crowns of glory, dressed in garments of splendor (all these are eschatological terms), and cleansed of all sin, men will stand in undying light together with angelic hosts and will sing together with the knowers, which is, as we said, a gnostic term.[29] Thus the human worm rises and joins the angels, and the longing for glory finally celebrates its victory, but only as a hope for the world to come.

Determinism, continued prophecy, angels, Messiah, and resurrection—in all these five problems, the Qumranis were set against the Sadducees, and in the first two, also against the Pharisees. In their way of life they resembled the Essenes, and apparently they were Essenes, except for their rejecting platonic dualism and maintaining a limited angelology. As to their place in the historical dialectic of Jewish thought, they were not at one with the Glory of apocalypse, which lifted man heavenward, nor with the Holiness of Wisdom, which however brought Wisdom as a metaphysical being down on earth. They followed the way of Holiness farther than any other group of that time. As to man's longing to know the future and the development of his laws, they offered a continued prophecy. Indeed, it was not the direct kind—this they in particular could no longer admit, just as they could not believe with the Pharisees in the power of human logic for the development of the law—but a prophecy based on prophecy, an echo (bat-kol) with an authority equal to that which it echoed.

One might apply then the talmudical phrase, "clear was the casket of wine, and they muddied it." For in addition to their ideological reservations, a personal bitterness seems to have driven them out of the national fold and to have made them utter harsh words against the leaders in Jerusalem,[30] particularly those words in the Damascus Document 6:10, that in time to come "they shall no more join the house of Judah." It was in this angry mood that they withdrew to the Judean deserts and fostered a love among themselves and a hate toward the rest of the people, regarding as sacred both this inner love and this external hate. Hence, we will understand a strange statement in Josephus' Wars (2:8). "The Essenes," he says, "are Jews by birth and love seems to reign among them more than among members of any other sect." [31] What is the meaning here of "Jews by birth," and how is this connected with the love that reigns among them? But these expressions imply their hostile estrangement from their people balanced by a warmer attitude toward each other. Josephus himself seems to have sympathy for this group, to whose philosophy he devotes much space.

Their wish was fulfilled. They were not joined to the house of Judah, and traces of the sect disappeared, until the coming of a generation of ingathering of the exiled and the stray.

◄ 5 ►

TANNAITIC SPECULATIONS

We are now coming to the period of the Tannaim, that is, to those sages who flourished during the first two centuries and whose statements compose the Mishnah and the Baraita. Banned, but nevertheless disturbing, the main problem of that period was the exploration of what is above this world and what was before Creation, and what is the bond between the above and below. Three controversies arose successively until there came the crisis and then a sharp turn.

THE FIRST CONTROVERSY:
THE SCHOOLS OF SHAMMAI AND HILLEL

"The Rabbis taught: the school of Shammai says, the heavens were created first and then was created the earth, for it is said, In the beginning God created the heavens and the earth; and the school of Hillel says, the earth was created first and then were created the heavens, for it is said, In the day when the Lord God made the earth and the heavens." [1] The discussion continues. The question is asked: How will the school of Shammai meet the verse cited by the school of Hillel, and how will the school of Hillel explain the verse adduced by the school of Shammai; but the view comes before the verses. Now this opinion of the Shammaites is maintained also by Philo who regards the heavens as the world of Ideas and as "the most holy dwell-

49

ing-place of manifest and visible gods"; and, therefore, because of their importance, they were created prior to the earth.[2] Similarly, Bet Shammai emphasizes the priority of the heavens in rank and dignity, as it is said, "The heaven is my throne, and the earth is my footstool" (Isa. 66:1), whereas Bet Hillel, denying the higher rank of the heavens, describes the world as a lower and an upper story, so that obviously the lower story comes first. Thus, this controversy takes on the aspect of an issue between Platonic idealism and Aristotelian realism. Bet Shammai accepts the theory of Ideas, and Bet Hillel rejects it.

There is another clash of opinion between these two schools which reinforces this issue. The school of Shammai says the thought (of creation) was at night and the deed by day, for it is said "in the *day* when the Lord God *made* the earth and the heavens," whereas the school of Hillel says, both the thought and deed were by day.[3] Obviously here too the verses were not the source of the view, but only its sanction, for according to Philo,[4] the Logos, i.e., the Thought, is the Idea of Ideas and therefore logically prior. This is the Shammaitic view of the Thought at night, so that Bet Shammai posits a cosmogonic scale: Thought, heaven, and earth; or Logos, ideas, worlds; but Bet Hillel rejects all mediation and all intermediary beings.

It should be noted that Bet Shammai gave thought priority to the deed in time and rank, but no explicit part in the creation of the world. Nevertheless, since the whole idea of the priority of Thought or Logos comes in the context of an attempt by Plato and Philo to connect the upper and lower worlds, this priority expresses the tendency of Glory, and this tendency then characterizes the school of Shammai. But it is this tendency which led, as we saw in apocalyptic literature, to ideas about man's ascent and apotheosis and to the change of the concept of Logos-God into that of Logos-Man, as was then current in various forms of Christological speculation; so that Bet Hillel recoiled from this tendency and followed the road of Holiness against all mediation.

And although the accepted opinion in legal matters is generally that of Bet Hillel, it is the philosophical view of Bet Shammai that triumphed. R. Johanan ben Zakkai speculated on the divine Chariot, which is essentially the Shammaitic Thought, and honored such speculations. He recognized, like Bet Hillel, the danger involved in this study leading to the deification of man, and he therefore ruled that one must not teach it unless the student was wise and able to speculate by himself. That is to say, he did *not* condemn it, but only *limited* it to the gifted few. And, therefore, when he heard his pupils converse in these mysteries, he said to them "you and your pupils and the pupils of your pupils are designated for the third division." [5]

And R. Eleazar ben Zadok reasoned that the life of him who makes improper use of the vessel (i.e., the Torah) with which this world and the world to come were created will be torn out from both worlds.[6] Here is already an identification. The Shammaitic Thought becomes the Torah, and it is given a task. It is called a vessel, or an instrument, of creation, exactly as Philo described the Logos. Here also we have an entrance to circles of ideas concerning the cosmogonic priority of the Torah and its being "a precious vessel"—ideas which became prominent afterwards. And, Nahum Ish Gam Zo learned from R. Eleazar ben Zadok and did not hesitate to maintain that the vessel be feared as much as its creator: "What is this which says: *et adonai eloheka tira*—'the Lord thy God thou shalt fear?' —Him and His Torah." [7]

Thus the school of Shammai posited two intermediary beings: Thought and heavens, and the divine Thought afterwards was conceived as the Torah and as a vessel. What about heavens? Can they too be understood as a vessel with reference to the earth? Here we come to the second controversy.

SECOND CONTROVERSY: R. ELIEZER BEN HYRCANUS AND R. JOSHUA BEN HANANIAH

"R. Eliezer says, whatever is in heaven was created from heaven, whatever is on the earth was created from earth. . . . R. Joshua says, whatever is in heaven or on earth was created only from heaven, and he infers it from the verse, 'For He saith to the snow, Be thou on the earth'" (Job 37:6).[8] This means that according to R. Eliezer the heavens had no part in the creation of the earth, but R. Joshua affirmed this creative role. R. Eliezer too apparently accepts the Shammaitic principle of the ranking priority of the heavens, but he follows Holiness in assuming an impassable border between the upper and the lower worlds and infers it from the verse "Praise ye the Lord from the heavens . . . Praise the Lord from the earth" (Ps. 148:2-7), signifying a separation. R. Joshua, on the other hand, adds to the ranking priority a creative power, and following Glory, he maintains a spiritual monism symbolized by heavenly snow.

Also, the same controversy is formulated differently. "R. Eliezer says: The world (i.e., the earth) was created from its center, for it is said, When the dust groweth into hardness, and the clods cleave fast together (Job 38:38). R. Joshua says, the world was created from its sides for it is said, 'For He saith to the snow, Be thou on the Earth.' " [9] A similar division of opinion between these two Tannaim obtains not only with reference to creation, but also as to the maintenance of the world. "Whence does the earth drink?" R. Eliezer says, from the waters, "and the waters rise from the earth to the sky and receive them as from a water bottle and no drop touches another." [10] Thus, even with reference to the supply of water, R. Eliezer maintains that the heavens and the earth are separate, while R. Joshua consistently maintains the dependency of the earth upon the heavens. And here R. Joshua introduces the concept of upper waters which will play so important a part in later Tannaitic speculation.

The different tendencies of these two men may also account for their discussion in the field of astronomy. The question is asked by what road the sun moves at night. R. Eliezer says, the world resembles a hall with the northern side not covered; and when the sun reaches the northwestern corner, it bends its course and ascends above the sky (where it returns to the east). R. Joshua says, the world resembles a tent, with the northern side covered; and when the sun reaches the northwestern corner, it goes around and returns behind the tent" (Baba Batra 25a). One can see that R. Eliezer, who zealously guards the borderline between heaven and earth, would keep the sun always in a celestial orbit, but R. Joshua, with his monistic tendency, would not object to the sun's descent from such a course.

Another account on this subject occurs in Bereshit Rabba 6:8: "How do the sun and the moon set in the sky? The Rabbis say, from the back of the sky and below (i.e., they move under the earth). R. Judah bar Il'ai said, from the back of the sky and upward" (i.e., above the sky). Here R. Judah bar Il'ai agrees with R. Eliezer, and the view of R. Joshua is not mentioned; but the general view of the Rabbis is different from both. This view of the Rabbis is strangely given as a non-Jewish view in Pesaḥim 94b, where we read: "The Jewish sages say, by day the sun moves below the sky, and at night above the sky [i.e., like R. Eliezer], and the non-Jewish sages say, by day the sun moves below the sky and at night under the earth." Thus, R. Eliezer's view becomes the official Jewish view; the general view of the Rabbis becomes the Gentile view: and the view of R. Joshua is not even mentioned. But R. Joshua does not stand alone. He is supported by the Greek thinker, Anaxagoras, who says that the heavenly bodies do not move under the earth but "round it as a cap turns round our head," and also by the patristic writer, Severianus, bishop of Gabala, who thinks that "the heaven is not a sphere but a tent or tabernacle and the sun does not pass under the earth at night but travels through the northern parts as if hidden by a wall." [11]

Holiness is a rationalistic tendency insisting on order in the universe, on law, and on nature; however, Glory mystically sees miracles and wonder. Hence, R. Eliezer maintains that the heavenly bodies did not cease moving during the days of the Flood, while according to R. Joshua their motion was suspended.[12] R. Eliezer says that the verse "that I made the children of Israel to dwell in booths" means real booths, but R. Akiba—a great follower of Glory—says that they were clouds of Glory.[13] R. Joshua also speaks of groups of angels created daily, who sing before God and then return to the river of fire.[14] In an attempt at rationalism, R. Eliezer explains the verse, as the power God imparted to Moses' eyes so that he saw from one end of the world to the other, and R. Joshua says God's *finger* became Metatron to Moses who showed him all the land of Israel.[15] Here R. Joshua created the concept of the finger of God, which played an important part afterwards. On the other hand, R. Eliezer ben Hyrcanus did not emphasize angels and intermediaries. Perhaps Bacher is right that the opinion ascribed to Aquilas the Convert, really belongs to his master, R. Joshua ben Hananiah. This thought that the world is full of the breath of life comes from Plato, who taught that the world is alive, and from Philolaus, who taught that the world breathes. Originally the idea was advanced by the Anaximenes who called it πνεῦμα which, like R. Joshua's *ruah*, combines the associations of both wind and spirit. At any rate such a thought fits into R. Joshua's spiritual monism.

THIRD CONTROVERSY:
R. ISHMAEL BEN ELISHA AND R. AKIBA

Let us first note that R. Eliezer ben Azariah, an opponent of R. Akiba, concurred with R. Eliezer ben Hyrkanus in favoring rationalism and Holiness. Once R. Akiba expounded: "One verse reads 'His *throne* was like the fiery flame,' and one verse reads 'the *thrones* were cast down'—one for justice and one for mercy. Said to him R. Eliezer ben Azariah: Akiba, what has thou to do with homiletics? Cease your speech and turn to legal matters, for one refers to the throne and one to the footstool, . . . as it is said, 'The heavens are my throne and the earth is my footstool.'" [17] Why did R. Eliezer ben Azariah here oppose R. Akiba? Not because of implied plurality, but rather because of an opposition to the hypostatization of the divine attributes of justice and mercy and to transforming them into intermediaries, in the same way that R. Hanina in *Bereshit Rabba* 8:4 spoke of the divine attribute of justice as of an angel. But even more sharply did R. Ishmael ben Elisha clash with R. Akiba in matters of speculative philosophy, and it is to these two opponents that we now turn.

Tradition maintains that R. Akiba *discoursed* [18] before R. Joshua ben Hananiah, who *discoursed* before R. Yohanan ben Zakkai. The Hebrew expression here for "discoursed" means "he engaged in esoteric knowledge," which according to our view is fundamentally Shammaitic speculation, i.e., the theory of emanations and intermediaries. R. Akiba maintained the priority of the heavens to the earth, like the school of Shammai.[19] He also accepted from R. Eleazar ben Zadok the epitaph "vessel" for the Torah, calling the Torah "a precious vessel," [20] which hints at the Shammaitic doctrine that Thought or Logos came first and adds the idea that thought was an instrument in creation. He prohibited the study of the divine Chariot, but he himself "entered the garden" or engaged in the study of esoteric philosophy, entered and came out in peace. On the other hand, R. Ishmael ben Elisha did not engage in such philosophy, permitted to study publicly "the work of the beginning," or cosmogony, and guarded the "holystic" borders between the above and the below.

Let us take as examples the following statements: "One verse reads: 'I have talked with you from heaven,' and another verse reads: 'And the Lord came down on Mount Sinai.' How can these two verses be harmonized? A third verse harmonizes: 'Out of heaven He made thee hear 'His voice that He might instruct thee; and upon earth He showed thee His great fire.' So says R. Ishmael. R. Akiba says, this teaches that He lowered the highest heavens to the top of the mountain and spoke with them from heaven. Rabbi (R. Judah ha-Nasi) says, if one of the servants of His servants (e.g., the sun) serves both in its place as well as in other places, how much more the glory of Him who said and the world came into being." [21] R. Ishmael belongs to the school of Holiness, the voice and the fire were separate, and there was no divine descent. R. Akiba belongs to the school of Glory and mystery: God indeed spoke from heaven, but he lowered heaven to the mountain top. Rabbi likewise tries to guard the borders, thus belonging to the school of R. Ishmael, and there was no descent. The same difference is seen in the following passage: "R. Eliezer says: While the King of Kings, the Holy One blessed be He, was on His couch in heaven, Mount Sinai was rising in fire. . . . R. Akiba says, while the King of Kings of Kings, the Holy One, blessed be He, was on His couch in heaven, the *glory* of the Lord was resting on Mount Sinai." [22] One can see here in the words of R. Eliezer a consistent refusal to express descent.

Similarly, with reference to the miraculous, as against the rational, and to a certain degree of emanation, we may cite the following passage. "And all the people saw the voices and the flames—they saw the seen and heard the heard. So says R. Ishmael. R. Akiba says, they saw and heard the seen. And every word came forth out of the mouth of God and engraved itself on the tablets, as it is said, the voice of the Lord cleaveth the flames of fire." [23] And here we have the beginning of the speculative concept of the "voice of God" which we will meet later in connection with Ben Azzai.

Again similarly: "This month is unto you—R. Ishmael said, Moses showed the new moon to Israel . . . R. Akiba says, this is one of the three things with which Moses had difficulty and God showed them all with the finger." [24] This also shows that R. Akiba received from R. Joshua ben Hananiah the concept of the "finger," about which more anon.

This blurring of the border between the above and the below is involved also in the controversy between R. Ishmael and R. Akiba concerning angels. "Man did eat the bread of the mighty—the bread which the ministering angels eat. These are the words of R. Akiba. When these words were said before R. Ishmael, he said, go out and tell Akiba, Akiba, you erred. Do the ministering angels eat bread?" [25] Similarly, " 'By them shall the birds of heaven have their habitation'— R. Akiba says these are the ministering angels. Said to him R. Ishmael, cease your speech and turn to legal matters. It is a bird that rests on trees, which praise the Holy One, blessed be He." [26] Thus, also with reference to angels, R. Ishmael's approach is that of Holiness, and that of R. Akiba—Glory.

And to the extent that R. Akiba tried to bring the upper world nearer to man, he also tried to lift man to the heights and first of all to exalt Israel whom he called children of God. No individual stands higher than the people of Israel. Even with Moses God spoke only because of the merit of Israel.[27] And the whole book of Song of Songs is a love song between God and Israel.

Not only Israel, but also all men are exalted by R. Akiba. "Beloved is man, for he was created in the Image [of God]; it is by special love that he was created in the Image (*Abot* III, 18), and anyone who sheds blood is charged as if he diminished the image." [28] To such an extent R. Akiba permitted himself to indulge in the apotheosis of man. It is not only that man is the image of God, but God becomes, as it were, the image of man. And therefore it seems that the reading in *Shir ha-Shirim Rabba* I, 46: "R. Pappus expounded: Behold, the man has become as one of us—like the Only One of the world. Said to him R. Akiba: Enough for you, Pappus: Said to him R. Pappus: How then do you interpret 'like one of us'? He said to him: Like one of the ministering angels"—is correct, even though there is another version in *Bereshit Rabba* 21:5, in which R. Akiba objects to the elevation of man even to the rank of angels.[29] Similarly, in *Sanhedrin* 38b, R. Akiba speaks about two thrones in heaven, one for God and one for David, and he is rebuked for this by R. Jose—a rebuke which conveys a recoil from Christological associations. It is therefore possible that the marvelous anonymous words in the *Mekilta* on Exod. 17:6: "Behold I stand before thee there—God said to him, wherever you find the impression of human feet, there I am before thee"—have their origin in the school of R. Akiba.[30]

Similarly, in matters eschatological, we note the fundamental difference between these two sages. R. Akiba deals freely with these problems. The term "Glory," which denotes for him the Shekinah or the divine Presence, means for him, as in the Apocrypha and the Dead Sea Scrolls, also the world to come, where man is transformed and elevated. The righteous sit in booths of clouds of Glory.[30a] The wicked are judged in Hell only—twelve months. Also, the word "day," according to R. Akiba, refers to the world to come. It is the day which shall be wholly a Sabbath and rest in the life everlasting. R. Yohanan ben Zakkai spoke about a feast as a parable for the Hereafter. With R. Akiba it is already an eschatological term: "all is ready for the meal." [31]

And in all these eschatological matters there is no statement by R. Ishmael ben Elisha. He was too realistic to entertain apocalyptic reveries that blur the line, even though only for the end of days, between man and divinity.

THE CRISIS: BEN AZZAI AND BEN ZOMA

"Four entered the garden, Ben Azzai and Ben Zoma, Aher and R. Akiba. Said to them R. Akiba: When you reach the stones of pure marble, do not say, water, water! Because it is said (Ps. 101:7); 'He that telleth lies shall not tarry in my sight.' Ben Azzai looked and died. Concerning him the Bible says (Ps. 116:15): Precious in the sight of the Lord is the death of his saints. . . . Ben Zoma looked and became demented. . . . Aher cut down the shoots. R. Akiba went out in peace." [32] The whole passage is mysterious, but particularly mysterious is R. Akiba's caution against saying "water, water!" What is the meaning of it?

This event of the "four who entered" constituted a crisis in the history of the Shammaitic doctrine concerning intermediary beings. As long as these beings were posited in limited cases, or even in the administration of the world, or even as a primordial matter in the creation of the world, the Rabbis tolerated them. But when they affected the unity of the creator by being conceived as *partners of creation*, let alone as creators in their own right, in the manner of gnostic speculations which were rife in those days, Judaism recoiled. An abyss was torn open. Such a crisis occurred in the case of two of the four who entered. Aher went to the extreme and adopted a belief in Metatron and in Persian dualism (*Hagigah* 15a). But in the case of Ben Azzai and Ben Zoma, there have been transmitted hints that seem to have reference to "water, water."

Both Ben Zoma and Ben Azzai interpreted the verse in Ps. 29:3, "the voice of the Lord is upon the waters," to mean that the voice of the Holy One, blessed be He, became Metatron on the waters, *directing* them to gather in one place.[33] But by this statement they did no harm. R. Akiba too explained, as we saw, the expression "the voice of the Lord cleaveth flames of fire" to mean that the voice of God at the revelation of Sinai was a visible being. And even before R. Akiba, R. Joshua ben Hananiah said: "The finger of God became Metatron to Moses and showed him the whole land." [34] The Voice or Metatron is the Philonic Logos, and the affirmation of it on levels other than creation Judaism did not condemn.

But now we are coming to Ben Zoma separately. Let us cite the whole passage.

The story is that once R. Joshua was walking on the road and Ben Zoma came towards him and did not greet him. He said to him, whence and whither, Ben Zoma? The latter replied. I was gazing at the work of creation, and there was not between the upper waters and the lower waters even a hand-breadth; for it is said, and the spirit of the Lord was hovering on the face of the waters, and it is said, as an eagle stirreth up her nest, fluttereth over her young. Just as the eagle, flying over her nest, touches and touches not, so there is not between the upper waters and the lower waters even a hand-breadth. At that time R. Joshua said to his students, Ben Zoma is already outside. In a short time he was taken away.[35]

We read and we are astonished. Wherein was Ben Zoma at fault? Was it not the doctrine of R. Joshua himself, as we have seen, that all draw from the upper waters, that "the clouds rise from the earth to the sky and receive them as from the mouth of a water-bottle?" And after Ben Zoma, R. Levi also taught: "The upper waters are masculine, and the lower waters are feminine; and the former say to the latter, receive us, you are God's creatures and we are His messengers. At once they receive them." [86] This idea, which also occurs in En. 54:8, is certainly reminiscent of gnostic sexual conceptions of spheres or aeons; yet the sages did not seem to protest.

But you must note that Ben Zoma conceives of the upper waters not as a physical element, but *as the spirit of God* hovering over the lower waters. Comparing this idea with the teaching of Simon Magus, the Samaritan gnostic, we will see the meaning of Ben Zoma's statement. The teaching of Simon Magus was as follows: From infinite fire there emanated mind and thought, voice and name, understanding and consideration. These six principles with their infinite source constitute the supreme, heptadic world. The middle world is also composed of three pairs, together with their source which is thought, or the holy spirit. These are heaven and earth, sun and moon, air and water. The lower world came into being by the holy spirit, which is found in its entirety in every principle and which hovered over the lower waters, even as it is said, and the spirit of God was hovering on the face of the waters.[37] Thus, the middle world, in its chain of principles, ends with water, and the lower world begins with water, so that between the upper and the lower waters there is not even a hand-breadth. And the upper waters carry the holy spirit, and it is this which hovers over the lower waters. So, Ben Zoma's view becomes identical, even as to the verse to which it attaches itself, with the view of Simon Magus the gnostic concerning an emanated *creative* power. Hence R. Joshua winced: Ben Zoma is already outside.

This conception of a creative intermediary confronts us also in another statement. " 'And God made the firmament'—this is one of the verses with which Ben Zoma stormed the world. And God made?! Is it not by his word that things were created? For it is said (Ps. 33:6): By the word of the Lord the heavens were made; and all the host of them by the breath of his mouth." [38] And the question is what was Ben Zoma's own attitude in this contradiction? And the answer is clear: the word of the Lord (the Logos) or the spirit of his mouth (the holy spirit, the upper waters). It is this which made the firmament; that is to say, there is a demiurgus. According to Justin Martyr, Plato too identified the spirit of God hovering over the face of the waters with the third spirit (God-Logos-spirit), and therefore "the third on the third" (on water which was gathered on the third day).[39]

Elisha ben Abuiah must have gone further. Perhaps he, like the gnostics, lost the supreme deity altogether as a creative power. But all these thoughts which began modestly with the school of Shammai caused the Tannaim to recoil from the line of Glory. R. Akiba himself cautioned his students: "When you reach the stones of pure marble, do not say water, water!"

THE TURN

The crisis of the "four who entered" crushed speculative philosophy; and most of the Tannaim, the students and the descendants of the students of R. Akiba, until Rabbi and his generation, withdrew to the road of Holiness, except a few like R. Simon ben Yohai and R. Natan.

R. Jose ben Halafta conceived of divine transcendence as the fundamental difference between the container and the contained. "God is the space of the world, and the world is not His space." [40] But this in itself does not prove the dominance of Holiness, for Simon Magus and Philo,[41] who followed Glory, uttered similar expressions. R. Eliezer ben Jacob emphasized transcendence more profoundly by interpreting. "I am God Almighty [Shaddai]—I am He of whose divinity the world and its fulness is not worthy [Kedai]." [42] And R. Eliazar ben R. Jose emphasizes God's physical and spiritual inaccessibility by adding to Akiba's statement, saying, "the ministering angels not only cannot see the Shekinah but also cannot hear and do not know where the Shekinah is." [43] And R. Meir finds the ontological marvel in this that in spite of God's greatness, filling all heaven and earth, he nevertheless confines himself between the two staves of the Ark.[44] Note that R. Meir does not say with R. Akiba and Ben Azzai "between the two Cherubim." Why? Because the Cherubim were taken as symbols of metaphysical forms, by Philo [45] and others, and perhaps also by those two Tannaim, and R. Meir no longer admitted such forces.

More expressive from the standpoint of transcendence is the declaration of R. Jose ben Halafta: "The Shekinah never came down, and Moses and Elijah never ascended to heaven." [46] In this declaration this Rabbi negated entirely the literature of Ascensions current in his day. And one must remember that R. Jose placed Moses on a higher level than the patriarchs and even the ministering angels. In this regard, R. Joshua ben Korhah [47] and Rabbi opposed him, apprehensive perhaps of the idea of a man-God.[48] But he refused for this very reason to accept that Moses ascended, in order to maintain a sharp line between the above and the below, between heaven and man. R. Judah ha-Nasi also agrees with R. Jose that the Shekinah did not descend, did not *have* to descend. The sun shines above and illuminates below.[49]

And the Platonic idealism which was symbolically expressed in the Shammaitic formula "the heavens were created first" was entirely abandoned. R. Meir, it is true, speaks much about angels and Seraphim; but these are not creative forces, only creatures that are sent, and the divine family. The upper waters are not a creative metaphysical being, not the spirit of God hovering, as Ben Zoma thought, but physically suspended in the air by divine command.[50] Justice and mercy are not two thrones, that is, they are not ideal beings, as R. Akiba thought, but two attributes of God Who is good.[51] However, the gnostics taught that God the creator is right but not good, just but not merciful. And R. Judah bar Il'ai, like the school of Hillel, decided that the earth was created first.[52] And R. Eleazar, son of R. Simon ben Yohai, held that the heaven and the earth are equal in rank—again in disagreement with Bet Shammai. R. Judah bar Il'ai, it is true, accepts the priority of the Torah and interprets Ps. 8:30 "I was by him as one brought up [amon] with him.," to mean "I was by him as an architect [uman]." [53] However, all the demiurgic character of the Torah is not expressed by him in an active way, as in the Wisdom of Solomon, but only passively, so that only God is the creator: "God looked into the Torah and created the world." [54] The question how did God say to Moses "*this* month" or "this new moon," when He spoke to him only by day, R. Eleazar ben Shamu'a answered rationalistically: He spoke to him by day at dusk,[55] whereas his master R. Akiba had answered: He showed it to Moses with His finger, that is, through an emanated force.

Only R. Simon ben Yohai still inclined toward the idealistic Shammaitic school: "I wonder how the masters of the world, Bet Shammai and Bet Hillel, differ on the order of the creation of heaven and earth. But Thought was both by day and at night, and work was at sunset." [56] This means that Thought was prior, but heaven and earth were created together.[57] He thus differs from Bet Shammai, but only in that he maintains one intermediary being, Thought or Logos, and not Logos as apart from the Ideas. But essentially this is a Shammaitic tendency. Also, when he says that the mountain Morijah corresponds with the heavenly temple,[58] there is a hint at Platonic Forms. R. Natan ha-Babli, at the end of this period, likewise maintained that the temple below corresponded with the Temple on high, and that the Ark was in a line with the throne of glory.[59] R. Natan ha-Babli was much influenced by Greek science and philosophy. His saying "the middle is honored" [60] is Pythagorean, quoted by Aristotle in his *De Caelo*, 293d, 20, and taken over by the Stoics and used by Saadia in the introduction to the fourth treatise in *Emunot we-De'ot*. And when R. Simon ben Yoḥai describes how God's word went forth from the right side of God to the left side of Israel, surrounding the camp of Israel . . . and coming forth from the right of Israel to the left side of God, whereupon God received it on his right side and engraved it on the tablet [61]—there is again an idealistic conception of the Voice or the Logos.

A consciousness of Holiness agrees with a pessimistic outlook on the world and on man. "Cease ye from man . . . for wherein is he to be accounted of?" (Isa. 2:22). As in the Dead Sea Scrolls, so in R. Jose ben Halafta's thinking, there is a fatalistic outlook combined with Holiness. There are set periods that are good or evil, and also set places. There are periods for prayer, there are special hours, there is an auspicious day, and there is an inauspicious day.[62] R. Judah bar Il'ai looks pessimistically at the moral powers of man. This world was created with the letter *he* because it is like an *exedra*, i.e., closed on three sides and open on the fourth, like the letter *he*, and whosoever wishes to go astray may do so. Yet the left leg of this letter is suspended so as to leave a place for him to return in penitence. He cannot return the way he went out,[63] for he needs the help of heaven. Thus R. Akiba's formula, that permission (to do good or evil) is granted, shrank. And the consciousness of human sinfulness began to grow in the mind of the last Tannaim, so that the felicity of the world to come was conceived by R. Judah bar Il'ai in a vision of the evil temptation being slaughtered.[64] R. Reuben ben Iẓtrobli shows how man is ruled by the evil inclination from the very beginning of his formation.[65] Rabbi composes a prayer against the destructive Satan and against the evil inclination.[66] And the entire direction of life becomes otherworldly, this world having no intrinsic value. According to R. Jacob, it is only a vestibule wherein man must prepare himself so as to enter the banquet hall.[67] According to Rabbi, there is even an opposition between the two worlds, and man must choose either the pleasures of this world or those of the next.[68] There is no place for both. Only few Tannaim, like R. Simon ben Menasia, who said: "the Sabbath is for you"—the Sabbath is delivered to you, but you are not delivered to the Sabbath,[69] or Bar Ḳappara who said that the Nazarite, because he deprived himself of wine, is called a sinner,[70] still called for an affirmation of life.

The consciousness of sinfulness carries with it, by contrast, a veneration for the *zaddiq* or the one who is righteous. The whole world was created only for the righteous. The *zaddiq* rules throughout the world.[71] R. Simon ben Yoḥai, the man of Glory, indulges in speculation about the supernatural happiness of the righteous ones in the world to come, when their faces will resemble the sun, the moon, and the stars; and, playing upon the biblical phrase "fulness (*sova'*) of joy" (Ps. 16:11), he interprets it to mean seven (*sheva'*) joys,[72] evidently under the influence of IV Ezra 7:75-101, which describes the seven joys of the *zaddiq* when he is ready to behold the face of Shekinah.

Thus speculative philosophy weakened when the four entered the garden. The Tannaim then began to draw tighter the line of Holiness between the higher and lower worlds.

▲
◄ 6 ►
▼

THE WORLD VIEW OF THE AMORAIM

In the talmudical period that en-
sued, interest in the speculative philosophy diminished among the
Palestinian Amoraim, and even more among those in Babylonia. The
legal element, or Halakah, came to dominate powerfully, and the
heavens became a *yeshiva* and a court on high, and God and His
heavenly court differed as to what is ritually clean or unclean.[1] As to
the fundamental controversy between Bet Shammai and Bet Hillel—
whether the heavens were created first or the earth, which according
to our view carried with it the question as to the existence of the
Logos and intermediaries—only faint memories of it were left. R.
Joḥanan adopted a compromise that the heavens and the earth were
created together (*Bereshit Rabba* 12:12; but compare his statement
in *Bereshit Rabba* 1:15)—an idea which is philosophically opposed
mainly to Bet Shammai. Also R. Abbahu and R. Judah bar Simon
thought that they were created simultaneously (*Bereshit Rabba* 2:2;
but compare the statement of R. Judah bar Pazi who is identical with
R. Judah bar Simon, in *Jer. Hagigah* 77, top of column d). "R. Simon,
in the name of R. Joshua ben Levi, said, the Lord jested with the
ministering angels when He told them that the most essential is
above. Whence do we know it? It is said (Ps. 148:13) His glory is
above earth and heaven. First earth, then heaven." (*Bamidbar Rabba*
12:8). Also R. Nehemiah, of Kefar Sihin, taught: The earth was
created on the first day, as is the opinion of Bet Hillel . . . and the

sky on the second. R. Azariah, on the other hand, maintained that the heavens were created on the first, thus agreeing with Bet Shammai, and the earth on the third (*Bereshit Rabba* 12:5). R. Yizhak, also, took a Shammaitic stand. "Said R. Yizhak, flesh-and-blood builds a palace; first he builds the lower story and then he builds the upper story. But the Holy One, blessed be He, first he created the upper world, the heavens, and only then the earth" (*Tanhuma Bereshit* 4). But all these sayings did not assume the form of a philosophical controversy, as in the Tannaitic period, and did not lead to any conclusions. Among the Babylonian Amoraim, the whole controversy seems to have been forgotten. See *Bereshit Rabba* 12:11 (and compare *Qohelet Rabba* 3:26) where R. Joseph and R. Nahman, the Babylonians, together with R. Judan of Palestine, maintain that all things in heaven and earth come from the earth—which negates both the superearthly monism of R. Joshua and the dualism of R. Eliezer and, at any rate, rejects Platonic-Shammaitic idealism.

Also, the idea of the upper waters, which brought about the isolation of Ben Zoma and the crisis of the four who entered, lingered on in the Amoraitic period, but lacked speculative sharpness. R. Johanan and Resh Lakish accepted the view of R. Joshua that the earth drinks of the upper waters and not of the oceanic waters, as R. Eliezer thought. They differ only in this, that according to R. Johanan the clouds too come from heaven, while Resh Lakish thinks that the clouds come from below (*Bereshit Rabba* 13:11). According to R. Johanan the primeval waters are divided: half in the heaven and half in the ocean (*Bereshit Rabba* 4:5); however, R. Simon ben Pazi says the upper waters were more than the lower waters by thirty sextarii (a sextarius is about a pint), for it is said *bein mayim lemayim* (between the waters and the waters), and the letter *lamed* from the word *lemayim* equals thirty. This number thirty probably carries gnostic meaning, reminiscent of the thirty aeons of the upper world (see below, n. 29). Also Rabba hints at the upper waters, or the abyss on high, when he relates: "I saw Ridya [name of the angel of rain]; he looks like a third-grown calf, and his lips are parted, and stands between the lower abyss and the abyss on high" (*Ta'anit* 25b). The name *Ridya* also means plowing and therefore indicates the magic connection between plowing, or the plowing bull, and rain. Examples of such a belief one can find in James G. Frazer's *Golden Bough* (New York, 1923), pp. 70-71. The statement of R. Levi—"The upper waters are masculine and the lower feminine; and the upper say to the lower waters: Receive us, you are the creatures of the Holy One, blessed be

He, and we are His messengers. At once they receive them" (*Bere-shit Rabba* 13:13)—we mentioned in the previous chapter. But particularly important is the statement of R. Hosha'iah. "High as the empty space between the earth and the sky is the empty space between the sky and the upper waters." R. Tanhuma agrees with it and ends: "This means that the upper waters are suspended by divine command" (*Bereshit Rabba* 4:3). This idea that the upper waters are suspended by command is that of R. Meir (*Bereshit Rabba* 4:4), and was meant to reject the opinion of Ben Zoma that the upper waters *hover* over the lower waters, which means that they are a force in creation, or an intermediary.

One cannot therefore speak of philosophical controversies in the Amoraic period. Nevertheless, owing to their clashes with parties and sects, the Amoraim arrived at three important clarifications: the negation of attributes, the negation of intermediaries, and the negation of man-God. This constitutes their contribution to the history of Jewish thought.

ATTRIBUTES

Certainly, many anthropomorphic passages in the Gemara were originally meant only as a parable and a veiled idea, as the same Amora who anthropomorphizes in one place attacks anthropomorphisms in another place. Two examples. One is the case of R. Samuel bar Nahman. In *Shemot Rabba* 47:11 and *Tanhuma Ki Tisa* 37, he says, "the two tablets of the law were six handbreadths long, six wide, and Moses seized two handbreadths, *the Shekinah—two handbreadths*, and there were two in between, and from there Moses received the rays of glory"; but in *Menahot* 86b, we read: "Said R. Samuel bar Nahmani: Command the Children of Israel, that they bring unto thee pure olive oil beaten for the light—unto thee, and not unto me, no need have I for the light"—which emphasizes the spirituality of God. Another example is R. Hama bar Hanina. In *Baba Mezi'a* 86b, he interprets: "What is the meaning of the expression 'in the heat of the day?' It was the third day after Abraham's circumcision, and the Holy One, blessed be He, came to inquire after his peace. The Holy One, blessed be He, drew the sun out of its sheath in order not to have him molested by visitors . . . he went forth *and saw God standing at the door*" (italics added). Whereas in *Sota* 14b, he asks: "What is the meaning of 'after the Lord God ye shall walk?' Can man walk after the Shekinah? Is it not written 'For the Lord thy God is a consuming fire, a jealous God?' It can only mean follow the attributes of the Holy One, blessed be He." Thus in the *Aggadah*, too, there is *halakah* and *aggadah*, and one must differentiate between them. One may note the *halakah of aggadah* in sayings like that of Ḥizkiyyah ben R. Ḥiyya: The ears are made to hear what they can hear and the eyes —to see what they can see (*Shoher Tob* 1:4); or like this of Hizkiyyah: Happy prophets who can represent the creator in the form of the creature (*loc. cit.*, and similarly R. Judan in *Bereshit Rabba* 27:1); or like that of the outstanding adherent of transcendence, R. Hanina bar Hama, in *Shoher Tob* 1:50, and of R. Abbahu in *Megillah* 21a, and of others: "Were it not for the written verse, one could not utter it." Here is an explicit recoil from anthropomorphism.

Together with a denial of corporealism, this transcendence implies also a negation of the category of time. Following Philo and the Tanna R. Jose ben Halafta,[2] R. Ammi explains: Why do we call the Holy One, blessed be He, place (*maḳom*)? Because He is the place of the world, and the world is not His place, or, in the formulation of R. Yizhak Nappaḥa, the Holy One, blessed be He, is the dwelling place of His world, and His world is not His dwelling place (*Bereshit Rabba* 68:10). It is true that space as measure still applies, for even according to R. Johanan, who remarked on Ps. 8:4: "When I consider thy heavens, the work of thy fingers," that all the heavens amount only to one finger of God,[3] we still have not left behind us the category of space! But God is dominant over this category. R. Abbahu also refers to this mystery of divine contraction, which we have already met in the opinion of R. Akiba and Ben Azzai.[4] He wonders: He about whom it is written God is greatly feared in the assembly of the saints (Ps. 89:8) leaves His counselors and descends, *contracting* His divine presence below! (*Pesikta, Buber,* 152:1). Also R. Johanan expounded, "Moses said before the Holy One, blessed be He: Lord of the Universe, behold, the heavens and the heavens of heavens do not contain thee, how then dost thou say they shall make unto me a sanctuary? And the Holy One, blessed be He, answered him: Moses, not as thou thinkest, but only twenty boards in the north and twenty in the south and eight in the west and I will descend and contract my divine presence below" (*Pesikta* 20:1; 61:2). The Amoraim no longer dared to accept the view of R. Jose ben Halafta and Rabbi that the Shekinah never came down; but R. Joshua ben Levi explains the matter by saying, it is as if the Height of the world (i.e., the Most High) bent down, for it is said and the Lord descended in a cloud.[5] Thus all the contradictions become both acceptable and dissolved in the mystery of "as if," so that R. Judah bar Simon well understands: The Holy One, blessed be He, appears far off but there is none nearer than He . . . See how high is He above His world, and yet man enters the synagogue and stands behind a stand and prays silently and the Holy One, blessed be He, listens (*Jer. Berakot* 13a). Both outside of space and in space—this is the mystery of divine transcendence.

And divine transcendence includes also His being above *all* attributes. The classical expression for this "holyistic" attitude was presented by one of the earliest Amoraim already mentioned, R. Ḥanina bar Ḥama. "A man went down to the praying desk in the presence of R. Ḥanina, and said God, the great, mighty, revered, majestic, powerful, feared, strong, brave, sure, honored. R. Ḥanina waited until the man finished. When he finished, R. Ḥanina said to him: Have you come to the end of the praises of your Lord? It is like a king of flesh and blood who had a million gold denars and people praised him that he had silver! Is it not an insult to him?" (*Berakot* 33b).[6] God not only defies description, but also comprehension, that is, He is above all categories. Nor is this simply the opinion of a single individual, for it also occurs under the names of R. Johanan, R. Jonatan, R. Huna in the name of Rab, R. Abbahu, and others (*Jer. Berakot*, beginning of chapter 9). And R. Berechiah says, "The Holy One, blessed be He, said to David, praise me howsoever you desire and I will pardon your praising, for none can find one of the many kinds of the praises of God (*Shoḥer Tob* 88). And R. Judah of Kefar Niburayya, and some say of Kefar Nibbur Ḥayil, finds the indescribability of God implied in the verse "unto thee silence is praise" (*Megillah* 18a). And all this already touches on the theory of attributes of the Middle Ages.

But God's indescribability notwithstanding, R. Tanḥuma knows that the good is God (*Pesikta Rabbati* 142:2), just as Plato called God *agathos*, the good, and just as R. Meir and R. Perida called Him Good (*Jer. Hagigah* 77c; *Menahot* 53b; and see Matt. 19:17), and R. Akiba taught the world is ruled with divine goodness (*Abot* 3:19), and R. Simon ben Halafta called God "the goodness of the world." [7] R. Johanan called all the thirteen attributes of God "thirteen attributes of mercy" (*Pesikta, Buber,* 57:1), and Resh Lakish maintained that when Israel takes the *shofar* and blows, God arises from the throne of justice and sits on the throne of mercy (*Pesikta* 151:2). For just such a reference to two thrones, R. Akiba was rebuked by R. Eliezer ben Azariah (*Hagigah* 14a), very likely because of the implied hypostatization of the attributes; but in the period of the Amoraim they no longer feared it, perhaps because the juxtaposition of the word throne to justice or mercy had already become a cliché. And R. Johanan remarks on Exod. 10:1, "For I have hardened his heart": "This provides sectaries with grounds for arguing that Pharoah had no means of repenting" (Shemot Rabba 13:4); and these sectaries are the gnostics who claimed that the God of Israel is the creator and the God of justice and judgment, but not the God of goodness and mercy, and that only the Supreme Being is the God of love. But R. Simon teaches us that the term "love" means the divine presence.[8] R. Haninah bar Papa calls God "father"[9] and R. Levi and R. Aha call God re'a, "friend" (Hagigah 7a, Vayyikra Rabba 27:6), and R. Jose ben R. Hanina, "my beloved," and there is the frequently used word rahamana, "the merciful." Perhaps it is all summed up in R. Simlai's interpretation of Deut. 4:7: "For what nation is there so great, who hath God so nigh unto them—nigh with all kinds of nighness" (Jer. Berakot 13a). And in keeping with these expressions of divine nearness, there is also an attempt at vindicating creation, that is, if its positive side is good, then its other aspect, which is generally regarded negatively as evil inclination, suffering, or death, is very good; and man himself, in Hebrew adam, has for his anagram the Hebrew word meod, "very," i.e., "very good" (Bereshit Rabba 9:7-12). All this is the opposite of gnostic pessimism which regarded both creation and creator as intrinsically evil.

On the other hand, there were some who defended the superiority of justice. Thus, commenting on the Mishnah in Berakot 33b, "He who says, thy mercies extend to a nest of birds, must be silenced," the Gemara explains that it is because he makes compassion the source of the divine laws, which are only decrees. R. Hanina bar Hama, the consistent follower of Holiness, says that God's seal is truth (Shabbat 55a), which means a necessary relation between man's deeds and his destiny, and that he who says, God is loose in dealing out justice, his life shall be let loose (Baba Kamma 50a and somewhat similarly in Jer. Beza end of chapter 3), and that God deals with those around Him (the righteous) very strictly (Yebamot 121b). And sometimes R. Hanina differentiates: God is good to all—in this world; but in the world to come—do good, O Lord, unto the good (Shoher Tob 22:1).

INTERMEDIARIES

There are four kinds of intermediary forces: Logos, Platonic Ideas, Torah, and angels.

The Logos or the Word was regarded as an entity in itself. R. Joḥanan uses the expression "the Word (*dibbur*) returned before the Holy One, blessed be He, and said, O Lord of the universe" (*Shir ha-Shirim Rabba* 5:16), which shows that it is a separate being, or the expression "an angel took the Word from before God . . . and went around with it to every one of Israel" (*ibid.*, 1:13). The Word itself was an angel. And He put a *word* in the mouth of Balaam—R. Eleazar says an angel (*Sanhedrin* 105b), and in this R. Eleazar follows Philo who calls Logos *angelos*, or *archangelos;* [10] R. Berechiah differentiates between Logos and other angels: the fire of Logos is greater than that of angels, for the angels are only of the fire from underneath the throne of glory, from the river of fire . . . but the fire of Logos comes from the right hand of God (*Pesikta Rabbati* 155b). The many references which identify Bezalel with Wisdom, for example, those of Rab and R. Jonathan ben Eleazar in *Berakot* 55a, and of R. Abba bar Kahana who says Wisdom built her house—this is Bezalel (*Vayyikra Rabba* 11:4), are all influenced by Philo who calls Logos the shadow of God [11] and hence Bezalel (literally, in the shadow of God). It is noteworthy that the Amoraim did not refrain from this use of this concept which was accepted by Christian theology.

The Tannaitic concept of vessels of fire descending from heaven resembles the thought found in Platonic Ideas and also occurs frequently in the Amoraic period. R. Jonathan ben Eleazar explains "the pure candlestick" (Exod. 31:8) as meaning that its form came down from a place of purity (*Menaḥot* 29a). R. Simon speaks of the tabernacle on high (*Pesikta Rabbati* 85, end). R. Yizḥak speaks of the image of Jacob engraved on the throne of glory.[12] And R. Berechiah says about the curtain, hanging before the holy of holies that "there was nowhere else in the world a praiseworthy form like it, and there was no form in the world that was not upon it, for it is said (Exod. 36:35), With cherubim made he it of cunning work, rows upon rows of forms." [12] The meaning of the Greek word *idea* is form, and R. Berechiah's meaning is that the curtain symbolized all the Ideas and the Idea of Ideas. Similarly, R. Tanhuma comments on Ps. 45:14, "In brilliant colors she is brought to the king." "What is the meaning of 'in brilliant colors?' This refers to the Tabernacle which had much embroidery [literally, covered with forms], as it is written, 'And the embroiderer in blue.' " [13] Perhaps also the statement of R. Joshua ben Levi in *Rosh ha-Shanah* 11b: "All the works of creation were created in their full-grown stature, with their consent, and in keeping with their own desire," is influenced by the theory of Ideas, and the meaning may be the desire of their Ideas. R. Hai Gaon discusses this statement and rejects such influence.[14] But it is supported by the other statements, all of which indicate such an influence.

The Torah, which preceded the world according to R. Joshua ben Levi by 974 generations (*Shabbat* 88b), and according to Resh Lakish by 2,000 years (*Bereshit Rabba* 8:2), and which according to R. Abba bar Kahana preceded even the throne of glory (*Bereshit Rabba* 1:5), filled two cosmogonic functions: one, as artisan or vessel, the other, as primordial matter or element.

The concept of vessel or instrument in creation is contained in the term, "a hidden preciousness," which is used by R. Joshua ben Levi with reference to the Torah [15] and which is reminiscent of R. Akiba's term for the Torah, "a precious vessel." R. Hosha'iah calls it an "artisan" and the "work tool of God." The Torah is the blueprint of the world into which God looked and created the world.[16] This statement is influenced by Philo who regards the Torah as the Intelligent World, after whose pattern this world was created. But there is in it also a reply to the gnostics. They posited an artisan or a demiurgus who created the world. R. Hosha'iah took over this term, but only in the sense of a tool or instrument.

But there were some who looked at the Torah in its second function, i.e., as the primordial matter of the universe. Among the Greeks, there were some who spoke of six elements of the world.[17] Philo (*De Opificio Mundi* I, 13) tried to prove, following Plato (*Republic* 546b), that six was the perfect number from the standpoint of creation. And Simon Magus, as we have seen, posited six principles. Clearly gnostic is the passage about six elements in *Shemot Rabba* 15:22: Three creations preceded the world: water, wind, and fire. The *water conceived and bore darkness, the fire conceived and bore light, the wind conceived and bore wisdom;* and by these six creatures the world is governed: by wind and wisdom and fire and light and darkness and water. Perhaps all this influenced R. Abbin, who interpreted six covered wagons (Num. 7:3) as corresponding to the six heavens (*Shir ha-Shirim Rabba* 6:10), not counting *seven* heavens, as is customary in the Apocrypha and in the Talmud (compare, *Ḥagigah* 12b). Also in Tannaitic literature we read: "One philosopher said to R. Gamaliel, Your God is a great artist but he found good dyes, and he mentioned six elements: chaos, void, darkness, wind, water, and abyss." R. Gamaliel's answer did not oppose the idea of elements, though it did reveal a great sensitivity to this subject which concerns the foundations of the work of creation and touches upon the question of the Platonic hyle or beginningless matter. He rather accepted the idea of elements, but tried to prove that they too were created (*Bereshit Rabba* 1:9). Also R. Hama bar Hanina admitted six elements (*ibid.*, 10:3): Now R. Joshua ben Levi in the name of R. Levi also accepted the six elements, but to him they were simply the Torah. He who builds, he says, needs six things: water, soil, wood, stone, reeds, and iron . . . so the Torah preceded in the manner of these six precedences (*ibid.*, 1:11). The Torah then is that ἀρχή, that one world-ground, which the Milesian school in Greek philosophy sought in the physical world. Thus the Amoraim absorbed foreign ideas by translating them into Hebraic terms.

And since the Torah can be both a vessel and material for creation, there must be a secret power stored away in its letters, so that a door is here opened to gnostic magical influences. R. Abbahu in the name of R. Johanan thinks that the two worlds were created by means of two letters: This world by *he* and the world to come by *yod* (*Jer. Hagigah* 77c), but this thought was already expressed by R. Judah bar Il'ai in *Menahot* 29b. According to Rab, Bezalel knew how to combine letters with which heaven and earth were created (*Berakot* 55a). Joseph, who sanctified God's name in secret, was privileged, so that they added to him one letter of the name of God (the letter *he*); Judah, who sanctified God's name publicly, was privileged, so his name contains the whole name of God (*Sotat* 10b, 36b). And there begins to develop the belief in the theurgic power of the Name. Thus it is recorded that Gehazi, the prophet Elisha's servant, engraved a divine name in the mouth of the calf made by Jeroboam, and it proclaimed the first two of the Ten Commandments (*Sanhedrin* 107b); and Rabba relates that the sailors used to strike a gale on the sea with sticks engraved with divine names (*Baba Batra* 73a); and concerning R. Joshua ben Hananiah, the man of Glory and of Shammaitic speculations, the story went that in the course of debate with the elders of Athens he demonstrated his superiority by uttering a name, thus becoming suspended between heaven and earth (*Bekorot* 8b). One may add also with reference to these theurgic beliefs that R. Judah bar Simon thought that the tables of the law carried themselves because of the letters upon them, and that when the letters flew off they became heavy and broke (*Jer. Ta'anit* 68c). R. Eleazar ben Pedat believed that the sections of the Torah were not given in their proper order and that, were they given in their proper order, any one who read them would at once be enabled to create a world, to revive the dead, and to show wonders (*Shoḥer Tob* 3, beginning). All this already marks the beginning of the development of practical cabala.

As for the belief in angels, two tendencies appeared. One followed the road of revery and extension; the other feared the gnostic possibility of angels-creators and tried to limit this belief. Such a fear confronted the Amoraim in their controversy over when these angels were created. R. Johanan said on the second day; R. Hanina said on the fifth day. "And all admit that they were not created on the first day so that none should say Michael pulled on the south side of the sky, and Gabriel on the north, and the Holy One, blessed be He, stretched it in the center (*Bereshit Rabba* 1:4). In other words, none should entertain the notion that the angels had any part in creation. Hence, R. Johanan chose for the creation of the angels the second day. Similarly, R. Ḥama bar Ḥanina (*ibid.*, 11:10); but R. Ḥanina bar Ḥama, the consistent follower of Holiness, deferred their creation till the fifth day.

But the hierarchy begins even higher than angels. The highest intermediary is apparently the Shekinah or the Divine Presence, for in *Midrash Mishlei*,[18] the expression is used "the Shekinah stood before the Holy One, blessed be He," so that the Shekinah itself is not God, but an intermediary. After the Shekinah apparently comes the Holy Spirit, for in *Yoma* 21b we learn: These are the five things that mark the difference between the first and the second temple, for then they no longer existed . . . the Ark and the cover of the Ark and the Cherubim, the fire, the Shekinah, the Holy Spirit, and the Urim and Tummim; so that it appears that the Shekinah and the Holy Spirit are not identical. The Holy Spirit is higher than the Echo, for thus we learn: After the last prophets, Haggai, Zechariah, and Malaki, the Holy Spirit was removed from Israel, but they were still using the Echo (*Sanhedrin* 11a). That the Holy Spirit is higher than the angel can be inferred from the statement of R. Phinehas bar Ḥama: "God said to Israel, you caused your own downfall. Formerly you availed yourself of the Holy Spirit, now you are served only with an angel" (*Shemot Rabba* 32:1). And in the ranks of angels themselves there is a strict hierarchy, as appears from the statement of R. Abbin. "When man sleeps," he says, "the body speaks to the breath of life (*neshamah*), the breath of life to the soul (*nefesh*),[19] the soul to the angel, the angel to the Cherub, the Cherub to the Winged One—who is this?—the Seraph, and the Seraph carries the word and tells it before the Creator." [20]

Under the gnostic influences, angels and the categories of angels increased, and, as in apocryphal literature, they acquired distinct personalities. During the first temple, they were *only* messengers, or rather manifestations of God. Now they begin to develop a will of their own. In the Bible, God speaks to the angel; now the direction is reversed. We read: "the ministering angels said before God." They offer advice and influence the divine being.[21] Sometimes they are about to act on their own free will, and we meet with such a phrase as "the ministering angels wanted to push him." [22] Sometimes two angels engage in an argument, as in *Baba Batra* 75a: "I will make thy pinnacles of *kadkod*," said R. Samuel bar Nahmani: "There is a dispute [as to the meaning of *kadkod*] between two angels in heaven. . . . One says [*kadkod* means] onyx; and the other says jasper. The Holy One, blessed be He, said unto them: Let it be as this one [says] and as that one" (*kedein u-kdein*—a play on the word *kadkod*).

And angels become more material. Every angel holds the measure of one-third of the world, so that when Jacob saw four angels he saw the size of the world and a third (*Bereshit Rabba* 88:17). He is half water and half fire and has five faces (*Shir ha-Shirim Rabba* 3:20). According to R. Samuel bar Nahman, angels, like men, need charity from one another.[23] And the angel is mortal. Moses wanted to slay *af* and *hemah* (Anger and Wrath), and some say that he actually killed *hemah* (*Nedarim* 32a). And here, too, there is certainly much that should not be taken literally.

On the other hand, there emerges a critical attitude toward the angel cult which, up to that time, had found a propitious climate. This tendency is noticeable in the statement of R. Yizhak Nappaha: "When God descended on Sinai there descended with Him groups of angels, Michael and his group, Gabriel and his group. Some of the nations selected Michael for themselves, others—Gabriel. But Israel selected God. They said, 'my portion is the Lord, said my soul' " (*Debarim Rabba* 2, end). And R. Judah taught: "When trouble comes upon man, let him not cry out to Michael, nor to Gabriel. Let him cry out to Me and I shall answer him at once; as it is said (Joel 3:5): 'Whosoever shall call on the name of the Lord shall be delivered' " (*Jer. Berakot* 13a; *Shoher Tob* 4:3). And R. Hanina bar Hama, with his consistently rationalistic approach, opposes the opinion that the heavens praise God and expresses himself sharply: it is the movement of the sun that constitutes its praise of God (*Shoḥer Tob* 19:5).

MAN

The consciousness of an evil inclination and the sense of sinfulness, which, along with pessimism, characterized the Tannaitic period following the crisis of the "four who entered," filled the whole Amoraic period. Rab and Samuel differ as to whether the evil inclination resembles a fly or a grain of wheat (*Berakot* 61a). R. Huna warns: "Come and see how serious are sins. Before a man sins all creators are afraid of him . . . afterwards he is afraid of them." [24] Many prayers were instituted, to be recited before sleep, after waking, or after other prayers, against the rule of the evil inclination, the fermenting passion, the "leaven in the dough." [25] There arose, therefore, the question, if man must ask for mercy that he sin not, where is the doctrine of R. Akiba, "and the permission is granted," or as it was formulated by the man of strict rationalism and Holiness, R. Hanina bar Ḥama: All is in the hand of Heaven, except fear of Heaven (*Berakot* 33b)? Indeed R. Ḥanina bar Ḥama already perceived that man has a point of attack by saying, "Thou hast created in us the evil inclination and the guilt is not ours" (*Berakot* 32a). Raba also thought that Job sought to exempt the whole world from judgment because God created the evil inclination; but He also created the Torah with which to season it (*Baba Batra* 16a). Nevertheless, if man has to pray against sin, his moral life is not his own.

The answer given to the problem of free will was: it is true that man is naturally weak and needs help from heaven in his struggle with evil, but there is a first step which is free and subject to choice. Afterwards, for the next steps, there is already help from on high. "Man defiles himself a little, and *they* let him defile himself much . . . man sanctifies himself a little, and *they* let him sanctify himself much" (*Yoma* 39a). "In the way that man chooses to walk, *they* lead him" (*Makkot* 10b). Resh Lakish says, if he comes to defile himself, they open the door to him; if he comes to cleanse himself, they help him (*Abodah Zarah* 55a). And R. Johanan says, man should always ask for mercy that they should strengthen his powers and that he may not have enemies on high (*Sanhedrin* 44b). So there is choice, but it is limited to the choice of the first step. Therefore, women should not say, we will not take our children to synagogue, because if their constellation indicates their being scholars they will be scholars anyway (*Jer Ḥallah* 52b). R. Jeremiah says, a man should not say

God will keep me away from sin,[26] because there is something that still depends on himself, namely, the beginning.

As in the close of the Tannaitic period, so now, and even to a greater degree, under the dominating consciousness of guilt, the *zaddiq*, or the righteous person, rises in esteem. True, the guilt-consciousness carries with it a sense of decline. "If the former generations were children of angels, then we are children of men, and if the former generations were children of men, then we are like asses" (*Shabbat* 112b, *Jer. Shekalim*, chapter 5, beginning). R. Johanan says, better the nail of the former generations than the belly of the new generations (*Yoma* 9b),[27] and R. Johanan follows his own principle, for in *Erubin* 53a he says, the heart of the former generations was like the entrance to the *Ulam* or the hall of the temple; of the latter generation, like the entrance to the temple; ours, like the hole of a needle. But there is in every generation a minimal number of *zaddiqim*, or righteous, upon whom the world stands.[28] According to R. Simon ben Jehozadak, this number is forty-five (*Hullin* 92a); according to R. Joshua ben Levi, it is thirty, as it is said, so shall be (*yiyeh* numerically equals thirty) thy seed. "When Israel is privileged there are eighteen in the land of Israel and twelve in the Diaspora" (*Shoher Tob* 5). Others agree with this opinion.[29] But Abbayye thinks: the world is never less than thirty-six *zaddiqim* that greet the Shekinah in every generation, for it is said, happy they who wait for Him (*Sanhedrin* 97b. Hebrew *lo*, which means for Him, equals thirty-six). And R. Johanan says, even for the sake of one *zaddiq* the world exists, as it is said, and the righteous is the foundation of the world (*Yoma* 38b).[30]

The Amoraim seem to vie with each other in an apotheosis of these righteous. Raba says if the righteous wanted they could create the world (*Sanhedrin* 65b). The righteous are destined to revive the dead (*Pesahim* 68b). God will place the compartment of the righteous inside of that of the ministering angels, and the ministering angels will inquire of them, what hath God wrought? What hath God taught you? (*Jer. Shabbat* 8d). Greater are the deeds of the righteous than the creation of heaven and earth (*Ketubot* 5a). R. Eleazar ben Pedat said the righteous are destined for a time when people will greet them with *kadosh*, holy, as they say before the Holy One, blessed be He (*Baba Batra* 75b). R. Johanan said the righteous are greater than the ministering angels (*Sanhedrin* 93a), and the time will come when the righteous will be called by the name of God (*Baba Batra* 75b). R. Phinehas bar Hama interprets Gen. 49:2, "and hearken *unto Israel* your father," *El* (God) is Israel your father; just as God creates worlds and destroys them, so your father creates worlds (*Bereshit Rabba* 98:4). So also believes R. Aḥa in the name of R. Eleazar. "Whence do we know that God called Jacob God, for it is said (Gen. 33:20) and he called it *El-elohe-Israel*" (*Megillah* 18:1), evidently reading: the God of Israel called him *El*, God. And R. Ḥannin thinks that Elijah never tasted the taste of death (*Bereshit Rabba* 21:5). All this shows the Glory-tendency of raising man nearer to divinity.

But in opposition to all these, the rationalists among the Amoraim kept strict guard of the border line between the above and the below. First among them is the consistent follower of Holiness, R. Ḥanina bar Ḥama, who, together with Resh Lakish, refused to take the expression "sons of God" in Gen. 6:2 ("and the sons of God saw the daughters of man that they were fair") in a mythological sense, but interpreted it to mean only that they lived long without pain and suffering (*Bereshit Rabba* 26:8). Then R. Hosha'iah told a tale, implicitly opposing the concept of man-God in Christian theology, that when God created Adam the ministering angels mistook him and wished to say before him Holy. What did God do? He cast upon him a slumber and all knew that he was man (*Bereshit Rabba* 8:9). R. Abbahu emphasized the *death* of Enoch, as against Christians who claimed we do not find that Enoch died (*ibid.*, 25:1);[31] and "if a man will tell thee, I am God, he lies; I am son of man, he shall regret it; I will rise to heaven, he will not fulfill it" (*Jer. Ta'anit* 65b).[32] R. Tanḥuma too emphasized the mortality of all men. "What man," he said, "is there like Moses who spoke with his creator face to face, and yet afterwards—Behold, thy days approach that thou must die" (*Debarim Rabba* 9:4). And according to R. Berechiah, Adam too was mortal from the start, and it is a false charge that he brought death into the world (*Tanḥuma Vayyesheb* 4).[33] And thus did Amoraic thought, in its critical stream, withdraw from all the apocalyptic literature of ascension.

With these three negations: the negation of attributes, the negation of intermediaries, and the negation of God-man, Jewish thought returned to its initial protest of Holiness; but this time its protest was directed not only against material monism, but also against dualism itself if internal distinctions are blurred. With these three negations, it arrived at the very heart of the discussions of the Middle Ages.

IN CONCLUSION

Greek philosophy begins with a quest for a single primordial element: water, air, or fire, and is willing to leave the rest to natural development. Hebraic thought leaves nothing to development, but keeps the divine being continuously at work until the first Sabbatical stars appear in the firmament and all is done.

For such a consciousness, it is natural that all its clashing thoughts should unfold over the relation that exists between its ever-present Object and itself. Two schools came into being: one sought to emphasize distance, the other longed for nearness; and it was around both schools, and under the strain of both pulls, that the elliptic curve of Hebraic thought was formed.

Of the two—the mystic longing for Glory and the rationalistic caution of Holiness—the first seems to have been more fruitful. Out of its vagueness, it projected glittering ideas of ascent and intermediation that played important parts on the stage of world philosophy and religion. Perhaps they needed a larger platform than that offered by their own birthplace to run their course and play themselves out. At any rate, Holiness always arrived and removed the ladders, leaving a sense of sinfulness and a feeling of a fall. The heart always knew when a new period came and the old circle closed.

Judaism then is not a religion of rest. It does not stretch out its arms: Come to me, ye weary ones, and find rest. It is not a desire for Nirvana. It is all tension. It is a field of soul-polarity. It is a deep experience and an endless going. It does not offer rest. Instead, it presents moral demands in which there is an idealistic longing for the impossible which is nevertheless a duty, as in the religious experience: Be ye holy, for I am holy. It is a divine morality imposed upon a human creature, the infinite pressed into the finite.

PHILOSOPHY OF BIBLICAL ETHICS

part II

SOURCE AND SANCTION

The Hebrew people, as it entered
its prophetic period, appeared like Socrates on the historic scene. That
great Athenian lived at a time when Homeric fatalism still reigned,
one generation transmitting to another the burden of its destiny, and
when philosophy was a chaos of relativistic sophism, crystalized by
Protagoras in his maxim: Man (i.e., the individual) is the measure
of all things. So, all truth is subjective; there is no absolute truth,
even in morals. In reaction to this, Socrates first turned the axis of
thought away from fruitless and uncertain speculations about the
physical origin of the world to moral questions, which alone touch
human life. Secondly, he sought some solid foundation of universal
truth for an ethical system to inspire man with certainty, dignity, and
freedom. Similarly, the Hebrew people began its historic work because
there were arbitrary deities—and divine arbitrariness and veiled fatalism
have the same dark effect on man—and because there had reached
man only unsure and inconsistent voices as to the whereabouts of the
right path. He knew he had to do something; he must find grace in
someone's eyes in heaven, or be the target of empyreal thunderbolts.
But what exactly do those above desire? To ascertain this, there were
moral laws given by the gods. Watching over the universal order,
there was, for example, Shamash, the sun-god of the Babylonian world,
who gave Hammurabi a code of laws, and Sin, the moon-god. Some
gods were even designated by ethical names such as law and righteous-

ness. Also, in the Western-Semitic world, there was a god named Zedeq (righteousness), as is shown by the names Melchizedek (Gen. 14:18; Ps. 110:4) and Adonizedek (Josh. 10:1). But these moral laws had no absolute validity, no unqualified bindingness, for the gods themselves practiced deceit and treachery.[1] It was against this background that the Hebrew people proclaimed not only a moral absolute which was equally binding upon heaven and earth, but also man's moral freedom and stature. And the question that arises is: How did they arrive at this sovereign morality which inflamed their lives with such a prophetic passion?

There are some who think that the first steps of Hebraic thought were a movement from monotheism to ethics. First, the Jew attained to the idea of divine oneness; and, as there are both good and evil in the world, one must conclude that the good comes from God and the evil comes as a punishment for sin—and hence, ethical monotheism. But this hardly explains the dominant moral passion of the Bible. In fact, we saw that other gods also propounded moral laws, yet lacked that emphasis. There were also other ancient peoples who had arrived at monotheism, a kind of idolatrous, i.e., physical, monotheism, such as that of Amenhotep IV in fourteenth-century Egypt, but they did not attain to such pan-ethicism. Moreover, why assume that the good is from God and the evil is punishment? Perhaps both come from God arbitrarily? Doesn't this assumption introduce an element of absolute goodness in God not warranted by His oneness, so that it is a clear case of begging the question? Therefore, there seem to have been other factors operative in the formation of ancient Hebrew thinking. Some think that the desert played its part, the outer monotony diverting attention to inner speculation. Others think that the economic stress of living in the wilderness forced its inhabitants to unite, thus developing their social thinking.[2] But this view, too, is doubtful because there were other ethnic groups that roamed the Arabian and other deserts. Why did not they attain to the concept of absolute moralism?

On the basis of the original Hebraic protest, suggested in the first part of this work, another explanation presents itself. We pointed to the fact that the biblical stress is not on the numerical oneness of God, but on his qualitative uniqueness, on his transcendence, on his being above and beyond any shape or image ("You have seen no image"), and that the gravest sin, deserving the direst punishment, is that of making a statue or a molten image. This means that the emphasis was, and in fact continued to be in talmudic thought, on the immateriality and metaphysicality of God. This was true also, in a more rationalistic form, among medieval Jews, Christians, and Moslems, in so far as they were all biblically inspired. Now this concept, this Hebraic protest, initially was only negative: no image! But the concept demanded also some positive, although metaphysical, meaning: "Show me thy glory," or "What is his name? What shall I tell them?" And the concept responded to the need—"I will cause all my *goodness* to pass before thee" (Exod. 33:19) and "Lord, Lord, God merciful and gracious" (Exod. 34:6)—with positive attributes, almost all denoting mercy. God, then, is goodness, even as several centuries later Plato names him *agathos*—the good—a term that is not as organic to the rest of Plato's philosophy as it is here to the Bible, where it is the heart and soul of all the laws and of the entire national chronicle.

This conception of God as good and merciful, i.e., as ethical, was also formed by powerful and searing early memories, historical or semi-historical, of the bondage in Egypt. This experience so deeply engraved itself on the national consciousness that it left its impress on feasts and seasons, on the very opening of the Ten Commandments which are Judaism in miniature, and on many primary ethical laws: "And you shall love the stranger for you were strangers in the land of Egypt" (Deut. 10:19). Out of the misty past of the people there resounded throughout the Bible the outcry of Israel in Egypt—an outcry for mercy and redemption which helped to form the *positive* aspect of God as mercy and justice, God as ethics. And it is noteworthy that all through the Bible the human or national outcry is as if magically connected with the stirring of heavenly mercy. Thus two factors shaped biblical theology: a metaphysical protest and an historic experience. The first is Holiness; the second is Glory.

Looking at the wider scene, we may discern in man's approach to God three different dimensions of the God-concept: all-powerful, all-knowing, and all-righteous, or power, wisdom, and ethics. Each people has its own characteristic approach to the absolute, and that approach dominates perhaps the development of each people's thinking and history. Islam took the approach of power, so that its orthodoxy fought against the rationalistic *mutazilah* and was ready to ascribe to God even the power of the absurd, like turning yesterday into tomorrow and violating processes of arithmetic, in order to avoid any limitation of God's ability. Greek philosophy leaned to the idea that God is all reason, so that he becomes only a self-thinking thought, a thinker and a thinking and a thought all in one, taking no interest in human life at all. But Judaism took the absolutely ethical approach: "Shall not the judge of all the earth do justice?" (Gen. 18:25); hence, king as well as peasant must bend to justice: "Thou art the man!" (II Sam. 12:7). It is true that Job (and Ecclesiastes) dared to question the third dimension. He accepted the infinite power and also the wisdom of God, but His morality he saw no trace of in his suffering. But God appeared in the storm, unrolling some truly majestical poems of nature, and Job knelt: "I have spoken and understood not; things too wonderful for me which I knew not" (Job 42:3), and the dimension remained with all its intensity.

Hence, the course of early Hebrew thinking was not from monotheism to ethics, but just the reverse, from ethics to monotheism. It is not that God is one and therefore ethical, but ethical—the absolutely ethical—and therefore one, for two kinds of morality would constitute relativity. And, furthermore, because the God of Israel was conceived, as we have seen, with no other characteristics, attributes, or being but morality, but goodness, we may form a two-way proposition: God is ethics, and ethics—as an abstract absolute—is God. Indeed, in many places in the Pentateuch, as in Lev. 19, where one ethical imperative after another ends with the words, "I am the Lord," we seem to catch the voice of the moral command itself proclaiming: I am the Lord, I am the Lord.[3] Thus the concept of God moves out of the ontic into the axiological realm, into that of values; or better, He mysteriously unites in his divinity the two worlds: being and value. This is reminiscent of the profound saying of Euclid of Megara that the Socratic goodness is the Being which Parmenides posited as the foundation of the world. Such a thought is not a stranger to later Jewish speculation, for the cabala identified concepts from the realm of values, such as loving-kindness, power, and beauty, with spheres of Being. And when God appeared to Moses, saying: "I have surely seen the affliction of my people which are in Egypt and have heard their cry by reason of their taskmasters; for I know their sorrows" (Gen. 3:7), he revealed himself as I AM, that is, the Being of God, his ontic meaning, is his hearing of the cry, is his goodness, his axiological being. The difference between the biblical thought and that of Euclid of Megara is that according to the latter goodness is an axiological *immanent* being, whereas in the Bible, it is still a transcendent being, goodness that is nothing else but goodness and yet *is*. And we should note here that this concept of God as abstract morality, as pure ethicalness, as that mystery of contradiction involved in an identity of value with being, constitutes the core of biblical ethics and contains an answer to many problems and difficulties.

There is, however, a great difference between the biblical God-concept and the *agathos* which is the highest idea in the Platonic system. *Agathos* exists for itself, sheds light out of itself upon itself, and is entirely passive with reference to the world, for, as stated in the beginning of this work, the elements of work and doing never entered into Greek theological meditation. The Greeks were ashamed of doing, so that in the frame of Hebraic activistic thinking, one cannot regard *agathos* as a god at all. But the Hebraic God creates and does all; in all his nature he is interested and involved in all human doings, as he is absolute morality. He knocks, in a manner not found in any other literature, on all the windows of man: know me, recognize me, admit me! Why is he so interested to be known? Now it is clear. The transcendentally ethical longs by his very nature to clothe himself in human acts and relations because these constitute his concrete existence and meaning. It is out of this divine longing for reality that the various parts of doctrinal theology flow, for such a God must create a world to serve as a field of operation for his ethical-ness. So, from God's standpoint, he is *eternally* a creator of time. And he must reveal himself, because without a Mount Sinai, the sun is blind, i.e., without beams. And he is always provident and watchful; unlike the Platonic *agathos* and Aristotle's pure Form, he is a "God of seeing" (Gen. 16:13). Hence, God has a necessary function in the life of man. He is not an intruder into our little world, making laws for us to obey. He is invited by our suffering. The outcry calls into the I AM. His laws of mercy and goodness are our quest and our own legislation. Man needs God who needs man. Otherwise, the God of Israel would have long flown away and vanished in the wide heavens of metaphysics. Perhaps this is what happened to Buddhism. Man and God are tied to each other unto eternity. "Thou hast avouched the Lord this day . . . and the Lord has avouched thee" (Deut. 26:17-18). The ethical absolute is therefore both transcendent and immanent, so that the two schools of biblical thought, Holiness and Glory, here coalesce and are one.

This being the nature of God, how does man communicate with him to know his will? How does man know what is ethical? It is not through intellectual cognition, as Socrates and later Greek philosophers taught. This intellectualism, as we shall see, is not Judaism. "I am the Lord" is the voice of the categorical imperative itself on all the highest heights of biblical ethics. There is, therefore, another knowledge which is supersensual and superrational, a special moral knowledge, a metaphysical self-identification. But in order to understand this, we must for a moment look into the psychology of ethics, into the meaning of the self, the subjective self, without which there is no moral responsibility, no intention or obligation.

Inscribed over the gate of the Delphic oracle was the command which Socrates emphasized with his entire personality: "Know thyself." And over the gate of Judaism was inscribed: "Know the God of thy father" (I Chron. 28:9), "In all thy ways know Him" (Ps. 3:6). And both commands are unachievable. How can we know our personal self, the I, which is the *subject* of our thinking, when thinking, by its very process, turns it into an object, so the I vanishes at the very moment of our thinking, becoming a me? The snake turns into a staff as soon as you touch its tail. It is possible that Descartes too failed in his proof, "I think, therefore I am," because the "I think" in the moment of self-consciousness becomes a "methinks." The subject becomes an object, which can therefore in Descartes' moment of general doubt be an illusion, but never the "I AM," which is the subject of thought and the quest of the proof. It seems then that there is no way to circumvent the object and to arrive at his back again, the I, except in the ethical moment, in the struggle between two ways of action, when we take a stand: This is the way, and thus I act, and for all the consequences of this act I, and I alone, am responsible. Or in the soul-shaking moment of regret, when the deed is done, and you roll in the dust: Woe to you, miserable I, that you locked against yourself all the gates of heaven and chose to wallow among the cattle. Only in such a moral moment, in the assumption of the heavy yoke of responsibility, is there contact with the I: Thus I *act*, and therefore I am. But there is still another question: Why does the I act thus and not otherwise? What is the cause and source of confidence of my action or decision? Let us turn to the second command, to know God. And again—how? For God is conceivable only as the I AM, the subject of the world, while intellectual cognition leads to an object, the object of the cognition, but by no means to an I. And the answer is, and now in all its fulness, through a moral-metaphysical act, through a juncture of the Delphic self with the biblical I AM, who is sheer Ethics. For knowledge, as Hebraically conceived, as is shown by its meaning in the Hebrew language, is not merely a mental going forth of a subject to an object, but a whole-souled *union* of subject with subject. And hence "Knowledge of God," which in the Bible means ethical knowledge, is a union of the human I with the divine I, so that for the space of a moment man becomes God and gives unto himself moral laws. Only such suprarational or extrarational knowledge provides the metaphysical self-identification implied in the passages: "And ye shall be like unto God knowing good and evil," "Behold man has become like one of us knowing good and evil," and in the words of all prophets: "Thus said the Lord." And only this moral-metaphysical self-identification, as God is ethics itself, provides us with that Kantian autonomy, morality for the sake of morality, which alone constitutes a moral act, for it never moves out of the ethical sphere and therefore ceases to be obedience and becomes self-legislation. Thus the moral choice is a mystic union expressible in the formula I-I, and it leaves, like all mystic experiences, a strangely happy feeling in its wake. It is a feeling of conquest of separation and aloneness, and it constitutes a return to primeval oneness with the All.

There is then a basic difference between psychological self-searching and an ethical experience. When I observe myself, my self, psychologically, I become an object to myself, losing my self under the very beam of self-inspection, and the effort fails. Ethically, however, I join the cosmic I, forming an I-I, so that I am again my subject, only with wider reaches and metaphysical implications. I become my own moral legislator, for it is only a free self that can legislate moral laws, but all objects are bound and determined by the thinking object. Hence, the moral self is the religious self, a conscious spark of a great flame: Thus said the Lord. The moment of ethical crisis is therefore a mystical experience.

Already a gulf opens up between Israel and Greece, the gulf of Greek intellectualism. According to Socrates, the source of morality is knowledge. To know the good is to do the good, for the moral good only means that it is good for us, and no one harms himself out of his own free will. When evil occurs, it can only be an error in judgment, like an error in arithmetic or in geometry. Yehudah Halevi in his *Kuzari* clearly discerns and criticizes this intellectualistic approach, concluding with a triumphant outcry: See the difference between the God of Abraham and the God of Aristotle! Plato did see the turmoil of passions of the human body, but even he could not free himself from the Socratic view; hence, he construed the moral struggle to be between passion and intellect and invited philosophers to be the rulers. Aristotle, who already opposed the Socratic principle, nevertheless entrusted the intellect with the fixation of the mean, wherein alone lies virtue. As for the Stoics, the moral is only the intellect determining itself theoretically and practically; and nature is all reason, so that obedience to nature is morality. Thus, according to all these thinkers, there is no morality as a special precinct for action and decision, and there is no room for contrition and shame, for self-purification and elevation. It is all a mistake in calculus, and one should take better care in the future.

Over against this there is the biblical view, which is somewhat as follows. At first only God knew good and evil, and the mind which was given to man to rule therewith over "the fish of the sea and the fowl of heaven and the cattle and over all the earth," the scientific mind, was inadequate to attain to moral discernments,[4] for moral cognition is "the knowledge of God," seeing through God, seeing morality through Morality, and is therefore autonomous. And, evil is not a blunder but a disturbance of all worlds, which deprives divine ethicalness of existence or concreteness. This is the metaphysical meaning of morality and the secret of the ethical flame in the Bible. And this kind of cognition, the identification of I-I, or, as we have said, the ability to see morality through Morality, was at first withheld from man. He only had to hear and obey.

But for better or worse, it was just that divine forbidden secret that man strove to attain, because he wanted to be like God, he wanted to be God. This is implied in the very first story of man, that of the Tree of Knowledge, as a vision of wish fulfillment in the concept of God's image, and in the chapters of the fallen angels and the Tower of Babel. Sartre is right: "Man is a being that strives to be God," and again "He is mainly a will to be God." [5] All the opening chapters of Genesis are a confirmation of this view. While in the Greek myth there is the motif of the gods' jealously of man, here, in the story of Genesis, the motif is man's jealousy of God. God is the start and datum; and man, like Prometheus, plucked the heavenly secret, swallowed it, and became like God. Then the Hebrew drama of man against God began, consisting of one catastrophic episode after another, until God Himself, who had just seen that all he had made was very good, realized that there was a stubborn wickedness and an evil instinct in the heart of man (Gen. 6:5; 8:21; Deut. 31:21). Thus an unforeseen element was discovered, the instinct, and the moral experience was now conceived as a struggle, pitiably frail and therefore deserving patience in heaven, in which, the instinct disrupts the I-1.

Kant posited the concept of practical reason, i.e., the moral will, and Fichte emphasized that there is a knowledge that comes, unaided by reason, out of the will which morally directs man; and in this, they were both nearer to biblical Judaism than to Hellenism.

We tried to show that the biblical God-concept is a purely moral concept, that moral choice is not identical with reason but with the "I am the Lord," the voice of a metaphysical ethicalness, a categorical command not dependent upon reason or any goal beyond it. Therefore, biblical morality is autonomous; it exists for its own sake; it is morality seen through Morality, which is God.

To be sure there are many passages that do mention reward and punishment. Indeed, the prophets based all their previsions concerning men and nations on what we called moral causality or the inescapable chain of crime and punishment. But this does not contradict the principle of ethics as the voice of the ethical Absolute. Surely there are consequences in accordance with the moral nature of the deed, but the deed must be done for its own sake.[6] Perhaps this will explain why the Bible does not emphasize individual rewards, but rather those of the group, like rain in its due season. The collective personality is a collective product and may therefore receive reward, but the individual is the ethical *subject* and must therefore aim at morality itself in order for his act to be purely moral. Kant himself believed in the triumph and final justification of the moral order and therefore postulated the existence of God as a guarantee, but the act itself must not aim at triumph. And even the Book of Proverbs, which frequently holds forth material reward, repudiates intellectualism and utilitarianism and warns us: "Trust in the Lord with all thine heart; and lean not unto thine own understanding." Not the intellect, which always asks why and to what end, questions entirely heteronomous, is the moral guide, but the voice within the heart which is, in the moment of mystical identification, truly a divine voice. This is the thought that runs like a thread through all the sapiential literature. In passages where the fear of the Lord is the beginning of wisdom or knowledge and is the very essence of wisdom (Ps. 101:10; Prov. 1:7; 9:10; 15:33; Job 28:28) knowledge and wisdom refer to ethics; and the fear of the Lord, the absolute Ethicalness, is the only motif, the voice above that speaks within, the transcendent-immanent.

Here then is an answer to scholars [7] who think that biblical ethics is heteronomous, based on obedience and therefore only religious, and the opposite of Greek and modern philosophy where ethics is based on human reason and therefore autonomous. The reverse is true. It is just the identification of morals with reason that deprives them of autonomy. Witness Greek ethics which is entirely intellectualistic and endaemonistic, a quest of happiness as the starting point and direction for the quest of the good. Intellectualism also deprives morals of metaphysical breadth and that deep lyricism which the soul enjoys during its struggle and decision, and makes the doing of evil a mere blunder. Furthermore, biblical obedience is not directed to an external but to an inner voice, the transcendent-immanent voice of the I-I, and is therefore autonomous. Again in this biblical conception of obedience, we catch the tension of Holiness and Glory.

What then is the source and sanction of biblical ethics? Not the dictates of reason in quest of happiness, but the hearing of the "I am the Lord" in the voice of the categorical imperative, an intuitive knowledge of the good as a self-revelation and concretization of the Absolute Good, a correlation of the individual deed with the Infinite which thus confers upon the deed and upon man metaphysical implications. Is biblical ethics then religious, or, if counterpoint it be, autonomous? Certainly religious, because it springs from God and in its effectiveness returns unto Him; but since God Himself is conceived as value-being, that is, in no other terms than pure ethicalness, the source and sanction operates within the ethical sphere and is therefore internal, autonomous.[8]

And in every moral moment, in every struggle which ends in moral decision, the stature of man reaches the heavens, and the first dream, to be like God, to be God, comes to fulfillment. "Behold man has become like one of us." He becomes a subject; and, through his union with the subject of all being, it is he himself that legislates in pure freedom his moral laws and confers upon divinity concreteness and existence.

STATIONS ON THE WAY

We have seen that Hebraic thought, under the influence of the Holiness tendency to lift the deity above all contact and description, found no positive content for the God-concept other than abstract ethicalness, so that the supreme being is the supreme value. Ontology and axiology are identical in the flame of their Hebraic origin. A contributing factor to this ethical conception was the early experience of the Israelites in Egypt, that outcry which pierced the heavens and stamped itself on the laws and festivals of that people and on the very opening of the decalogue itself. The unjust suffering discovered a deity which is all justice and the protector of the persecuted. It was not fear which made the gods—it certainly did not shape the image of the Hebraic God—but injustice; man cried out because he was oppressed and persecuted. The antithesis below created the thesis above.

We have also seen that in the moment of choice and decision man identifies himself with the absolute morality which is the divine being. He hears the voice of his spirit and feels with all his might that this is the voice of the Absolute. Hence the finality of decision and the authoritativeness of a moral step. This identification we have called I-I. No relativistic intellect, and no motive or calculus, prevails at that moment. There is an atmosphere of pure and autonomous morality, emanating from a contact of Glory and a mutual, miraculous approaching of man and God. Hence, after a moral choice, the feeling

of deep satisfaction lingers, similar to the elation experienced in that
moment when immersed in a higher purity. Thus, the two fundamental tendencies combine in the moral moment: Holiness pushes ever
upward, and Glory creates an exalted sense of contact, of achievement.

The restlessness and dynamism found in biblical ethics are what
distinguish it from Greek ethics—the ever going forward, the feeling
that I have not yet arrived, that the way is yet long from the I to the I.
It is an infinitely idealistic ethics, full of tension and drama, even like
the theology of this people. This becomes clear wherever we turn in
the realm of biblical ethics, and especially in the consideration of the
cardinal virtues: justice, mercy, love, and holiness—four concepts that
indicate rungs in a spiritual ladder, or stations on the road, clearly
distinguishable from their parallels in Greek thought, the four cardinal
platonic virtues.

JUSTICE

God is justice. "Justice and judgment are the habitations of thy
throne" (Ps. 89:14). "Righteousness and judgment are the habitation
of his throne" (Ps. 97:2). Justice is called the way of God: "And they
shall keep the way of the Lord, to do justice and judgment" (Gen.
18:19). Man could not see—and Holiness did not let him see—the
One on the throne, only the throne, not Him Who walks on the way,
only the way, until the way became identified with God, and the
throne with the Sitter thereon; and justice was kindled into a flame
as in no other people: "The Lord our righteousness" (Jer. 23:6;
33:16).

This identification of justice with God necessarily projected
God's infinity also on the concept of justice, removing justice from
the category of relativity, since God is the exact antipodes of relativity,
and giving it objective significance. Justice is that which is inherently
just. It dwells in the depth of the deed itself, without regard to the
persons between whom this relation obtains. It is an algebraic equation, and one may substitute X and Y for the proper names without
affecting the equation. This indeed constitutes the majesty of justice:
it is abstract and absolute, and the subject is in back of the just deed,
not ethically in the deed itself. Boaz may or may not be present in the
field; the poor women go and glean after the reapers. Hence, justice is
an abstract and absolute relation between *one object and another*.
This is the first step on the moral road, and it already indicates the
divine sovereignty of morality. Thus, out of this identification of
justice with the Absolute, there emanate two great principles: (1) jus-

tice is due all men, and (2) justice *concerns* all men. The first principle is extensive; the second, intensive.

Biblical justice is extensive or universal in that it knows no economic, social, or political barriers, and sees on all human faces the image of God, so that, as bearer of this image, no man is more human than another. That is why, according to Ben Azzai, the verse in Gen. 5:1: "This is the book of the generations of man . . . in the likeness of God made He him" is a greater principle even than "And thou shalt love thy neighbor as thyself," cited by R. Akiba as the great principle in the law.[1] There is something greater than to love your neighbor and that is to think him God-like. Nor does it seem that R. Akiba really differs with Ben Azzai, for he himself teaches that "man is beloved in being created in the image." [2] This explains the care taken throughout the Bible for the poor, the orphan, and the widow that they be not crushed under the heavy wheels of life, and the existence of the seven agrarian laws designated as gifts to the poor: gleaning, i.e., ears of corn fallen from the hand of the gleaner, forgotten sheaves in the field, corners of the fields, grapes left on the vines, grapes fallen from the gleaner, the tithe every third year, and all that grows of itself during the Sabbatical year, in addition to other social legislation which, for example, prohibited a man's selling himself for all his life because of poverty, losing forever one's heritage, and exacting interest on loans. And the object of care became the object of affection, and the word "poor" became synonymous with humble and just to such an extent that sometimes a halo of divinity appears to surround the head of the poor.[3] There arose, therefore, a danger of a distortion of justice in favor of the poor, and we have the strange and revealing command: "Neither shalt thou countenance a poor man in his cause" (Exod. 23:33), and "Thou shalt not respect the person of the poor, nor honor the person of the great" (Lev. 19:15)—the poor becoming equal with the great as possible objects of favoritism.

Justice also seeks to protect the alien, who perhaps has no relative or friend to defend him. "One law shall be to him that is home-born, and unto the stranger that sojourneth among you" (Exod. 12:49). One should note particularly the deeply humane feelings behind such verses as "Thou shalt neither vex a stranger nor oppress him: for ye were strangers in the land of Egypt" (Exod. 22:21). "Also thou shalt not oppress a stranger: for ye know the heart of a stranger, seeing ye were strangers in the land of Egypt" (Exod. 23:9). A natural development might have been the opposite course, a hatred for Egypt and for all aliens; yet the Bible was concerned that those humane promptings that came during the suffering should endure after it, demanding even what seems to be above human capacity: "And thou shalt *love* him as thyself; for ye were strangers in the land of Egypt" (Lev. 19:34). Hermann Cohen thinks that in this attitude toward the alien man discovered the concept of humanity, that which transcends political borders; but this attitude is directly connected with the identification that lies at the basis of biblical ethics: I-I. The Supreme Ethicalness must be infinite because it has no other attributes which could by their separate being delimit it. Hence, the ethical ideal cannot be other than without limits and borders. Hebrew justice is necessarily universal.

The same humane attitude is evinced toward slavery. The Code of Hammurabi (paragraph 199) imposes a penalty on one who smites the eye or the tooth of *someone else's servant*, because the servant is conceived as property,[4] but in the Bible we read: "And if a man smite the eye of *his servant*, or the eye of his maid, that it perish; he shall let him go free for his eye's sake. And if he smite out his manservant's tooth, or his maidservant's tooth; he shall let him go free for his tooth's sake" (Exod. 21:26-27), because he is conceived as a person.[5] We therefore have the law, of which it took the world thousands of years to take notice: "Thou shalt not deliver unto his master the servant which is escaped from his master unto thee. He shall dwell with thee, even among you, in that place which he shall choose in one of thy gates, where it liketh him best: thou shalt not oppress him" (Deut. 23:15-16), and as an echo of it, Prov. 30:10: "Slander not a servant unto his master, lest he curse thee and thou be found guilty" [6]—all this as distinguished from the Code of Hammurabi (paragraph 16): "He who hides an escaping servant must be put to death." And there is an apparent contempt in the Bible for the servant who bends his back and begs: "I love my master . . . I will not go out free" (Exod. 21:5-6).

And in general, biblical justice tolerates no economic or social verticality: "And the loftiness of man shall be bowed down" (Isa. 2:13). It is a universalism that also embraces international relations, if alas not yet in reality, then in vision: "Nation shall not lift up sword against nation" (Isa. 2:4; Mic. 4:3). "In that day shall Israel be the third with Egypt and with Assyria, even a blessing in the midst of the land: Whom the Lord of hosts shall bless, saying, Blessed be Egypt my people, and Assyria the work of my hands, and Israel mine inheritance" (Isa. 19:24-25). "Neither let the son of the stranger, that hath joined himself to the Lord, speak saying, The Lord hath utterly separated me from his people . . . for mine house shall be called a house of prayer for all people" (Isa. 56:3-7). In a similar vein Solomon speaks in his prayer at the inauguration of the Temple in I Kings 8:41-43, and Zephaniah in his vision in chapter 3:9. The Book of Jonah is entirely witness to this moral universality. Indeed, the whole biblical conception of the beginnings of Israel was instrumentalistic; for after the successive human falls, as told in the first eleven chapters of Genesis, from the high level of "Behold it is very good," God began to search for a light for the nations, a whole people to be the guide, and he chose Abraham for this universal, Messianic aim. This may be the meaning of Isa. 42:21, namely, that God wished for the sake of *His* own triumph that *Israel* shall magnify the law in the world. All this springs necessarily from the infinity of God, who is conceived only in terms of justice, so that justice itself is infinite, boundless, all-human.

Biblical justice is also infinite from the standpoint of intensity. In the first place, it is concerned not only with action, but also with thoughts and feelings behind and prior to the actions. It reaches down to the depths of man and demands pure springs. Some deny this, thinking that biblical ethics is entirely external, that it knows only manifest sins, but not those hiding inside of man, and that even the tenth commandment, "Thou shalt not covet," which is apparently all a matter of the heart, is to be understood as "Thou shalt not try to obtain," as a caution against an act. See the views discussed by Th. C. Vriezen in his *An Outline of Old Testament Theology*, pp. 330 ff. But the following citations will suffice to prove the opposite:

"Thou shalt not hate thy brother in thine heart" (Lev. 19:17).

"Forasmuch as this people drew near me with their mouth, and with their lips do honor me, but have removed their heart from me, and their fear toward me is taught by the precept of man" (Isa. 29:13).

"Let the wicked forsake his way, and the unrighteous man his thoughts" (Isa. 55:7).

"And let none of you imagine evil against his brother in your heart" (Zech. 7:10).

"And let none of you imagine evil in your hearts against his neighbor" (Zech. 8:17).

"The fool hath said in his heart, there is no God" (Ps. 14:1; 53:2).

"Lord, who shall abide in thy tabernacle? Who shall dwell in thy holy hill? He that walketh uprightly, and worketh righteousness, and speaketh truth in his heart" (Ps. 15:1-2).

"Who shall ascend into the hill of the Lord? Or who shall stand in his holy place? He that hath clean hands and a pure heart, who hath not lifted up his soul with vanity" (Ps. 24:3-4).

"Behold, thou desireth truth in the inward parts: and in the hidden part thou shalt make me to know wisdom" (Ps. 51:6).

"Create in me a clean heart, O God; and renew a right spirit within me" (Ps. 51:10).

"The sacrifices of God are a broken spirit: a broken and a contrite heart, O God, thou will not despise" (Ps. 51:17).

"A forward heart shall depart from me . . . him that hath an high look and a proud heart will not I suffer" (Ps. 101:4-5).

Vriezen himself seeks a compromise. Biblical morality is concerned with man's disposition, but there are no "sins of thought," as apart from the sinfulness of the act. "By the act the sin becomes manifest, and the command is transgressed." There are no sins of thought, because "something abstract and spiritual does not exist in Hebraic thought." He also distinguishes between sins of thought and sins of the heart. But there are difficulties in this view. First, in biblical psychology, sins of thought and sins of the heart can only be the same thing, for the heart is the seat of thoughts. Secondly, if the Bible speaks so fervently of a pure heart, there must be the vivid fear of an impure heart or sins of thought. These obviously cannot be included among transgressions punishable by law, but the repeated commands against them makes them inherently sinful. Any interpretation to the contrary goes unnecessarily against the text. Thirdly, one may take issue, as some do, with an extreme position that "something abstract and spiritual does not exist in Hebraic thought," when the constant and vehement protest against any image hardly sustains it; but this question will be discussed in later chapters. Our conclusion must be, therefore, that biblical ethics is also deeply spiritual, seeking a pure heart and inner truth.

But the infinite intensity expresses itself mainly in the glow of its passion for justice and in its recoil from misdeeds occurring anywhere in the world. It is worthwhile here to cast a glance at Greek thought. There too God is *agathos*, good, but cold and passive. Man strives to be like him, but no promptings come from above.[7] God is not an efficient, but a final, cause. He moves the world only as an ideal inspires imitation or longing. In the Bible, however, divine justice is active and infinitely concerned in human life. "For the Lord thy God is a consuming fire, even a jealous God" (Deut. 4:29). We may call it the principle of involvement, meaning that God is Himself involved in what man does below—a principle which, as we shall see, touches the very heart of biblical ethics, and which is opposed, as emphasized in various places in the Bible,[8] to the deistic view, *creavit et abiit*, He created and walked off. This is the idea of divine jealousy, which the Bible stresses and which many failed to understand and even scorned without discerning its moral truth. Infinite justice, serving as a pattern for human striving, must be what it is, without compromises and retreats, because it is infinite. What assurances were there in the world were it not for ethical logic somewhere in the universe? But the whole essence of God in the Bible, of this consuming fire that is His goodness, inevitably requires a world as a field of operation for His being. Hence, there appears the biblical phenomenon, unique in world literature, that God implores times without number: Be wise and know me, that He so continuously knocks on the windows of the world and the human soul, seeking to enter.[9] Also, He desires a sanctuary below: "That I may dwell among them" (Exod. 25:8). "And I will dwell among the children of Israel, and will be their God" (Exod. 29:45). "And I will dwell in the midst of them forever" (Ezek. 43:9). The great Nought [10] needs man for the existence and the advancement of His ethical essence, so that human justice is a divine event, and human history turns into a theogony. Every good deed is a "sanctification of the name," and advancement of His becoming, and every evil deed is a "profanation of the name," a retardation of His becoming, or, as R. Akiba expressed it, a diminution of the Image (*Bereshit Rabba* 34:20). You must, therefore, be concerned in justice; you must feel *involved* in it with all your being, not only when the matter touches you directly, when you stand in the center, but also when it does not touch you directly, when somewhere outside of your sphere a crime is committed, a deceit or treachery occurs. In the ethical universe you are always in the center, and everything concerns you. As classical examples of this moral sensitivity and involvement, one thinks of Moses ("Wherefore smitest thou thy fellow?"), Phinehas, and Elijah.

It follows that there is collective responsibility for the maintenance of the good, for all are concerned in the continuance of the Divine Presence, in the moral advancement toward the ideal. Jeremiah and Ezekiel did not deny collective *responsibility*, but collective punishment. "Every one shall die for his own iniquity" (Jer. 31:30). "The soul that sinneth it shall die" (Ezek. 18:4). Similarly, Deut.

24:16: "Every man shall be put to death for his own sin." But Ezekiel himself warned: "Son of man, I have made thee a watchman unto the house of Israel . . . when I say unto the wicked, Thou shalt surely die; and thou givest him not warning . . . the same wicked man shall die in his iniquity; but his blood will I require at thine hand . . . yet if thou warn the wicked, and he turn not from his wickedness . . . he shall die in his iniquity; but thou hast delivered thy soul" (Ezek. 3:17 ff.). This means the existence of group responsibility. Therefore, "Thou shalt in any wise rebuke thy neighbor, and not suffer sin upon him" (Lev. 19:17), and "Rebuke a wise man, and he will love thee" (Prov. 9:8). And if a man runs after another to slay him, you are in duty bound to jump into the situation and save the pursued one, even if you have to kill the pursuer, even as it says: "Neither shalt thou stand against the blood of thy neighbor: I am the Lord" (Lev. 19:16; see also *Sifra ad loc.*, and *Sanhedrin* 73a). And the whole biblical section about the beheaded heifer (Deut. 21:1-9) is intended to emphasize this principle of collective responsibility: The entire city must see itself in the shadow of guilt when a slain person is found in a neighboring field. It is in this respect that Moses reveals his deepest characteristic, by his moral outcry re-echoing throughout all ages: "Wicked one, why dost thou smite?" This is the principle of involvement or the moral "jealousy" on the human side, that whatever man does anywhere is ultimately of concern to you, for justice is God, and God is that which is of concern to your deepest depths. Therefore, the prophets delivered their "burdens" concerning foreign countries as well, for the whole world is morally one personality, one unitary and integral field of operation for the Absolute Ethicalness, and Jeremiah wailed: "Woe is me, my mother, that thou hast borne me a man of strife and a man of contention to the whole earth" (Jer. 15:10). But such is the lot and destiny of every ethical man; he is ethically implicated in all things.

Let us again cast a glance at the Greek world. From the extensive standpoint, we miss there the sense of equality and infinity. There the ideal society, as in the social visions of Plato and Aristotle, is a pyramid cut widthwise—as in the physiological division into head, heart, and liver—into rulers, soldiers, and workmen. The state cares for the education and the well-being of the two higher classes and leaves for the broad base, which is the lowest class, only one task: to work and provide the material needs of the state. The philosophers, it is true, spoke of equality, yet not of arithmetic equality (one is like another), but of the geometric kind (to every man according to his position), so that we have again relativity. And from the intensive standpoint, we have seen that the Greek philosophical god is self-centered and indifferent to human acts, unlike the biblical concept of "a consuming fire, even a jealous God."

More penetrating, however, is the difference in the understanding of the term "justice" itself. In Plato, it means only a harmony of the three human faculties: wisdom, will, and passions, so that one faculty does not grow at the expense of another. This is similar to his concept of geometric equality or the social contract of Thomas Hobbes. Justice, therefore, is not a certain attitude toward someone else, but toward oneself; and it is not really an ethical, but an esthetic or political term in the sphere of psychology. The same is true of political justice because it too is only a harmony among the three political classes: rulers, soldiers, and workmen, which parallel the physiological trichotomy. Aristotle meant by "justice" the middle road or the mean. All extremes are vices; only the mean is justice, i.e., something of both extremes,[11] what Horace called *aurea mediocritas*; so we have again symmetry and harmony, an inner compromise and peace. In contrast to this, biblical justice knows no compromise or peace. It is not a calculation of the equidistant road between two extremes—a calculation so characteristic of Greek intellectualism. It is itself a passion, an irrational and whole-souled flame. It looks askance at the marble-calmness of harmony and stands tense on the watchtower. It is extreme ad infinitum. It knows not when to stop or withdraw. "Justice, justice, thou shalt pursue" (Deut. 16:20). You must run after justice and give it its due, since you are always responsible. "Son of man, I have made thee a watchman." Amos saw justice like a flood of mighty waters: "But let judgment run down as waters, and righteousness as a mighty stream" (Amos 5:24). Jeremiah explains: "Then I said, I will not make mention of him, nor speak any more in his name. But his word was in mine heart as a burning fire shut up in my bones, and I was weary with forbearing, and I could not stay" (Jer. 20:9). And if we remember that God was conceived only in terms of justice, then this fire of justice in the heart of man becomes in itself a religious experience, and ethics and worship become completely identical. We then understand the spirit of the prophets in their demand of a religion which should be mainly justice and righteousness.[12]

Perhaps we can explain the difference between the Greek approach and the biblical in terms both artistic and metaphysical. The Greeks were captured by form (harmony, the middle road), and this means finiteness and space, as in the Greek statues, over all of which hovers a spirit of limitation, completeness, and supreme, static calm. There is nothing beyond beauty to intrude and disturb. Even conceptualism, which the Greeks introduced into logic, and about which more is to be said later,[13] is essentially a quest of this esthetic finality, the closed circle which embraces and includes all, without a residue. The Jews, however, were captivated by a vision of an infinite road, namely, time, so that essentially every object is a piece of living time, over which was thrown a curtain of form. They look behind the veil, where there are no walls or partitions, and winds blow from far off spaces. Hence, they are characterized by an anticonceptualism, that is to say, by the moral storm inside the individual: "Let the law pierce the mountain!" This biblical view, not plastic but historical, makes room for epochal changes, for Messianism, for incessant straining toward world-redemption.

MERCY

Not all world-thinkers looked at the attribute of mercy favorably. Plato criticized the tragic drama because it stirs and develops compassion in the heart of the beholder, instead of indurating and shielding him against disturbances from without and from within—which reminds us of the Stoic ideal of apathy. Aristotle, it is true, admitted tragedies, but only for the sake of catharsis, that is to say, to awaken in the heart feelings of terror and mercy so as to *free* it, to empty it, of them. Spinoza banished pity by his determinism. La Rochefoucauld regarded it as egoistic, the perception of our own pain in the pain of others. Even Immanuel Kant could not find in pity any ethical foundation, because it springs from feeling, and furthermore it is only self-love. And Nietzsche follows in the aristocratic footsteps of Plato. All of them saw in pity an irrational foundation, a disturbing factor for the rationalistic calm of man, a going out of the ivory tower of Greek intellectualism into the uncertain and frightening outdoors. This is how philosophy abandoned the emotions. What do we really know of emotions? And what do we know about what to do with them?

In the atmosphere of the Bible, there is no fear of irrationalism or of emotions. The whole ethical sphere is here beyond rationalism, and is entirely devoted to the development and refinement of emotions. The conception of God draws largely from the element of mercy. Among the thirteen attributes of God,[14] only the last is strict justice; all the others are expressions of mercy. Rachel was the chosen one of Jacob, the woman that drew to herself so much love and mercy, the mother that cried over her children in Ramah; nevertheless, "And when the Lord saw that Leah was hated, he opened her womb" (Gen. 29:31). God is the ideal and dream of man. And the entrance to ethics is paved with stones of theology.

Infinite idealism is here revealed in its two directions. The first is the dimension of width. We have already mentioned, in connection with justice, the "seven gifts to the poor," which also belong here to the station of mercy. These gifts constitute an intermediate territory between mercy and justice. They are the part of mercy in justice. They are mercy because the rich took nothing from the poor and owed nothing to any particular person. But they are also justice because they do not manifest themselves in a personal contact between the giver and the taker, and also because the one who has owes, nevertheless, somewhere in the realm of higher ethics, to the one who has not. The poor have in a certain sense a claim of ownership on the property of the rich: "Withhold not good from them to whom it is due" (literally: from its owner. Prov. 3:27).[15] It is also to be noted that both semantically and psychologically one virtue shades over into another: *zedeq* (justice) into *zedaqah* (charity, and hence mercy), already in the book of *Tobit*,[16] and *rahamim* (mercy) is in itself rich with meanings of womb (*rehem*) and love, as in *erhamka adonai*, I love thee, O Lord (Ps. 18:2). It passes over into the next virtue when it becomes intensified and inflamed, so that all the fundamental concepts in the sphere of ethics constitute a colorful spectrum, and goodness in general becomes not a sporadic group of virtues, but a unified and integrated pattern. At any rate, this command of charity and mercy is, according to Maimonides, one of the positive commands of the Torah, for it is said "That shalt surely give him" (Deut. 15:10), and we must be careful to observe this command more than all other positive commandments (*Yad Hazaqah*, "Mattenot Aniyyim" 10:1). According to Rav Assi, charity is as important as all other commandments put together (*Baba Batra* 9a). And when Job delivered his oath that he did no wrong, he proclaimed: "If I have withheld the poor from their desire, or have caused the eyes of the widow to fail, or have eaten my morsel myself alone, and the fatherless hath not eaten thereof . . . if I have seen any perish for want of clothing, or any poor without covering" (Job 31:16-22). The aim must always be "There shall be no poor among you" (Deut. 15:4). This surely is a Messianic vision. Poverty will always accompany society like a heavy shadow. "For the poor shall never cease out of the land"; nevertheless, or perhaps just because of it, *"Therefore* I command thee, saying, Thou shalt open thine hand wide unto thy brother, to thy poor, and to thy needy, in thy land" (Deut. 15:11). The unrealizability of an ideal does not at all affect the truth of an ideal or the recognition of our duties toward it. This is the very soul of Jewish Messianism.

The enemy too is worthy of your mercy. "If thou meet thine enemy's ox or his ass going astray, thou shalt surely bring it back to him again. If thou see the ass of him that hateth thee lying under his burden . . . thou shalt surely help him" (Exod. 23:4-5). Your enemy's hatred of you does not justify your hatred of him because mercy, like justice, is absolute and springs from itself, not from considerations of what preceded in a personal framework. These verses also emphasize mercy toward the suffering of animals. Toward animals there is no justice, only mercy. Hence, it might seem that justice is greater than mercy, for it is more human, more related to the divine Image. But the divine Image also unveils itself on the one that has mercy.

It is worth noting how many laws there are in the Bible intended to foster this special kind of mercy: (1) "If a bird's nest chance to be before thee . . . thou shalt not take the dam with the young" (Deut. 22:6-7); (2) "And whether it be cow or ewe, ye shall not kill it and her young both in one day" (Lev. 22:28); (3) "Thou shalt not seethe a kid in his mother's milk"—for reasons of mercy, according to Abrabanel and Luzzatto (Exod. 23:19; 34:26; Deut. 14:21); (4) "And on the seventh day thou shalt rest: that thine ox and thine ass may rest" (Exod. 23:12); and (5) "Thou shalt not muzzle the ox when he treadeth out the corn" (Deut. 25:4). And there are many other verses expressive of this feeling: "A righteous man regardeth the life of his beast" (Prov. 12:10); "O Lord, thou preservest man and beast" (Ps. 36:6); "and his tender mercies are over all his works" (Ps. 145:9).[17] And that universalistic book called Jonah ends on a crescendo of warm humaneness: "And should I not spare Nineveh, that great city, wherein are more than sixscore thousand persons that cannot discern between their right hand and their left hand; and also much cattle."

On the verse, "Thou shalt not muzzle the mouth of the ox," St. Paul queries: "Doth God take care for oxen?" (I Cor. 9:9). But mercy reveals its sheerest beauty when it goes forth without hope of recognition, gratitude, or return. It is like Josiah Royce's loyalty, a virtue in itself, irrespective of the nature of the recipient thereof. Even in wartime, when trumpets blasted, man was required to remember that he was still man and that he was not to wipe even then the image of God from off his face. Also, officers immediately dismissed from the battlefield anyone who had built a new house and had not dedicated it, who had planted a vineyard and had not yet eaten thereof, who had betrothed a wife and had not taken her (Deut. 20:5-7)—all in order not to deprive a man of something which filled his heart with anticipatory joy during the peace. This is indeed what Judah the Maccabee did in his war with the Syrians (I *Hasmoneans* 3:56). And during the siege no fruit tree was to be destroyed: "Are the trees in the field men that they should be besieged by you?" (Deut. 20:20). One should note also the consideration and tenderness the law shows toward the captive female in the time of war (Deut. 21:10-13).

This infinite idealism also manifests itself intensively in the dimension of depth. The man who takes pity becomes as if by fate fastened to the poor, and he must make easier for him the process of receiving aid, until the helper and the helped become one shoulder for carrying the burden of poverty. An example of this is the article pledged as security for a debt. It was forbidden that the lender enter the house of the poor to take the pledge: he had to stand and wait outside, as if *he* were the poor. If the pledge were a raiment, the lender was to return it each day when the sun went down: "For that is his covering only, it is his raiment for his skin: wherein shall he sleep? And it shall come to pass, when he crieth unto me that I will hear" (Exod. 22:27; see also Deut. 24:10-13) [18]—that cry which, like the primal one imbedded in the Jewish memory by Egyptian bondage, constitutes a cosmic event, opening the gates of mercy above. One poor man cries out and the whole existence is shaken! It was such dealings with the poor, the enlistment of sympathy and wisdom so as to avoid humiliating him in the course of helping him, that the Psalmist referred to with: "Blessed is he that *considereth* the poor" (Ps. 41:1), for, as stated, the attitude to the sufferer was accompanied by a feeling of respect and deference, even by something like a sense of divine presence, of holy ground. Perhaps this complex feeling was also the basis of the respect enjoined toward the old and tired: "Thou shalt rise up before the hoary head, and honor the face of the old man, and fear thy God: I am the Lord" (Lev. 19:32).

These two virtues, justice and mercy, do not conflict with each other. There is room for the two: "To do justly and to love mercy" (Mic. 6:8), each in its own sphere. For intentional murder, the

Bible says: "Thine eye shall have no pity" (a characteristic Deuteronomic phrase; see Deut. 7:16; 13:9; 19:13, 21; 25:12), and "Thou
shalt take him from mine altar, that he may die" (Exod. 21:14).
There is no place here for pity. But the Biblical philosophy of punishment is not only to deter, even though this motive too exists: "And
those which remain shall hear, and fear, and shall henceforth commit no more any such evil among you" (Deut. 19:20), but also to
"put the evil away from among you"—a reason recurring frequently
in the Book of Deuteronomy, which seems particularly interested in
the why of punishment. This second reason seeks to guard the law
of moral causality—a crime in the moral nature of the universe draws
punishment—a law on which biblical prophecy foretelling the destiny
of individuals and peoples is founded, and without which there is no
orientation and all is chaos. Hence the midrash warns that "man must
not be more liberal than the Law" (*Bamidbar Rabba* 21:6), and R.
Hanina teaches: "If a man says that the Holy One, blessed be He, is
lax in the execution of justice, his life shall be outlawed, for it is
stated, He is the Rock, his work is perfect, for all his ways are judgment" (*Baba Qamma* 50a; *Jer. Bezah* 62a). There is no denial of
mercy and forgiveness which are the essence and spirit of the Bible.
Indeed, when Moses interceded for the Israelites who accepted the
evil report of the ten spies, he said: "And now, I pray thee, let the
power of the Lord be great, according as thou hast spoken, saying,
The Lord is slow to anger and plenteous in loving-kindness" (Num.
14:17-18)—thus indicating that mercy is a greater power and requires
a greater effort than justice. Justice is logical; mercy combats logic. R.
Hanina's statement means only that too dilated a concept of divine
forgiveness is apt to dim justice and moral causality and blunt the
sharp sense of responsibility.

Similarly, when there is a litigation between rich and poor, there
is no room for compassion. "Neither shalt thou countenance a poor
man in this cause" (Exod. 23:3). "Thou shalt not respect the person
of the poor" (Lev. 19:15). A judge must judge justly because, if he
favors the poor, he robs the rich, who in this case are just. No one
can be merciful at the expense of others. This means not that justice
is greater than mercy, but that mercy belongs to justice and has no
right to intrude in the law, or, as R. Akiba expressed it sharply: "There
is no mercy in law" (*Ketubut* 84a), and as R. Eliezer, son of R. Jose
ha-Gelili, proclaimed: "Let the law cut through the mountain"
(*Yebamot* 92a; *Sanhedrin* 6b). Thus we have two spheres; the legal

and the non-legal; and only where the law does not apply is there room for mercy.

But it should be noted that in the talmudic period there came into being the concept, "inside the line of the law," which allowed mercy in some situations to inject itself into the domain of law until it too became law. Here is an example: "Some porters [negligently] broke a barrel of wine belonging to Rabba, son of R. Huna. Thereupon he seized their garments; so they went and complained to Rab. 'Return them their garments,' he ordered. 'Is that the law?' he inquired. 'Even so,' he rejoined: *That thou mayest walk in the way of good men*' (Prov. 2:20). Their garments having been returned, they observed, 'We are poor men, have worked all day, and are in need: are we to get nothing?' 'Go and pay them,' he ordered. 'Is that the law?' he asked. 'Even so,' was his reply: *and keep the path of the righteous*' " (*Loc. cit.* See *Baba Mezi'a* 83a). Did Rab go against the explicit verse: "Neither shalt thou countenance a poor man in his cause?" No, the verse remains a general rule. But there are the few, the good and the righteous, who are subject to another law, the *law* of mercy. The new features of the concept of "inside the line of law" are two: (1) a breach in the absolute and objective wall of justice, offering a place for relativity, and (2) a recognition of a gap between law and morality, and "Jerusalem was destroyed only . . . because they based their judgment [strictly] upon biblical law, and did not go beyond the requirements of the law" (*Baba Mezi'a* 30b). It is interesting that Rab, who admits mercy into the sphere of law, follows his own line of thought when he answers the question, What does God pray? with: "May it be my will that my mercy may suppress my anger, and that my mercy may prevail over my [other] attributes, so that I may deal with my children in the attribute of mercy, and enter on their behalf inside the line of law" (*Berakot* 7a). So again we see how theology and ethics influence each other.

This idea that—in any case according to Rab—the attribute of mercy is superior to that of justice was constantly weighed in Hebrew literature. We have seen how the prophets themselves were divided in this respect into two camps. Amos and Isaiah were inclined to Holiness or justice, and Hosea, Jeremiah, and Ezekiel favored Glory or loving-kindness. In the talmudic period, R. Akiba was apparently inclined to law and justice, and Rab, to mercy. And in modern Hebrew literature, Samuel David Luzzatto saw the essence of Judaism in mercy, and Ahad ha-Am, in justice. But perhaps one should not seek monism, or one single basis, in biblical ethics because we thereby introduce statics, abstraction, and limitation, which, as will become clearer later, are not in keeping with the spirit of the Bible. In this spirit, the ethical life is conceived as a road, and on the road there are stations, and in each station there is something of the next; otherwise—that is, without a dim awareness of something more, still hidden in the distance—there would be no push or drive to walk onward. Indeed, from a psychological-ethical view, there is progress from justice to mercy, as there is from mercy to the next station. Justice is rational and objective. Even when it burns as a prophetic torch, it burns *personally* in an impersonal and objective fire. It strives to be independent of the nature of the men involved, of the identity of litigant A or B, to be, as stated, an algebraic equation of two unknown quantities, or a fixed relation between an *object* and an *object*. Not so mercy. Here one side has no claim on the other. Nothing is owing him from me. And if it is owing, then not particularly from me, but from all mankind. "If thy brother be waxen poor"—*thy* brother? Not exactly. The sufferer accuses all society, in which there are the poor and the deprived, and he who has mercy is the priest who offers his incense to atone for all mankind. He, therefore, represents mankind and juts out of it, so that we already have a subject. True, it is still rudimental, hylic, like a statue half rising out of the marble, because it is still wrapped up in nameless mankind; but there are already the first stirrings of the "I," the shaping of an emotion, the beginning of an identification, even though partial. It is not yet "with all thy heart" of the love for God, nor "like thyself" of the love for your neighbor. One cannot say, "And thou shalt pity thy neighbor as thyself," because, first, your neighbor as an object of pity is only an object, and identification, as we shall see, demands much more, and secondly, because there is no "as thyself," no self-pity in the normal course, as man to himself is not an *object*. Nevertheless, something of the awakening of an "I," of a subject, already exists in the heart of one who pities. And on the other hand, the pitied one is *only* an object because the eyes of the pitier are fastened on the wound, the pain, or the humiliation. He does not ask who and what is the sufferer: is he righteous or wicked, priest or lay, friend or foe, man or beast, a stray ox, an ass crouching under a burden. He sees only the suffering—and this, indeed, is all the greatness of the pitier, being touched by nameless, universal suffering, pure suffering. He is not interested in history or biography. He lives entirely in the present, irremovably concentrated in one point—the wound or the pain. He does not share in someone's sorrow—how incorrect and disrespectful is this current expression, which suggests robbing the sorrow of others, something of sin and conceit together. The pitier is a pure stirring and an outpouring, a heavenly mercy. Thus, we already have progress on the road. Justice is a relation between object and object; pity—between *subject* and object.

LOVE

In the concept of love, the ethical dialectics of the Bible reaches its apex. In it, the prayers of all ages meet. Here too the extent is infinite. "And thou shalt love thy neighbor as thyself, I am the Lord" (Lev. 19:18), and "neighbor" here, as elsewhere in the Bible, means man in general. Moreover, in this particular context, immediately after the expression, "Thou shalt not avenge, nor bear any grudge," the words "thy neighbor" can only refer to the enemy. The Gospel, it is true, claimed the origination of the ethics of love for the enemy (cf. Matt. 5:38, 40, 43-44; Luke 6:35). But the principle of nonresistance is clearly enunciated in the majestic poem of the servant of the Lord: "I gave my back to the smiters, and my cheeks to them that plucked off the hair. I did not hide my face from shame and spitting" (Isa. 50:6). As for a positive ethics toward the enemy, the following citations may suffice:

"If thou meet thine enemy's ox or his ass going astray, thou shalt surely bring it back to him again. If thou see the ass of him that hateth thee under his burden, and wouldst forbear to help him, thou shalt surely help with him" (Exod. 23:4-5).

"Thou shalt not hate thy brother in thine heart: thou shalt not in any wise rebuke thy neighbor, and not suffer sin upon him. Thou shalt not avenge, nor bear any grudge against the children of thy people, but thou shalt love thy neighbor as thyself: I am the Lord" (Lev. 19:17-18).

"For if a man find his enemy, will he let him go well away? wherefore the Lord reward thee good for that thou hast done unto me this day" (I Sam. 24:20).

"If I rewarded evil unto him that was at peace with me; (yea, I have delivered him that without cause is mine enemy)" (Ps. 7:5).

"Say not thou, I will recompense evil; but wait on the Lord, and he shall save thee" (Prov. 20:22).

"Rejoice not when thine enemy falleth, and let not thine heart be glad when he stumbleth" (Prov. 24:17).

"Say not, I will do so to him as he hath done to me; I will render to the man according to his work" (Prov. 24:29).

"If thine enemy be hungry, give him bread to eat; and if he be thirsty, give him water to drink" (Prov. 25:21; Rom. 12:20).

"If I rejoiced at the destruction of him that hated me, or lifted up myself when evil found him: Neither have I suffered my mouth to sin by wishing a curse to his soul" (Job 31:29-30).[19]

Love extends also to the alien. "But the stranger that dwelleth with you shall be unto you as one born among you, and thou shalt love him as thyself" (Lev. 19:34). "Love ye therefore the stranger: for ye were strangers in the land of Egypt" (Deut. 10:19). Aristotle speculates whether one can grant friendship to more than one person, and here we are bidden to love all men. Kant thinks that love cannot be a duty because one cannot command love, and here it is a positive command: Try. You must seek to fulfill even this impossible demand. Thus, we again have infinite idealism as the general characteristic of biblical ethics.

One should note particularly the mystery and wonder involved in the love urged in "And thou shalt love thy neighbor as thyself." Justice, we have seen, is a relation between object and object. Mercy is a relation between subject and object. Now comes love, as a relation between subject and subject—"as thyself"—a relation in which the personality on each side reveals itself in beauty. It preserves, on the one hand, the subject of the beloved. Logic says, love takes an object, even as you turn the known, by the very process of knowledge, into an object. But there are two kinds of knowledge. One kind impoverishes the known: so many petals to a flower, such a height to the stem, such and such a shape, and that is all. And there is a knowledge—a Hebraic knowledge, which means union—which deepens and enriches, enters and reveals the subject, and identifies itself with it. It circumvents the object and comes over directly behind it, to the "I." Deep unto deep calling, I to I. True, I think *thee*, but I love in thee the I, the free subject, the deciding personality. Love is creative. It works on the beloved and changes him to an ideal; and at the same time the same action goes forth from the beloved to the lover, so that two ideal forms are folded in an embrace, and the whole world stands and sings, "It is good." And love guards also over the subject of the lover. True, with Plato, love is an affection, a subjection to an external stimulus. Cratylus explains that the word Eros is derived from the word ἐσρῶν, a streaming inward from the outside.[20] The same psychology of emotions we have in Aristotle: they are all due to external stimuli. This indeed is one of the factors in the construction of a negative theology in the philosophy of Maimonides and his predecessors, as one cannot postulate a divine reception of an external influence. Not so in the Bible. Here love is internal in origin and hence the command "And thou shalt love." It depends on you. The I stands as freedom against freedom. True, in the concept of mercy, he who has mercy is influenced by external suffering, stirred and activated by it. Here, however, there reigns perfect freedom because there is no love where there is compulsion, and there is no external factor. I love the beloved not because of any fair virtue or mark of beauty, but my love is complete and causeless love. The whole I meets the whole I without any remainder; and where there is I, there is freedom and choice because the I *is* freedom and choice. Nevertheless, the choice is so deep and absolute that it is experienced as necessity, as *fatum*. Thus we say in English, "I fell in love." And in this feeling of freedom, so deep and entire that it seems like fatalism, the chains of causality break asunder. The I rises on each side in all its radiance and freedom. This is the mystery of "And thou shalt love thy neighbor as thyself": I-I, freedom against freedom, causeless love.

There is an oriental tale: A prince loved a princess, but was not accepted. Day by day he came to her shut window, introducing himself: I am the possessor of all the golden treasures of the country, or I am a prince of the tenth generation, or I am the composer of a thousand fables. So it went, day by day, but she never appeared. One morning he came and said: I am thou, and at once the window opened. This is the East: self-deletion. The West is self-assertion. But in the Bible there is the irrational combination of distance and union, I-I, "as thyself," the miracle and wonder of Holiness and Glory together.

What if the interests of the two I's, riveted together in the I-I, clash? Obviously, one must not sacrifice the interests of the neighbor because then the "as thyself" will prove to be "less than thyself." You must therefore ignore your own interests because Satan knew well: "Skin for skin, yea, all that a man hath will he give for his life" (Job 2:4); and if you love your neighbor as yourself, you will give all for his life. No interpretation of "as thyself" is possible other than "more than thyself," i.e., self-sacrifice. And David well discerned the *religious* holiness of such a love, when, after he said, "Oh that one would give me drink of the water of the well of Beth-lehem," and in response his three "mighty men" broke through the Philistine camp, drew water, and brought it to him, he refused to drink it "and poured it out unto the Lord" (II Sam. 23:16). Self-sacrifice to a neighbor becomes a sacrifice to God, and the two loves become identical. This is infinite love, which, with reference to God, expresses itself in the phrase "with all thy heart and with all thy soul and with all thy might," and which has the same ideal intensity with reference to the neighbor. No other interpretation is possible. And all this stands in sharp contrast to the Platonic harmony, to the Aristotelian mean, and to Stoic apathy. It also differs from Kant's rigoristic declaration: "If I would see my friend fleeing from a pursuer and hiding in my house, and I would know that if I lied and said 'he did not enter my house,' I would save him from death—even then I would not lie." Is this really ethical? Would the Bible approve of such callous rigidity? Does it not record with apparent approval the opposite action? "And the woman took the two men, and hid them, and said thus: There came men unto me, but I wist not whence they were" (Josh. 2:4). Does not the beauty of morality unfold itself not only in bodily, but also in spiritual, self-sacrifice, in the sacrifice of all precious virtues for the sake of the life of a neighbor? Have there been no cases where love shone forth in all its infiniteness through self-desecration, and our hearts responded with deepest admiration?

This understanding of love of one's neighbor Christianity adopted. "Greater love hath no man than this, that a man lay down his life for his friend" (John 15:13). "And thou shalt love thy neighbor more than thy life" (Bar. 19:15). It is therefore regrettable that Ahad ha-Am in his Hebrew essay *Al shetei ha-seippim* ("Between Two Opinions"), because of his general rationalistic approach, interpreted Judaism only in terms of objective justice, taking a critical attitude toward the moral quality of mercy and love. Because of this approach, he was constrained to insist on exactness: "as thyself," and not "more than thyself." But the expression "as thyself" is meant to extend love to its highest power, i.e., to infinity, and not to suspend subtle scales on which to weigh every feeling to determine if it is "as thyself" or a little more.

Ahad ha-Am finds support in the words of R. Akiba: "If two are travelling on a journey, and one has a pitcher of water, if both drink, they will both die, but if one drinks, he can reach civilization— Ben Patura lectured: It is better that both should drink and die, rather than one should behold his companion's death. Until R. Akiba came and taught: 'that thy brother may live with thee' (Lev. 25:36): thy life takes precedence over his life" (*Baba Mezi'a*, and with variants in *Sifra* on Lev. 25:36).[21] But R. Akiba is consistent. We already saw that he rendered his decision: There is no pity in law, refusing to mix rule with compassion or with love, law with "inside the line of law." Observe that Ben Patura "lectured" or "preached" (*darash*) and used the expression "it is better," but R. Akiba "taught" (*limmed*). Thus, Ben Patura proposed the ethical view, and R. Akiba propounded the law. For himself, he too took the ethical approach: "All my life I was anxious to fulfill the law of 'with all thy soul' (*Jer. Berakot* 14b); and 'with all thy soul' of the love of God and 'as thyself' of the love of a neighbor are the same." And when R. Akiba was confined in a prison-house, and the prison keeper took his severely-limited portion of water and poured out half of it so that what was left would not suffice for both washing his hands and for drinking, he risked his life and used the water for washing his hands, saying: "*It is better* that I myself should die than that I should transgress against the opinion of my colleagues" (*Erubin* 21:2).

Ahad ha-Am also revealed this rationalistic tendency in connection with the old question of whether "And thou shalt love thy neighbor" should be interpreted in a positive or a negative manner. There is no doubt that this command should be understood as it reads, positively and not negatively, love and not not-hate, because why should we force ourselves to assume otherwise? And why should we differentiate between "And thou shalt love thy neighbor" and "And thou shalt love the Lord thy God"? Is the meaning there too negative? Ahad ha-Am finds it difficult to orient himself in positive love, just as it was difficult for Kant to admit love as duty. Too much wine ferments in it for it to be kept in the narrow barrel of rationalistic justice. This is why, according to Ahad ha-Am, Hillel gave a negative interpretation: "What is hateful unto thee do not do unto others" (*Sabbat* 31a and also *Johanan ben Uzziel*), but the Gospel taught the positive form, which again, according to him, is really an inverted egotism: "Therefore all things whatsoever ye would that men should do to you, do ye even so to them: for this is the law and the prophets" (Matt. 7:12), "And as ye would that men should do to you, do ye also to them likewise" (Luke 6:31). The answer is: (1) Hillel did not offer his negative interpretation as a commentary on the biblical verse, to which indeed he does not refer, (2) Hillel, too, as a man of law concerned with acts, gave necessarily a juridical definition, i.e., to refrain from acts of hate, again assuming the gap between law and ethics, and (3) Hillel—and this is the point in the talmudic context— was less demanding than Shammai of the pagan who would learn the whole Torah while standing on one foot, offering not the rigorous ideal but the easier minimal basis in the form of the abolition of hateful deeds, without intending this to supersede the height and the glory of the biblical ethics which the "commentary" is to unfold. Note indeed that Jesus, in his Sermon on the Mount, did not maintain that he originated it but that "this is the law and the prophets" (Matt. 7:12). Incidentally, both Saadia Gaon in his philosophical work, *Emunot we-De'ot* (III, 1), and Abraham ibn Ezra in his commentary (*ad loc.*) take the verse explicitly in a positive sense, as indeed is its literal meaning. As to Ahad ha-Am's fundamental contention, that the negative form is nearer to rational and objective justice, is it not to be assumed that all moral negatives spring from a constant moral positive, from the demand that even when one's life is not engaged in actual deeds it must still be *devoted* and awake? Thou shalt not murder means that all during his life man must watch over himself not to murder, not to be capable of murder, and this watchfulness is all. We emphasize too much the difference, which is essentially verbal, between positive and negative, when even the negative may not be wholly a return to justice, when it too may assume in biblical ethics a character of infinite idealism **and** of incessant self-refinement of the subject.

And before we proceed to the fourth concept, we must tarry for a moment over a phenomenon which I think requires attention. The love of one's neighbor is urged in Leviticus and Deuteronomy, both of which are priestly in character, but does not occur even once in the prophetical books. Ethical demands are the breath and life of the prophets. "Wash you, make you clean, put away the evil of your doings from before mine eyes, cease to do evil; Learn to do well, seek judgment, relieve the oppressed, judge the fatherless, plead for the widow" (Isa. 1:16-17). This is an impetuous torrent, but not a word is devoted to the pinnacle of biblical ethics, the love of one's neighbor. This love shines forth only from the borders of priesthood. Note also that man's love of God and God's love of man are both concentrated in Deuteronomy, and only hints of them are scattered in the other books.[22] It seems that one must emend the prevalent notion that the priests constituted no ideologically original, but only a compromising, power, and hence the struggle between the two classes, priests and prophets. In the first place, there was no such class struggle. The prophets frequently showed a positive attitude toward the priests [23] and warred only against the overemphasis of sacrifices at the expense of morality. But the main point is that the concept of love appears only in the priestly books, which shows that the great priests were not only interested in the cult, but also in a degree of morality higher than which there is none. And this should be no surprise, considering their educational function, which has not received its due attention.

In the Books of Leviticus and Deuteronomy, the priest occupies a more prominent place than the prophet. The prophet comes to displace the Canaanitish observers of time and diviners; he foretells the future (Deut. 18:14-15, 22), whereas the priest sits together with the judge to decide in matters "between blood and blood, between plea and plea, between stroke and stroke, being matters of controversy within thy gates" (Deut. 17:8). Nor should one confine the priestly influence to rendering juridical verdicts, and so differentiate between theory and practice; for just as there is "theory leading to practice," so is there practice leading to theory. The word "Torah," which in many places means justice and righteousness, was reserved particularly for the law of the priests. "According to the Torah which they shall teach thee, and according to the judgment which they shall teach thee, thou shalt do" (Deut. 17:11). "For the Torah shall not perish from the priest, nor counsel from the wise, nor the word from the prophet" (Jer. 18:18). "Then shall they seek a vision of the prophet, but the Torah shall perish from the priest and counsel from the ancients" (Ezek. 7:26). "For the priest's lips should keep knowledge and they should seek Torah at his mouth, for he is the messenger of the Lord of hosts" (Mal. 2:7).[24]

The priests were also responsible for some spiritual upheavals of the people. Probably the reforms of Hezekiah, and certainly those of Josiah, were due to them. It may be assumed, therefore, that they exercised a great educational influence, and one may regard the command, "And thou shalt love thy neighbor as thyself," as their contribution to biblical ethics. This urging of mutual love is in keeping with the general spirit of joy that overwhelmed the people at the time of such sacrifices as thank-offering, peace-offerings, and the paschal lamb, and especially during the feast of ingathering. The joy expressed itself in dances accompanied by instrumental music. There were communal feasts to which were invited the Levite, the alien, the orphan, and the widow, and there were marches to the temple. "I went with them," recalls the Psalmist longingly, "to the house of God, with the voice of joy and praise, with a multitude that kept holyday" (Ps. 42:4).[25] On the other hand, Hosea seems to have looked askance at such emotional outbursts, seeing in them an imitation of Baalistic cult: "Rejoice not, O Israel, for joy, as other people" (Hos. 9:1). Therefore, the prophets, if we take this view, were more restrained. And as they appeared always at the time of moral loosening in order to chastise and warn, they pointed to the desecration of the very first bases of morality: justice and kindness. The prophets were, therefore, an Apollonian element, and the priests, a Dionysian element. The prophets were Holiness; the priests, Glory. And the two together constituted the color and tension of biblical ethics.

HOLINESS

Holiness, too, seems to have had its main roots in priestly circles because it occurs most frequently in the Book of Leviticus and in the Book of Ezekiel the priest. Sometimes it is synonymous with the priesthood: "a kingdom of priests and a holy nation." [26] And in this concept of Holiness we have also in Hebrew the reflexive form, *hitqadesh*, self-sanctification, man's working upon himself. What is the meaning of this concept?

Holiness is the internal dimension of ethical life. All concepts dealt with heretofore pointed to deeds and relations outside, to someone else; this concept points to man's own self, to the soul-background. All the previous were social; this one alone carries within itself all individual ethics. It is like a deep accompanying melody to all the previous virtues and has two internal aspects: man vis-à-vis the world, and man vis-à-vis himself.

The original meaning of the term is to be *separated* and devoted to God and therefore to live as though in the presence of God: "For the Lord thy God walketh in the midst of thy camp . . . therefore shall thy camp be holy" (Deut. 23:15), a feeling similar to that of the Psalmist: "I have set the Lord always before me" (Ps. 16:8). This sense of divine presence creates two tendencies: one formal and the other moral. The formal tendency, designated explicitly as Holiness, manifests itself in a ritualistic or ceremonious separateness, viz., through dietary laws (Lev. 20:25), the Sabbath (Exod. 31:13; Ezek. 20:12), sexual limitations (Lev. 20:7-24), or fringes on the garment (Num. 15:38, 41). There appears in all this a striving to build a separate order, a holy people, which by its aloofness will be a clearer light to the nations. In this respect, Holiness serves as a sociological-political frame on a theocratic background. As for the second, or moral tendency, it is an emphasis on the *metaphysical* importance of the previous ethical values: justice, mercy, and love. It may be said that the holy man is stretched and tortured on the diagonal of a right angle, one side of which is toward the world, and the other is aimed at God. He is the bridge and the mutual beckoning between the two sides, and the angle is his soul. As God is conceived only in abstract ethical terms, infinite ethicalness, because there are no other attributes to limit it, this perception called Holiness imposes upon man the heavy task of realizing or making God concrete in moral acts, to clothe Him, as it were, with being. Hence, there exists a deep earnestness toward life, the sense of responsibility. Holiness means grave responsibility: "For he is an holy God: he is a jealous God" (Josh. 24:19), for all the upper worlds depend on man. This responsibility stands and faces man in Leviticus and in Ezekiel—but also in Amos 2:7: "To profane my holy name"—in the form of a choice between sanctification of the Name and profanation of the Name, between the enlargement of the deity and the reverse, the diminution of the Image. Hence, Holiness is neither the negation of life, nor its affirmation, but its sanctification, making of it vestures for divinity. In other words, the holy person is not really separate and apart. On the contrary, he stands with all his being in the midst of the stream of life and sanctifies it, apotheosizes it, through justice, mercy, and love. The sanctification of the Name and the sanctification of life mean the same thing. In this sanctifying act, man becomes the counterpoint of the Greek tragic hero. Both are cosmic, heaven-reaching, heroes. But whereas the Greek hero stands against the gods, struggling with the chains of their arbitrary destiny, the Hebraic hero struggles with chains from below and *for the sake of* the world above. And higher forces awake and share his suffering, as was the case when the Hebrew people went into exile, and when angels wept and let their tears fall into the eyes of Isaac, bound on the altar. The holy man then becomes the center of the world; heavenly eyes watch him; he himself becomes of heaven, a supernatural force. He sanctifies the Name, and he himself becomes sanctified, not tragic, not at all tragic, in fact always triumphant, but also holy, a metaphysical power in the embrace of snakes, Laocoön.

The background of such acts is not the ethics of relativity, neither that of Protagoras who regards the *individual* man as the measure of all things, nor the generally Greek ethics which measures the good by the degree of happiness to which it leads—no two concepts are more antipodal than relativity and Holiness—nor the pragmatic variety or the calculations of what the Talmud calls the neutral type: "mine is mine and thine is thine," which the Talmud also designates as the Sodom-type (*Abot* 5:13), but a sense of a moral mystery embracing all, penetrating all, and posing eternal demands—demands that draw their validity and authority from that mystery itself, in which they are fixed like the stars in the night. Intellectual thinking needs a solid rock outside of itself upon which to set the sole of its moral foot. Else on what does it stand? Even Ecclesiastes, the Skeptic, knew that "he hath set the *world* in their heart" (Eccles. 3:11), where Rashi explains the Hebrew word for "world," as meaning not-knowing, a secret or a mystery. That is to say, Holiness is also a rigorous moral autonomy, a secret, for every intellectual process refers not to a thing itself but to its borders and relations. The concept, like Zebulun, dwells "at the haven of the sea" (Gen. 49:13), but Holiness dips in the sea itself, and out of its depth it looks at all things. And this perception of an infinite secret begets modesty and reserve, a "walking humbly" (Mic. 6:8). As Isaiah, who belonged to the Holiness school, expressed it: "And the loftiness of man shall be bowed down, and the haughtiness of men shall be made low: and the Lord alone shall be exalted on that day" (Isa. 2:17); and Kierkegaard learned from Isaiah in saying that modesty means to live in the presence of God, and man may be defined as capable of being ashamed. Alas, this perception of mystery is now completely evaporated, leaving man as though he had been thrown outside through a window, abandoned and nakedly alone, yet lightheaded unto dizziness. As for modesty, no generation has surpassed ours in penetrating the physical secrets surrounding us, and no generation has displayed more arrogance—shall we say: scientific arrogance?—toward the world. We strut with our soiled boots into Being, and with one sweep of our hand we want to remove all its seven veils. Gone is the sense of mystery and with it the sense of modesty and open-eyed reserve that belong to the holy man.

But Holiness is an attitude of seriousness not only toward life but also to ourselves. If the Holyistic approach says God is infinite, i.e., always higher, then the holiness of man means that he too is always higher, always beyond himself—what Nietzsche understood well, but not the Greeks. They spoke of virtues and perfections and habits, i.e., static conditions resulting from self-training and practice. Aristotle in his *Nicomachean Ethics* (II, 1103a, 15) states that ethics (ἠθική) is derived from (ἔθος) or habit. The Bible, however, knows no such perfections, high levels above which there are no more hills and mountains and no more heights to climb. "For there is no man that sinneth not" (I Kings 8:46). "For there is not a just man upon earth, that doeth good, and sinneth not" (Eccles. 7:20). Holiness is, therefore, a dynamic consciousness of *imperfection* and unattaining. It is not a signpost of a fourth station. It accompanies man at each station, whispering to him: You still have not done enough justice, you still have not had enough mercy, you still have not loved with all your power. You still have to go on. To stand is to retreat. "He who does not add causes it to cease" (*Abot* 1:13), or as a Hasidic Rabbi once remarked: "If I thought at the end of a day that I still stand where I stood at the beginning of the day, I would not want to live any more." That Rabbi did not strive like Faust to be able to say to a moment: "Stay awhile, thou art so fair" because Holiness is never a condition, but a process and a march. Essentially there is no Holiness, but a self-sanctification, i.e., a going from one degree to another. Static, finished Holiness is an absurdity. "Ye shall therefore sanctify yourselves and ye shall be holy" (Lev. 11:44; 20:7), i.e., the condition lies in the process, the static—in the dynamics. It is a constant inner drive that robs man of his calm. It is the fire and flame of the previous concepts. It is their infinite dimension. And we should translate Lev. 19:2 thus: "Ye shall be holy"—ye shall be infinite—"For I the Lord your God am holy"—am infinite. This is the ethical idealism of the Bible. Greek philosophy, radiant with harmony and with the golden path, would have never grasped Hebraic Holiness in all its restlessness and infinity.

It should also be noted that just as there are degrees ad infinitum in Holiness, so there are degrees ad infinitum in *minus Holiness*, in moral degradation. The Talmud affirmed degrees in ritual uncleanness, and this is all the more true in uncleanness of the soul. *There*, no limits or numbers apply, and it is not correct that he who kills one is like him who kills a hundred, and he who kills a hundred is like him who kills a thousand. Punishment administered by man is indeed limited and does not admit any subtle variations to fit the variations of the crime. Ineed, it is from this human limitation that Saadia Gaon inferred the existence of another world, the Hereafter.[27] But there is no end to the abyss, just as there is no limit to the heavens, or, in other words, one cannot fully grasp the soul in its pure heavens and its deep dark chasms. In this, it is both inspiring and frightening.

And Holiness imparts to the moral life the quality of religion because, when man decides on a moral step in the absolute and authoritative spirit of "So said the Lord," i.e., in an identification of I-I, we have a moment of Glory, of revelation. But soon comes the sigh of Holiness: Not yet, always not yet; so that every ethical experience is a religious experience, a tension and a struggle between the joy of rising and the sorrow of distance.

◄9►

A PORTRAIT OF THE I

The human I has two forms of expression: the creative form and the ethical form. Outside of these two moments, the I can hardly be said to exist. Only in creation—it does not matter whether artistic or philosophical—and in ethical choice does the I emerge from its non-being. But there is a difference between the two forms. In creation the I works in hiding, like bees in the hive; and when the curtain rises, there is a seed, a disturbing rhythm, a flutter of a word. But in ethics, the I itself appears, struggles, and assumes responsibility: Thus I act, and all the consequences upon me.

Before we look at various aspects of the ethical I, we must make a terminological distinction. We spoke of the I-I both as a metaphysical identification, when in the moment of choice we identify ourselves with the ethical absolute or divinity and feel therefore the authoritativeness of our choice ("Thus said the Lord"); [1] and we spoke of the I-I as a social identification, when the I or the subject reaches out directly to another subject as subject and joins it, as in love. Our following discussion will be clearer if we differentiate between the two meanings by using for the divine subject the Hebrew word by which God introduces Himself in the opening of the decalogue on Mount-Sinai—the first personal pronoun *Anoki*: I, I am. We will therefore designate the metaphysical identification by I-*Anoki* and the social one—as before—by I-I.

THE INTERMITTENT I

The I-*Anoki*, or the metaphysical I which, in an ethical moment, is in union with the Absolute Ethicalness which is God or *Anoki*, must always stand on guard, for each situation presents itself as a unique entity, new and unitary. We do not first carve away all the individual details and then relate each situation to a moral principle which we have already acquired, but react to it as to an unrelatable unit. The situation as it is, with all its particulars and details, is prohibited, is robbery, is adultery. That is to say, moral reaction is immediate and not the result of logical abstraction and classification. Man must always be I-*Anoki*, self-legislator like God: ethically fresh and malleable, always morally instinctive and alert, as in war.

But here is the difficulty: the I of a human being is intermittent and erratic. It is no enduring substance, but rather volatile and transitory, without the strength of continuousness and persistence. No sooner does it complete its reaction than it closes its eyes and falls aslumber, a firefly in a midsummer night. Indeed, how long can man persist in the union-tension of I-*Anoki?* It follows, therefore, that in the intervals between decisions, man exists without the I, a mere biological creature, without a center, without an aim, without a frame of reference. Forward, backward, sideward—it is all the same; for without the *Anoki*, the I too disappears. Without the Infinite, all is monotony. And the whole aim of the Bible is to strengthen the moral I by reenforcing its attachment to the *Anoki*, by enfolding it in an atmosphere of holiness. "R. Hananiah ben 'Akashia says: The Holy One blessed be He, desired to make Israel worthy, therefore gave He to them the Law and many commandments; for it is said: The Lord was pleased, for His righteousness sake [or, better, for Israel's righteousness] to make the Law great and glorious" (*Makkot* 23b).

Not only does the human I lack permanent substance, but all substance. It is only a quasi-chain of actions, an activity without an actor, activity that moves of itself. We know the medieval philosophical view about the divine attributes, that they do not really describe God but only God's actions. Saadia Gaon endeavors to prove in his *Emunot we-De'ot*, second treatise, that God is a doer, an agent, but does not belong to any logical category, not even to that of substance. And Judah ha-Levi in his *Kuzari* IV, 25, says in his comments on the Book of Creation that God has no essence, i.e., not simply that we do not know His essence, but that He *has* no essence, "for the essence of anything is other than its being, whereas God—His being is His essence." [2] How are we to understand it? Only that God is a self-activeness, an activity without a substance, an activity which is in itself its whole substance, the whole personality—which constitutes the deepest mystery of all, and yet which emerges out of medieval rationalism, as if that entire rationalism was intended only to lead man to that mystery and leave him there, for beyond that there is no more road. Now the human I also appears as such an activeness, an activity without a substance, but also without continuity. The I must always create itself. And there is no habit or acquired perfection or Greek *hexis*. One can only develop an atmosphere through learning and good deeds in order to facilitate the metaphysical contact, but the I itself is not at hand, and there is nothing to habituate or to train. The I is not a rope-walker. It appears only in response to an ethical challenge of a given situation and disappears after the response. Thus, it too is only an activity without a substance, a nought in its Neoplatonic-cabalistic sense, a portion of divinity, a mystery hanging on to a greater mystery, or it is the greater mystery itself when it dwells within us, a revelation of *Glory*. "Awake up, my glory; awake, psaltery and harp" (Ps. 57:8). "To the end that my glory may sing praise to thee, and not be silent" (Ps. 30:13).

And here we arrive at a distinction between existence and being. The existentialists made various differentiations between these terms; our view sheds its own light. The existent has three characteristics: (1) it is external, because perceivable, and, therefore, (2) it is static. Even when we see a man running, it is static, as we perceive only the external movements and not the drive within which causes his hurriedness. And (3), it is an auxiliary verb, not only in the grammar of the language, but also in that of its essence. It is only a belongingness between the subject and the predicate; it is only a dash. Thus, if you abstract all the existents and speak about existence as such, you only have an auxiliary verb without any subject or predicate. In short, the concept "existent" is external, static, and empty.

It is not so with being, which represents an entirely different experience. (1) This concept is not external. We do not perceive being; we are it; we become a part of it. That is to say, being is never an object but always a subject. Perception reaches the inside of the being; it is an entrance into it. Hence, essentially, there are only two concepts that may be designated as being: God and I. Both are subjects only; otherwise one cannot grasp them at all. Both are all inwardness, as they have no outside at all. Therefore, (2) this concept is not static but active, more active than any other concept. The

Hebrew word for being, *havayah*, does not mean inert continuity but an event, almost an explosiveness, a becoming. "And God said, Let there be light" (Gen. 1:3). "For he said to the snow be earth" (Job 37:6). And, therefore, (3) it is not an auxiliary verb, a positive belongingness between a subject and a predicate, but a storm of action, a creation which is in itself all. It is God as I AM, and it is the human I in activity. Both create worlds, and both are depths of self-creation,[3] of becoming. With God, it is an eternal flame; with the I, it is a fleeting spark, a firefly.

We know that Kant tried to prove that there is no proof for the existence of God. Descartes tried to prove the existence of the I, and it seems that he too failed because all he proved was the existence of the I as an object, and therefore only the non-I.[4] But why, indeed, is every attempt to prove the existence of these two concepts disappointing? Because both are not existences but beings, because both reveal themselves only as I, and there is no approach to the I except through being, through Glory. Existence leads only to the thou, even inside of man himself.

All this makes perhaps somewhat clearer the mysterious confluence of I-*Anoki*, of the intermittent I.

THE SOCIAL I

The I awakes from its non-being when touched by infinite ethicalness. When the latter calls upon it: "Where art thou?" it answers here *I am*. When the calling voice passes, the I falls asleep. But this divine call comes in a given situation, when the I stands before another I, for in solitude there is no ethics. True, R. Hanina ben Teradion and R. Halafta ben Dosa thought that even if one sits alone the Divine Presence sometimes rests upon him (*Abot* 3, 2, 6); but only when he sits and is engaged in the law, i.e., in ethical meditation, in seeking ways to the neighbor. There is no Divine Presence in a void. "He who cannot live in society," says Aristotle, "or has no need for it because he is sufficient for himself, must be either a beast or a god."[5] This is not entirely correct, for even God, as we tried to prove,[6] needs society, needs man to realize his moral being, for which reason He created him. There remains, therefore, for this self-sufficient man only one identity, that of the beast, for the ethical I is all in all a social I, it is the relation of one I to another, and essentially not a relation but an identification, I-I. Thus only in "And thou shalt love thy neighbor as thyself" do I fulfill "And thou shalt love the Lord thy God."

Only in the I-I is manifested the I-*Anoki*. In the love of my neighbor
I draw divinity into being. And Spinoza was right: "The love of man
for God is only the love of man for man." All ethical experiences are,
therefore, at the high transit point, at the vertex of the pyramid,
where one personality goes over into another, metaphysical; and all
metaphysical experiences take place in an ethical situation.

But this I-I is not that empty love so much preached about, love
of humanity. First, humanity is an abstraction, and Judaism, as will be
further clarified, does not ethically favor abstractions. Love of humanity is not only a love of an abstraction, but also a swerve from the
neighbor, an address of a nonexistent addressee, doomed to lie in the
postoffice of the self, never to be delivered. Secondly, it is so easy to
pity or love humanity because to do so entails no actual obligations,
and also because the humanity imagined at that moment has nothing
but what stirs compassion or love. However, concrete man stands before you with all his stains and blemishes. Perhaps he is also a threat
to you or a competitor. And it is with reference to such a man that
the Bible demands "And thou shalt love." Love the individual and the
particular in your neighbor as yourself; for with reference to yourself,
your love is not directed toward the abstract humanity in you.

Moreover, I-I means that the I knows the thou, not as thou or as
he—which are both objects—but as an I. I know the pursuit in you of
justice, the stir in you of compassion, the dream in you of love, the
real I in you which comes into being only as I-*Anoki*; and it is in this
knowledge that I love you, so that all is again "And thou shalt love
the Lord," and again the love-triangle is closed. And only when there
is I-I is there room for the unity of plurality, or the plural unity,
we, and not under a psychological relation of I-Thou. From the
I-Thou, there will never come forth that expression of a proud blending, of an extended personality: We. And where there is We, there
is also room for the subjective correlate, Ye and They, as an extension
of I-I. All this means that it is only the I-I that can be employed and
extended in ethical speech and emotion, but I-Thou remains always
I-Thou, shrunken and riveted to its place, a surd, $\sqrt{2}$.

Accordingly, the ethical I of the Bible is not directly connected
with society, the people, or the state, but always indirectly through
man, and the moral correlate of the I is not primarily the organized
group, but another I. True, there are some reserved warnings to accept
and suffer the political framework: "Thou shalt not revile the Judge,
nor curse the ruler of thy people" (Exod. 22:28). "Curse not the
King, no not in thy thought; and curse not the rich in thy bedcham-

ber: for a bird in the air shall carry the voice, and that which hath wings shall tell the matter" (Eccles. 10:20). "I counsel thee to keep the king's commandments, and that in regard of the oath of God" (Ps. 8:3). And in the Psalms (80:18; 84:10; 89:19-20, 28) there are even verses that celebrate certain kings, and Psalm 45 was probably composed in honor of a royal wedding. But all these historico-literary expressions do not confirm the state as a primary moral force. On the contrary, the biblical sense of equality—so different from the spirit of the Platonic republic—recoiled from any dominance and tried to curb it. The individual has to control the state and not the reverse. "When thou art come unto the land . . . and shalt say, I will set a king over me, like as all the nations that are about me; Thou shalt in any wise set him king over thee. . . . But he shall not multiply horses. . . . Neither shall he multiply wives to himself. . . . Neither shall he greatly multiply to himself silver and gold . . . that he shall write him a copy of this law in a book. . . . That his heart be not lifted up above his brethren" (Deut. 17:14-26).

Furthermore, in the Code of Hammurabi there are many paragraphs, from 26 to 41, that define the duties and privileges of the army, the officers, and the tax-gatherers. But there is no mention in the Bible of such privileged publicans. And in general where are the tax laws in the Torah? Surely no state can exist without taxes.

The military spirit—and the militia is only next to the king—cannot be said to be fully developed in the Bible, if in the midst of military passion they were required to halt for a very humane moment to consider the feelings of anyone who had built a house and had not dedicated it, or had planted a vineyard and had not yet eaten of it, or had betrothed a wife and had not taken her, and, what is more, to consider the feelings of anyone who was fearful and fainthearted (Deut. 20:5-8). So again the individual juts out of the group. And the mightiest dream of the prophets was the elimination of the entire military parade: "Nation shall not lift up sword against nation, neither shall they learn war any more" (Isa. 2:4).

Also international or interstate politics and all international treaties and alliances were disfavored by the prophets, who tried with all their power to stop them, even in the time of national danger. "Take heed and be quiet, neither be fainthearted" (Isa. 7:4). "If ye will not believe, surely ye shall not be established" (Isa. 7:9). "For thus saith the Lord God, the Holy One of Israel: In repose and rest shall ye be saved; in quietness and in confidence shall be your strength" (Isa. 30:15). They worked for a different kind of international politics, to which Deutero-Isaiah gave the clearest expression, to be a light unto the nations, to make "a covenant of the people," which means a covenant with all mankind (Isa. 49:6, 8). Thus, the biblical state was not to be an end to itself, but an instrument in the spiritual shaping of all peoples. The Hebraic state was meant to fulfill a moral need of mankind.

Because the state was centered in cities and capitals, there is a looking askance at the urbanization of life: "Their land also is full of silver and gold. . . . Their land also is full of horses. . . . Their land also is full of idols. . . . And so is the earth-born bowed down, and the man brought low" (Isa. 2:7-9; and cf. also 3:16-24). "Woe to them that are at ease in Zion and trust in the mountain of Samaria. . . . That lie upon beds of ivory . . . that chant to the sound of the viol . . . that drink wine in bowls" (Amos 6:1-6). It is significant from this viewpoint that the Bible ascribes the building of the first city to Cain (Gen. 4:17), in contrast to the view of Aristotle that "He who first founded the state was the greatest of benefactors" (*Politics* I, 1253a, 30). And, therefore, there arose in Israel the Rechabites who forswore wine and cities and became lonely shepherds, and Jeremiah held them in great esteem (Jer. 35:12-19). Hence, one should not regard the Essenes, whose literature has in our generation risen from the caves, as entirely foreign to the spirit of Israel.

All this seems to prove that biblical ethics is apolitical, that it is not centered in the state but in the individual's relation to another individual or to himself. "Judge ye the fatherless, plead for the widow. . . ." "If thy brother be waxen poor . . . then thou shalt relieve him. . . ." "Ye shall be holy." It is an individualistic ethics, affecting the relations between persons, between one living man and another.

Accordingly, society consists simply of relations between individuals; and morally, there is no nation or state above or beyond these relations. Thus, man rises to the stature of dignity and freedom. The idea that man is I-*Anoki* itself lifts man not only above the biological category, but also above the social-organizational category. It is not society that makes the moral laws which man has to obey (therefore, he is not free, and *ipso facto* not moral), but man is the legislator. The aim of the Bible is to develop living, i.e., moral, men. "The living, the living, he shall praise thee" (Isa. 38:19). True, the Infinite Ethicalness requires society as a field for justice and other ethical values, but man remains the aim. Divinity is embodied; or shall we say, the divine metahistorical process is realized, not in the group, but in man.

Furthermore, man in the state is not a part of a whole, as Aristotle thought, but is in himself a whole; and many "wholes" are not more whole than one whole. The whole, like infinity, is not subject to addition or subtraction. Indeed, there is something of the infinite in the concept of wholeness. Surely there is room for many kinds of organizations and institutions, but first and foremost it is not in them that the ethical relation expresses itself. It expresses itself in all its fulness between one person and another, in the relations to the other living person. Freedom cannot be organized, nor can the I be institutionalized. It sometimes dies in institutions. Morality rests upon a purely human basis, on immediate human nearness: You are a man, and therefore you are my neighbor. It is this purely human and unorganized basis that constitutes an explanation for the utterly partitionless universalism of prophetic ethics.

It seems that the world in general was not capable of grasping this notion, i.e., the individual as an intrinsic value in a moral correlation. The East pointed with the finger of the Upanishads at the whole of nature and taught: *Tat twam asi*—all this is you, and you have to fuse with the All and lose yourself in it. The Greeks saw all in the state, and their phrase, "social animal," *zoon politikon*,[7] means really not social but political, starting its life in the family circle, but attaining its main development in the state. The four cardinal virtues of Plato carried special reference to the city-states: Courage, as resoluteness in battle; temperance, as a striving for peace; justice, as harmony among the three classes: rulers, soldiers, and workers; and wisdom, as proper political leadership. The whole platonic ethics was mainly political. It did not concern itself with the happiness of the individual, but with that of the state, in which alone individual happiness can be attained.[8] Aristotle, too, thought that the ethical virtues can attain their perfection only in the life of the state, which is the realization of man's highest good. He explicitly argued that the state is by nature prior to the individual and the family, "since the whole is of necessity prior to the part."[9] The Cynics and Cyrenaics were indifferent to politics, but they also surrendered the principle of concern and involvement which is the vital nerve of biblical ethics. The Stoics rose to a high degree of cosmopolitanism and to such loftly concepts that slaves too have human rights and that one must harbor pity and forgiveness even for the enemy, and thus, they helped prepare the atmosphere for the absorption of Hebraic thoughts in the name of Christianity. One should also take into consideration the Semitic influence in the formation of this school. They too saw the Logos that reveals itself in the universal laws of all mankind more than they saw the individual by himself. And modern German philosophy followed Greece. Only Nietzsche saw that the state and culture live at each other's expense; and only Kierkegaard saw the spiritual rights of the individual as against the demands and claims of the *polis*. And in this they were both influenced by the Bible.

Here is one of the gulfs between Israel and Greece: the tyranny of logic, or the passion of classification and abstraction. Whence springs this Greek neglect of the individual? From epistemological quests. The whole great body of Greek thinking began as a reaction to sophism, as a search for a firm basis of universal knowledge in distinction to the changing and confused percept. Hence, Socrates created the concept, Plato—the Idea, and Aristotle—the Form: all of which are based on classification and grouping, on the removal of the transient and living. Thus they posited, both logically and ontologically, a vertical order of concepts, so arranged, according to relations of species and genera, that the higher is the truer and the more ontic— what really readmits relativity into epistemology. At any rate, they entirely abandoned individuals and affirmed only the more general. Here they could have risen to the idea that mankind as a whole, which is the removal of all human individuation, is the highest concept and the highest truth. But Hellenic chauvinism prevented them from reaching this thought before the Stoics and checked the process when it reached the state. The state is the species or genus and therefore the whole human truth. This tyranny of the logic of classification is what caused the cult of the state and also the existence of social classes. Also the harmony they sought, both in ethics and in art, has something of the faith in the concept and its calm because the percept is an ever open stream of impressions. Thus they all fled from the individual to the general, and it may be that the spiritual sickness of our generation, to which existentialism points, began with Greek logic strengthened by medieval conceptualism.

On the other hand, the biblical mind is not analytical, does not abstract—the whole biblical language clearly proves it—does not draw the soul out of life, i.e., its individuality, its particularity. It is all based on the singular. Even when the Bible speaks in the plural, it really speaks to *every one* of us as singular and whole. And the Bible does not favor an ontological dialectic directed upward: individual, species, genus, and ultimately—by means of gradual abstraction or a leap—God, but rather a dialectic aimed downward: God and all the ideas in their strivings for concretization by and in individual man.

Perhaps one may discern here the difference between time and space. The concept is frozen. It already exists in all its completeness. It is, therefore, wholly present, i.e., space. The door is locked, and the whole family circle sits in eternal frigidness around the kindled fire of the concept. But this is not so with the individual or the precept, which is ever changing, ever showering upon you impressions of its details. This is time. This is alive and becoming. This is an endless stream in which one cannot bathe twice. Thus the difference between seeing the individual and the group indicates perhaps a deeper and more fundamental division than has so far been discussed. But about this we shall speak in the next chapter.

It should also be observed that this biblical nominalism tallies with a belief in choice and freedom. In logic, the individual is subservient to the concept, just as each part, according to Aristotle, is determined by the whole; and therefore it is necessitated and bound. In the Bible, however, there is no verticalism. Every man is infinite, free, and final; irreducible and unabstractable unto a concept, he is an image of God. Even the concept of humanity is nothing else than all men as they are, with all their individualities, so that every man is humanity.

Ahad ha-Am's view is entirely different from the individualistic view here presented. He maintains: "Judaism sees its goal not in the redemption of the individual man, but in the happiness and perfection of the group, the people, and, in 'the end of days,' in the whole human kind, i.e., a collective concept which has no defined concrete form" (see his essay "Between Two Opinions" *Kol Kitebei: Ahad ha-Am*, p. 372; also his essay "Flesh and Spirit," *op. cit.*, p. 350). We, on the other hand, have tried to show that the Bible aims at the individual man in his relation to another individual; and the road from man to mankind is shorter and more direct than it is from an intervening station, from nation to mankind. Platonic-Aristotelian ethics proves it, for it never attained to mankind.

Ahad ha-Am furthermore thinks that according to the Mosaic Law all generations form one chain: "the people is one throughout all its generations." The fathers have eaten sour grapes, and the children's teeth are set on edge. Only during the decay and destruction of the First Commonwealth, in the Books of Ezekiel, Ecclesiastes, and in several Psalms, did speculations arise as to why the just suffer.

Then the sages arrived at the idea that "this world is like unto a vestibule before the world to come" ("This is not the Way," *Kol Kitebe Ahad ha-Am* 1.6). But in the same Book of Deuteronomy, we read even more explicity: "The fathers shall not be put to death for the children, neither shall the children be put to death for the fathers" (24:16). And as for the world to come, this belief was not delayed because of a sense of nationalism, but because of a feeling of Messianism, as will be later explained.

Ahad ha-Am points to "the tendency to abstraction and to the negation of the concrete form, which is characteristic of Israel," in contrast to Christianity "which rests entirely on the pursuit of individual salvation" ("Between Two Opinions," *op. cit.*, p. 372). It seems that here too in Ahad ha-Am we have the influence of Greek intellectualism, which was captivated by logical abstraction and by the priority of the species or the genus to the individual and the singular. Judaism strives not toward the abstract but toward the concrete moral personality. Not society nor the people nor the state, *man* is the goal of divine history. There are no laws concerning the state, no chapter on taxation, no ceremonies of royalty. The Bible knows only the living individual. It is nominalistic.

THE STRUGGLING I

Greek intellectualism rests upon two assumptions: ethics is knowledge and the ethical good is the utilitarian good. From these two premises, it drew the conclusion: knowledge of the good leads necessarily to the doing of it, as no man willfully harms himself. Thus we have here an intellectual determinism and an absence of moral struggle. All is, as it were, at peace inside of man as on the radiant marble faces of the gods. In contrast to this, in the Bible man's knowledge of good and evil is the snake's achievement; and, indeed, after man ate of the fruit of knowledge the catastrophic sins began which led to the Flood, as if knowledge itself stirs contrary forces, as if it is human nature to fight what he knows.

This is the biblical approach to man: critical but permeated with hope for "the end of days." Man standing before a moral choice is not immediately free to act or even to choose; he must first struggle with a tendency to sin—a tendency whose first appearance suprised, as it were, God Himself. For at first "God saw every thing that he had made, and behold it was very good" (Gen. 1:31). Says the midrash, in *Bereshit Rabba* 9:14, the word *meod* (meaning "very") spells in a different order the word *adam* (meaning "man"). Man then is the "very," the superlative in creation. And suddenly there appears the imagination, or, better, the instinct: "And God saw that the wickedness of man was great in the earth, and that every imagination of the thoughts of the heart was only evil continually. And it repented the Lord." [10] With this discovery of the instinct, the human drama began, always revolving around sin, and always a radiant finger of redemption pointing toward "the end of days."

What is this instinct? With what exactly must man struggle? With himself. The instinct, according to the etymology of the Hebrew word for it (*yezer*), is the creation, the nature, the biology of man, and the moral I must overcome biology. "For that he also is flesh" (Gen. 6:3). "How much less in them that dwell in houses of clay, whose foundation is in the dust" (Job 4:19). Here the Bible is in agreement with Plato: [11] material body is the source of evil. Jeremiah stands stunned before corruption nestling in man: "The heart is deceitful above all things, and desperately wicked: who can know it?" (Jer. 17:9); Ezekiel looks forward to a new heart and a new spirit (18:31; 31:19; 36:26); and Deutero-Isaiah—to a new heaven and a new earth (56:17), as if there is no hope for man and the world as they are except their destruction. And the Psalmist penetrates even deeper and finds sinfulness in birth itself: "Behold, I was shapen in iniquity; and in sin did my mother conceive me" (Ps. 51:5), and Job joins him in despair: "Who can bring a clean thing out of an unclean? not one" (Job 14:4). "How much more abominable and filthy is man, which drinketh iniquity like water" (Job 15:14-16; and cf. 4, 17, 19). This attitude was accepted by the Essenes, with the exaggeration of self-loathing.[12] Christianity posited the degeneration of the nature of mankind, until it needed the self-sacrifice of Jesus. And Simone Weil stirs in us both admiration and recoil: "Wherever I am, I stain the silence of heaven and earth with my breath and my heartbeats." [13]

In the Bible, the presence of this instinct does not mean that there is no hope, but that there is struggle, and it is this struggle which constitutes man's freedom. Freedom is not the power to act according to moral advice, but the inward power to struggle for it. It is not so much the triumph as the battle. When the battle is done, freedom becomes a memory. Moreover, the moral I lives and becomes stronger in battle, just as it is weakened by each submission and surrender.

True, there are deterministic verses, but they can always be explained by the biblical tendency to ascribe all to God. Thus, for example, "The Lord thy God, he will go over before thee. . . . Joshua, he shall go over before thee" (Deut. 31:3), "And the Lord stirred up the spirit of Zerubbabel the son of Shealtiel . . . and they came and did work" (Hag. 1:14). The will of Zerubbabel, called his spirit, is ascribed to God without nullifying the nature of this will, and without entering into the niceties of logic, so that both were joined, free will and divinity. Interesting in this context is the fine insight of the midrash, which contains much psychological truth, remarking on Exod. 7:13: "In the account of the first five plagues the Torah does not state 'And he hardened Pharaoh's heart,' but 'And the heart of Pharaoh was hardened.' " [14] The meaning is that in the beginning the will is indeed in man's hands; but when man perseveres in misdeed, his heart is no longer his own. At any rate, all these verses can have no deterministic value in the field of ethics against the explicit declaration: "Behold, I set before you this day a blessing and a curse; A blessing if ye obey. . . . And a curse, if ye will not obey" (Deut. 11:26-27), "See I have set before thee this day life and good, and death and evil. . . . I have set before you life and death, blessing and cursing: therefore choose life" (Deut. 30:15-19), and against such expressions as Isa. 1:19-20: "If ye be willing and obedient. . . . But if ye refuse and rebel." This view of free will was adopted by the Pharisees, but the Essenes thought that all is decreed, and the Sadducees claimed that there is no decree in any area of human acts.[15] "All is seen but freedom is granted" (*Abot* 3:15). "Everything is in the hand of heaven except the fear of heaven, as it says, 'And now, Israel, what doth the Lord thy God require of thee but to fear' " (Deut. 10:12).[16]

Thus Judaism differs from the beliefs and opinions of other peoples: from Hinduism and Buddhism which believed in *karma*, the belief that deeds of man drag after him from one incarnation to another, without escape and without forgiveness or atonement; from Christianity which posited original sin and condemned the followers of Pelagius who denied it and maintained freedom; from Greece which was permeated with determinism, the determinism of Moira, the lady of the destinies; from Heraclitus in his aphorism: "The character of a person is his demon" (fate); [17] from Socratic intellectualism, and from the Stoics who held that all is a necessary manifestation of the Logos or the world-reason. It differs from both religion and science; religion tended to see in free will a reflection on the all-powerfulness of God, and science, the same with reference to its god, nature. Biblical thought rose above such fear through its fundamental assumption: I-*Anoki*. Let us explain further the assumption and its consequences.

The source of sadness and confusion is our *thinking* about our I. We seek it with all the power of our thought, and do not find it because, as an object of our thinking, it turns in the meantime into an it, an opaque object, something unspiritual, mute, and impenetrable; and all the living spirituality of the I, all its initiative and origination, all the primal powers—all is gone. Only in the moment of ethical decision, when the I makes a step and assumes responsibility, is it through and through I, it is all self, spiritual and free, without a particle of opaque objectivity. It is therefore a dark, deep source of gratification. Moreover, in our feeling of the moral I or the subject ("I decide thus and thus"), there is also a feeling of absolute authoritativeness, of being a part of the All-Subject in which it is contained.[18] This is the identification, I-*Anoki*. Under the inspiration of this identification, the prophets declared: "Thus said the Lord"—two voices in one speech, the voice of the self and the voice of the Absolute, neither one being primary or secondary, original or echo. This is the mystery of the identification. And here is also the feeling of freedom, for freedom is none other than divinity, pure subjectivity, a freshness of a moral approach without chains or past. God is always present, always causeless; and there is no greater joy in man than this moment of I-*Anoki*, of self-severance from the chain of causality, of breathing the divine air of pure present.

And where is this *Anoki*? How is it conceived in this self-identification? If entirely transcendent, then the I is no longer autonomous, does not judge according to itself but according to Someone above. It obeys and hence is again no longer I, but it. We must, therefore, say that God Himself is the I of man, that He is immanent in the moment of decision—"And I shall dwell in their midst." There are times when the sub-human I ceases to satisfy, and I turn to my deepest depths and see two roads, good and evil, and there is no strength to choose and to start going, and then—"Out of the depths have I cried to thee, O Lord," and out of my deep confusion and emptiness a small spring begins to flow and sing, and a strength rises in all fibers, and I gather courage and decide. That moment is one of inspiration, of a "breathing into," a grace, a help of heaven. But the heavens are in my depths, and God is my deepest I, and the choice is all my own. That is to say, man finds God in his depths immanently, but sees Him transcendently, infinitely.

Certainly Kant was right in his critique of all traditional proofs

of the existence of God. He was right because of a fundamental reason: each proof is a presentation of causes of a conclusion and leads
therefore to a contingent conclusion. We can phrase it also differently,
as in the case of the I: God is in all His essence a subject, *movens
non motum*; but under the process of thought, He turns into an it.[19]
There is, therefore, no absolute proof or absolute certainty except in
the heart, in the moment of identification. Nor can we accept the
negative theology which dominated in Arabic-Jewish-Christian circles
in the Middle Ages, that we can know only what God is not, not what
He is. What do we know about the boat in Maimonides' example
after all the gradual peeling of the negative attributes? [20] There *is* a
way to God which is all positive, but only one way, the ethical one:
"I will make all my goodness pass before thee" (Exod. 33:19).

And it is a way in which there is no decree, nor obedience, nor
even Kantian duty—all these make the good deed heteronomous and
rob it of its free moral soul—but self-legislation which is identical
with divine legislation, because of its absolute authoritativeness. The
divine law becomes my law. Thus Raba interprets the verse: "But his
delight is in the law of the Lord; and in *his* law doth he meditate day
and night" (Ps. 1:2) to mean the law of the Lord becomes the law
of man.[21] Moral recognition takes away from man the sense of subjection to external authority, giving him instead a feeling of free will,
a feeling that the law and the choice are his own. Simone Weil writes:
"Even if we could be like God, it would be better to be the soil that is
obedient to God," [22] and this again is startling, but also strange and
cold.

And if there is no obedience, because the moral legislation is
my own and therefore autonomous, then there are no guiding principles in morality. Every situation presents itself, as we have seen, in all
its entirety, and the I-*Anoki* does not relate it by abstracting its particularities to a general principle, e.g., "Thou shalt not steal," but
reacts to it as to a unit. This situation as it is in all its fulness is steal-
ing. This means that the moral reaction is immediate and direct, and
there is always freedom and choice and not a submission to some
abstract principle. Man is in all moral cases I-*Anoki*, "I have set the
Lord always before me" (Ps. 16:8), never in obedience to principles but in creation of principles. This is the meaning of the great
Kantian command: Act so that the maxim of thy conduct shall become a universal law. For man projects values by his deeds, although
he projects them *as* prior to his deeds. His creation is a discovery.
The values leap out of the waves of action in their full stature.

This free choice manifests itself particularly in the virtue of love, and it *must* be free. I *choose* to love, although the love overwhelms man as *fatum*. It is the revelation of my absolute freedom, freedom going forth to freedom. But it is revealed also in justice, though it is, as we have seen, objective. Man must flame subjectively like a torch in order to be objective in respect to the just.

And there is also a struggle, according to the prophetic view, *after* the deed, a kind of choice backward, when the severed I seeks its way in the dark back to *Anoki*, and voice calls unto voice. "Turn thou us unto thee, O Lord" (Lam. 5:21), "Return unto me and I will return unto thee" (Mal. 3:7). Those are the moments of regret and contrition. Is there any sense in regret? Can we pull out an aching tooth from the gums of the past? Some deny it. Buddhism posits *karma*. Christianity holds out only the self-sacrifice of Jesus (I John 4:8-10). The Greek myth sees that the sons not only are punished for the sins of their fathers, but also, what is more frightful, as in the house of Atreus, are doomed to commit evil deeds because of the evil deeds of their fathers, and there is no repentance or atonement, no breaking of the chain. Nor does regret have any place in Spinozistic ethics or in the scientific concept of causality.[23] But in the Bible sins are not only annulled by the retroactive power of repentance, but also turn in the reckoning into good deeds. "Great is repentance, for because of it premeditated sins are accounted as errors" (*Yoma* 86b). "If your sins be like scarlet they will become white as snow. If they be red like crimson they will become as wool" (Isa. 1:18). Under the flood of tears, our foul deeds are polished and even begin to shine. "In the place where the penitents stand even the wholly righteous cannot stand" (*Berakot* 34b). The wholly righteous do not have those polishing tears.

This idea of the power of regret reveals an unusual conception of time. If one can choose backward, to do good deeds in the past, then the past is not past. One can stretch forth his hand to deeds done yesterday and turn them like loaves of bread in the oven and make them look better. Also the linguistic phenomenon of the *Vav*-conversive in Hebrew reflects such a magic conception and the power of freedom of the ethical man. Only later, especially in Ecclesiastes did the concept of "time" (*zeman, 'et*) approach the meaning of *fatum*.

THE MESSIANIC I

In the Middle Ages, Hebraic thought—together with Islamic and Christian thought—changed its course. Lured by Greek wisdom, it conceived of God as a self-centered intellect,[24] without emotion, will, or change—all of which we associate with the very concept of life. It is not a question of anthropomorphism, for with the same amount of effort exerted to make comprehensible the intellectual essence of divinity, it would have been possible, and with greater originality and fertility, to explain God as a restless, moral will. And such an explanation would have been nearer to the origins of Hebraic thinking, for the biblical deity is not a frozen, pagan perfection, but a dynamic ethicalness, striving to carve through the human being as through a dark, rocky tunnel, a way to itself, to its ultimate embodiment in man. God is drama, the drama of all dramas, the song of all songs, of being in becoming, and not a marble statue, even if it be intellectual marble.

The Messianic vision, Israel's deepest contribution to the world's politico-religious thought, springs therefore necessarily from this concept of God as pure ethicalness because such a divinity necessitates the existence of man so as to translate into actuality the fulness of its moral being, i.e., the existence of a shining point at the end of the dark tunnel somewhere at the end of days. What is the image of this vision?

First, that biological factor, with which man has to wrestle in the moment of moral decision, will completely yield to the moral consciousness. "Then the wolf will lodge with the lamb, and the leopard will lie down with the kid" (Isa. 11:4-9; cf. 65:25). That is to say, all the brutality of man and beast will be rooted out; nature itself will be softened. "For behold, I am creating new heavens and a new earth; and the former things shall not be remembered" (Isa. 65:17). "I will give you a new heart, and will put within you a new spirit" (Ezek. 36:26; cf. 14:19). "Then will I pour out my spirit upon all flesh; your sons and daughters shall prophesy; your old men shall dream dreams, and your young men shall see visions" (Joel 2:28). Messiah himself will be endowed with moral zeal and supernatural insight. "He will smite the ruthless with the rod of his mouth, and with the breath of his lips will he slay the wicked" (Isa. 11:4). This may still be figurative, but Daniel already sees: "And lo! with the clouds of the heavens[25] there came one like a man, who advanced toward the Ancient of Days. . . . To him was given dominion, and glory, and kingly power, that all peoples, and nations, and tongues shall serve him; his dominion is an everlasting dominion" (Dan. 7:13-14). Certainly, there was a long development in the Messianic concept until it reached the apocalyptic character in Daniel and his successors; but there is already some degree of supernaturalness and superhumanness in Isa. 11. The Nietzschean thought that man must pass beyond himself is the basis of Hebraic Messianism.

Moreover, all the primeval dream of man to be like God,[26] revealing itself in the first episodes of Genesis, in the desire for the fruit of knowledge, in the intermingling of the daughters of man with the sons of God, and in the Tower of Babel, is embodied in the vision of Messiah, for God did not reject the dream itself. He rejected only the hasty leap, the breaking through to divinity at the very beginning. Man must be first expelled from the garden, for the way is yet long. One can note this intention of God also in the divine disapproval of human concentration in one place. The idea of such a concentration in the form of a city was ascribed to Cain. Later, in the Tower of Babel, the early language of man was broken up into a variety of tongues. And all seems to have followed a divine pattern: to inhabit the whole globe and begin the march of history. But that dream God Himself implanted in man. "Ye shall be holy for I am holy." He calls unto all men, not only to Moses, Ascend unto me, Ascend unto me. And the Pauline doctrine called "apocatastasis," that in the end God will be "everything to everyone" (1 Cor. 15:28) "that ye may be filled with the very fullness of God" (Eph. 3:19), that all will become divinity, is, therefore, a continuation of the thread of biblical speculation. Perhaps this is also the meaning of Zech. 14:9: "Then the Lord shall become king over all the earth. On that day the Lord shall be one; and his name one." The Hebrew word here for "one" (ehad) perhaps really means "alone," [27] that all will be divinity, infinite ethicalness.

But this divine fulness is necessarily the end of history, the saturation point of the hunger of becoming, when eternity will cut into time, and the two roads which started in the Beginning, the supernatural and the natural, will meet and the ellipse will close. This can come only at the end of days: first, because Holiness forbids a confusion of borders; and secondly, because the infinite ethicalness requires infinite time for its realization. Thus is created a dialectic situation, the Messianic dialectic. The "final" number of this infinite series constituting the divine and human moral tug is not man but God. Man strives to be God, for which reason there beckons to him his own supernatural image, the divinity of Messiah: "with the clouds of heaven" (Dan. 7:13). But what is this infinite? Not a certain number, for this would constitute a contradiction of meanings, but such a progession of numbers in which there is always a higher or lower number, and the term infinite describes the progression and not any particular number, which is always finite, so that the infinite is always finite.[28] Therefore, Messiah also, who is the "end" of an infinite progression, when he comes, must be finite, limited, human, never co-responding to the deepest longing of man to be like God. He is, therefore, always future, infinitely future, but not present. Man will always want to be God, and it will always be given to him to be only human. This is the tragic-optimistic-vital element of the Messianic I—always later, never now; never now, yet always later. Always faith, and always postponement: never this, because if this, there is no more ideal. We are torn between the will of the heart and the knowledge of the mind, between idealism and realism. This is the infinite idealism of biblical ethics. True, Platonic philosophy too speaks of clinging to the ideal, the Good, but that ideal is static, shining in its iciness; but the biblical ideal ("Be holy, for I am holy") is dynamic and dramatic. It weaves itself through the web and development of human morality and is always beyond it, always future. I AM above, and always I SHALL BE below, so that the idealism is dynamic and infinite. It is Holiness in process and Glory in target.

Here we have an explanation for the surprising absence of the Hereafter in the Bible.[29] It is not that the biblical mind is national, that man needs no individual reward in the Hereafter when he is satisfied with the reward promised to the nation in this world, as Ahad ha-Am thought,[30] for according to our view, biblical ethics is human-individualistic. But the Messianic vision delayed the coming of the faith in the Hereafter, since the vision is infinite and, therefore, this world cannot come to an end. In other words, heavenly infinity requires an infinite time to be materialized, and, consequently, an endlessness of *this* world. Hence, we find that the Messianic image is not clarified in the Bible, for he is an ideal in the infinite, never actual. The main feature is not he, but the road to him. Only in the apocalypse, when the biblical sense of the infinite was already blunted, perhaps by Greek influence, there emerges his detailed image together with a faith in the Hereafter. Essentially it is a different Messiah. In the Bible he is the ideal end of this endless world; but in Apocrypha, he opens the world to come. These are two different conceptions. The soul of biblical Messianism is futurity, horizons beyond horizons without number, and with the sense of the infinite we perceive it.

Thus the Messianic vision bends the axis of the human consciousness from the yesterday to the tomorrow. The I is not my past
but my future, not my history but my striving and my dream, and
horizons widen and open up endlessly as in spring. Truly the Messianic idea was springtime in the world-soul, for then began the long
march of man to himself, to his depth, at the command from above:
"Ye shall be holy, for I am holy." Ye shall be infinite, ever higher,
ever more beyond, for I am infinite. For there are depths in the heart
of man more than he knows, deeper than he can reach—divine depths.
"And I shall dwell among them." In those incomprehensible, infinite
depths, God and man meet, and the dream to be God—the final triumph of Glory, Glory's overtaking of Holiness—becomes realized in
the infinite, i.e., never ad infinitum. This is the Messianic dialectic—a
meeting and never—a convergence of parallel lines in the infinite.

But the ethical I not only walks toward Messiah; he is himself
already Messianic. The end of days throws backwards the blessed rays
of its ultimateness over all the times before it, even as the Sabbath
candles impart the light of their pure flames over the days of the
week, backward and forward. But this is true mainly because in an
infinite series the half too is infinite, even the smallest part is infinite,
so that every number in that series partakes of the nature of the
infinite. Thus, $\frac{\infty}{2} = \infty$. True, this only proves that the infinite is
not subject to mathematical operations; it does express, however,
the sense of the infinite in every step on the road to the infinite. And
this is Messiah. Every person in the march of generations has in him
something Messianic, some of the pains and exaltations of the Messianic days. "All Israel is holy," says the modern Hebrew poet,
Tschernichowsky, "thou art the Maccabean." Every day carries the
possibility and the responsibility of the immediate coming of Messiah.[31] "Sanctify yourselves therefore, and be ye holy" (Lev. 11:44).
Says Hermann Cohen: "The mere striving after holiness, in itself
sanctifies." And truly there is no finished and final holiness, a high
plateau attained after difficult efforts. There is only a self-sanctification,
a climbing on a steep mountain that loses itself in heaven, and there
is a bit of heaven at the fall of each foot, at each grasp of the hand.
It is noteworthy how over both Messianism and Holiness hovers the
mathematical mystery of a part in the infinite being itself infinite.

Biblical Messianism is a homeless road, a becoming and not
being. It is not plastic art but music, like the whole spirit of this
people, *steps* of Messiah. It weaves itself out not in place but in time,

and time is a vector, a direction, never finished, always a longing and a striving. "And it shall come to pass in the end of days." Time is the canvas upon which man embroiders his ethical self, his Messianic pattern. How did that Hasidic Rabbi express it? If I learned that at the end of the day I stood on the same rung that I stood on at the beginning, I would wish to live no more. And Socrates said: "The soul is always on trial."

From all this the image of man rises illuminated by a heavenly light. We have seen [32] that in the Psalms the question is asked twice: "What is man?" And two answers are given: one—"And thou hast made him a little lower than the angels" (literally, than God); and the other—"Man is like unto vanity." The first is Glory; the second—Holiness. Now paganism also took the stand that "man is like unto vanity." Thus, indeed, the chorus sings its second song in Sophocles' drama, Antigone, perhaps not because of Holiness, but because of the absence of Holiness, the absence of an infinite. All finite gods leave in the human heart an area of nothingness and despair. Homer speaks of "the wretched mortals" and of the life of misery which the gods fashion for them. Plato emphasizes that man was created to be a puppet or plaything of the gods.[33] And the problem of man in our days is again pagan, the problem of a moral man whose bracket I-Anoki was broken apart so that he lost the infinite, and consequently —how does Macbeth sing toward the end of the play?—"Out, out, brief candle! It is a tale told by an idiot, full of sound and fury, Signifying nothing." And over against this nihilism, biblical ethics sees in the life of man not an idiot's tale, but divine significance. God is not the antithesis of the world; on the contrary, He needs the world as a field of operation for His moral being, needs it in order to be. Thus, the world rises to the level of a divine necessity. And by the same token, man is not an epicyclical and absurd phenomenon. He carries, as it were, divinity on his shoulders until the end of days. His doings can be sanctifications of the Name or, the reverse, profanations, "lessening of the image." He can hasten or slow down redemption both above and below. He is endowed with super-cosmic significance. He was created, as the final prayer reads, "to perfect the world under the kingdom of the Almighty," which is the same as saying "to perfect the Almighty in the kingdom of the world."

Gorki has well said: "Man—there is in it a sound of pride." The Talmud saw more: "Every man must say, For my sake the world was created" (Sanhedrin 37a). Even more saw Isaiah: "For I have created him for my glory" (Isa. 43:7), and glory means manifestation.

◄ 10 ►

ISRAEL AND GREECE

The Jews knew about the existence
of Greece many centuries before Alexander of Macedonia passed
through the land of Israel and met, according to the legend, Simeon
the Just and other nobles of Jerusalem.[1] The Greeks are mentioned in
ancient biblical records. Gen. 10:2 mentions them among the sons of
Japhet. Ezekiel, in his lamentation for Tyre, states that they brought
slaves and vessels of brass to the Tyrian market: "They traded the
persons of men and vessels of brass in thy market" (Ezek. 27:13). Joel
too mentions them as slave merchants buying the captives of Judaea
from "Tyre, and Zidon, and all the coasts of Palestine" (Joel 4:6).
And Deutero-Isaiah (66:19) prophesies that those who will escape
the great judgment will go forth to the isles afar off, among them
Greece, "and they shall declare my glory among the Gentiles." And
behind these references are the Greek colonies in Asia Minor and the
cultural exchange in the development of script, language, and myth
between the Semitic peoples and the Greeks. Thus the waves of the
Mediterranean Sea carried spiritual cargoes from shore to shore and
mixed the climates around the basin. And when we read such a statement of Socrates as: "Then we ought neither to requite wrong with
wrong nor to do evil to anyone. . . . For I know that there are few
who believe or ever will believe this. Now those who believe, and
those who do not, have no common ground for discussion, but they
must necessarily, in view of their opinions, despise one another" [2]—

when we read these words, it seems as if a prophet of Judea meditates and motivates inwardly what he will soon glowingly pour out of his heart.[3] Certainly the Hebrews and the Greeks were far apart in general culture and in manner of expression, but near each other in their intent; perhaps far because near, because distances are particularly striking among near ones. These distances, to which we have already referred in previous chapters, are mainly three: deterministic intellectualism in Greece as against moral struggle in the Bible, the quest of harmony as against the sense of moral infinity, and classification and generalization as against the individual and the particular.

DETERMINISTIC INTELLECTUALISM

The Greek philosophers regarded the intellect not only as a power of observation but also as a moral guide. Socrates believed that knowledge and morality are one, as no man would do evil willfully, but only through ignorance. Plato strove for an intellectual aristocracy, for philosopher-kings. Aristotle already knew that the will can act against right insight and that it needs, therefore, moral fortification in order to overcome the passions,[4] but he nevertheless placed the dianoetic, or the intellectual-scientific, virtues higher than the practical kinds because the aim is higher than the means. He regarded the mean, or the middle road,[5] as the only right road, and only the wise man can locate it. The Stoics maintained that one should follow nature; but because nature is Logos, moral duty is obedience to reason. Thus they were all ready to submit, with a complete sense of security, to the guidance of intellect.

Now rationalistic ethics cannot be autonomous because every rationalistic approach by its very nature asks: why and wherefore? And this "wherefore" is always beyond the act in question, and, therefore, the act becomes heteronomous. It is not intrinsic morality —what Kant demanded with all the powers of his mind—but extrinsic. The good becomes the useful. "Is a dung basket beautiful then"— Socrates was asked. "Of course," he answered, "and a golden shield is ugly, if the one is well made for its special work and the other badly." [6] All Greek ethics was endaemonistic, egocentric. It was concerned primarily with the quest of the highest good, namely happiness —a word almost lacking in Hebrew. The Hebrew word *osher* is found only once in the Bible: "And Leah said, *Happy* am I, for the daughters will call me blessed" (Gen. 30:13), and the meaning there is not entirely clear. As for the plural form, *asherei*, as in "*Blessed* is the man that walketh not in the counsel of the ungodly" (Ps. 1:1), the meaning is not psychological but metaphysical, religious-ethical, well-rendered by "blessed." Nietzsche saw well the inferiority of utilitarian ethics, calling it slave-morality. "The ignoble character," he said, "may be distinguished by keeping benefit always within the range of vision," but the higher character, the noble one, is more irrational.

And rationalistic morality is also deterministic. The whole philosophy of the Socratic school aimed to free man from Homeric determinism, from fatalism, and yet it plunged into a determinism of a different kind, the intellectual kind. The knowledge of the good leads necessarily to the doing of the good, as no man, it is claimed, willfully does what harms him. He is unable consciously to do the opposite of the good, and there is no struggle with the instinct, and there is no choice. Knowledge or the lack of it determines the acts of man.[7]

On the other hand, the biblical view ascribes no authority to the rational power on the moral plane. Eating the fruit of the tree of knowledge did not hinder the outburst of catastrophic crimes that were quick to follow. On the contrary, it was itself a sin. And the Book of Proverbs, which represents calculated, practical wisdom, emphasizes, together with other sapiential books, that "the fear of the Lord is the beginning of wisdom," i.e., the beginning of ethics [8] (Prov. 1:7; and so also 9:10; 15:33). Similarly Ps. 111:10: "The beginning of wisdom is fear of the Lord," and Job 28:28: "Behold, the fear of the Lord, that is wisdom." [9] And the Book of Proverbs explicitly warns against intellectualism: "Trust in the Lord with all thine heart; and lean not unto thine own understanding" (Prov. 3:5). And since God is defined in the Bible only in terms of morality, the meaning of a saying like "The beginning of wisdom is the fear of the Lord" can only be that the motive in every question of conduct must be morality itself, infinite morality, morality which has no other aspects or motives that are apt to qualify and limit it, a morality which is pure and entire. In its ways we are commanded to go: "For with thee is the foundation of life; in thy light shall we see light" (Ps. 36:9). It is only in the light of the absolutely moral that we see concretely what is moral. The moral then is discerned only through itself—moral autonomy.

This infinite morality, moreover, does not force itself upon us from the outside. It enters into the depths and speaks to us from there, immanently: "Thus said the Lord," my voice is your voice, the voice of your depths, my command is your command. It is not I who makes the laws you are to obey: you yourself are the legislator, you yourself recognize in them, and through the inside of them, their rightness. "And in his law doth he meditate day and night" (Ps. 1:2) —the law is his, according to Raba, man's own. "When he learnt it becomes his law" (Rashi, *Kiddushin* 32b). Nor is it a means to the intellect, a means whereby the mind may be calm and peaceful, unattacked by storms of passions, and free to devote itself to higher thoughts. Here morality is the aim, in spite of the view of Maimonides, who followed Aristotle, that morality is only the third perfection, while the dianoetic virtues are the fourth and highest perfection.[10] And the God of the Bible is not a thinker, but "merciful and gracious." He is not a closed intellectual circle of thinker, thinking, and thought—all in one. In all the thirteen attributes of God in Exod. 34:6-7, there is not one of an intellectual nature. There is only moral panethicism. He is not "the mind concealed from all thought," but the concealed heart, *cor cordium.* And again it is to be regretted that the great minds of the Middle Ages deviated from their course, under the influence of Aristotelianism, and failed to weave on the original biblical thread and to develop the specific problems it entailed.

It follows then that biblical morality is not endaemonistic-heteronomous, as the approach is not rationalistic, not a quest of reason and benefit, but is wholly intrinsic morality, autonomy. Its criterion is in itself, in the exclusively moral absolute. And the great Kant regrettably erred here, not trying to look deeper, freer, into the spirit of the Bible. "I am the Lord"—sings each one of the moral commands in Lev. 19. Morality in all its entirety and purity is divinity itself, so that the moral value "lives itself out" on the moral plane, never visiting the life of utility. "Be not like servants that serve the master in order to receive reward" (*Abot* 1:3). Certainly, there is reward; there are practical consequences. "If thou wilt diligently hearken to the voice of the Lord thy God . . . I will put none of these diseases, which I have brought upon the Egyptians" (Exod. 15:26). "If ye be willing and obedient, ye shall eat the good of the land. But if ye refuse and rebel, ye shall be devoured with the sword" (Isa. 1:19-20). And the whole basis and guide of the prophets when they looked into the future of men and peoples—was it not what we called the "law of moral causality," namely that the wheels of history revolve in a fixed rhythm of crime and punishment? [11] But one should not confuse results with motives. The good is good intrinsically; it is the voice of God, the voice of absolute morality, without any hedonistic calculus. Greek philosophy was endaemonistic, a quest of happiness, while in the Bible there are values that stand higher than any striving for happiness. Morality proclaims "I am the Lord."

It should be observed that this moral recognition, since it is not rationalistic but intuitive, reaches where reason is unable to reach, to the eternalness of morals, to "I the Lord change not" (Mal. 3:6). For reason investigates the causes of things, which causes are logically prior, and, therefore, the conclusion must be temporal and contingent. But intuition sees the thing in its independence and causelessness, and, therefore, in its absoluteness, in its timelessness. Furthermore, reason is essentially an organizer. It relates things and ties them together: this is good for health, this makes for anxiety, this leads to happiness. It is entirely objective and descriptive, with nothing of its own to contribute. It is only the intuitive conscience that creates from itself, that occasionally judges an act as "free from punishment, yet forbidden" (Talmud). The mind gives form, establishes alliances, and intuition imparts value. This is so in morals, in esthetics, and also in the kingdom of science, insofar as truth is not only an assertion of relation and law but also an inner excitement and response: truth! Thus the three kingdoms are one in their inner source, the human voice in a silent universe.

And biblical ethics is not deterministic. Knowledge, or its opposite, ignorance, does not determine my action. There is also an instinct, and thanks to this evil instinct there is freedom, because I struggle and thus make the decision and the deed my own. The midrash is, therefore, right in saying "And behold it was *very* good"; this is the evil instinct (*Bereshit Rabba* 9:9). It challenges the will to choose, so that man becomes a field of battle between the Image and the instinct, between God and the snake. And the stakes are high. All depends on this battle. Every step is either a sanctification of the Name or a profanation of the Name, an increase of divinity or a "diminution of the Image," a hastening or a deferment of the Messianic day, of the meeting of the two parallel lines: Time and Eternity. And man, in whom this Manichaean struggle takes place, becomes a cosmic hero, a stage for a divine drama, a monodrama, and man in his stature reaches heavenward, instead of being, as in Plato, a plaything or a puppet in the hands of the gods. One may say, therefore, that the Bible plumbed greater depths in unveiling the instinct and the struggling will, and essentially this means that the Bible discovered morality both as a form of autonomous knowledge and as struggle and freedom, without which there can be no morality.

HARMONY AND INFINITY

The second divergence between Israel and Greece in the field of ethics reveals itself in the concept of justice. This concept (δίκη) was understood in Greek philosophy as harmony. In politics it is a balance of the three social classes: rulers, soldiers, and workers, and the individual is only a carrier of his class and, therefore, a part of this general harmony. This view of justice manifests itself particularly in man himself. Here it is a balance of the three souls or faculties of the soul: wisdom, will, and passions. In keeping with these three psychic powers, there are three cardinal virtues: wisdom, courage, and temperance, with the addition of the fourth virtue, justice, which is the symmetric blending of the others. Also the "mean," or the middle road of Aristotle, is nothing else than a compromise between the sharp challenges that life or the spirit within present to man.

In the shaping of this view, that the good is the middle road, various motives combined. Perhaps it was an attempt to gain the security afforded by appeasement and reconciliation, as in Rav Pappa's phrase: "The law is like both sides of the controversy" (Talmud). Or, it may have been due to a deeply concealed fear of life, life being apt to entangle you in responsibility for the consequences of your decision and choice and to upset your inner peace. For this reason, there developed later the two Greek schools, the Stoics and the Cynics, both of whom recommended apathy: Whatever happens, be not disturbed. But the harmonistic view of justice is mainly due to an esthetic approach toward the good. If beauty is a symmetry between sides, one side being mirrored and intensified in the other, a kind of hexameter in the Greek epic (the parallelism in the prophets is the opposite of this calm meter) reminiscent of the verse "God also hath set the one over against the other," or, perhaps deeper, of the verse "Male and female created he them," so that there is a frame of finiteness, of completeness and perfection, then why should not the same approach be applied to the powers and capacities of man? We should reject none of these human endowments, but bring them together and let them all play on one another, so that there would result a harmonious unit, symmetrical and balanced, an esthetic ethics, "good and comely" (Eccles. 5:18), καλὸν κἀγαθόν.

"Such is the right approach or introduction to love-matters," says Diotima in Plato's *Symposium.*

Beginning from obvious beauties he must for the sake of that highest beauty be ever climbing aloft, as on the rungs of a ladder, from one to two, and from two to all beautiful bodies; from personal beauty he proceeds to beautiful observances, from observance to beautiful learning, and from learning at last to that particular study which is concerned with the beautiful itself and that alone; so that in the end he comes to know the very essence of beauty.[12]

Thus, conduct becomes only a station on the road, and ethics loses itself as an independent domain somewhere on the way to the kingdom of beauty.

It may be worthwhile, in order to see the essential elements of the biblical view, to separate the threads that are woven into this esthetic-harmonistic approach. There are three threads: (1) egocentric psychologism, the harmonious development of all psychic forces, disregarding the relation with the neighbor which is of the essence in ethics, and its aim; (2) staticism, the marmoreal calm of the gods, perfection of virtues, or a harmony of perfections, and accordingly, a form and characteristic; (3) finiteness, finality, for every harmony is finite and final. All is according to weight and measure, neither more nor less. And all these are in complete and characteristic contrast to the biblical approach.

In the first place, here justice is a separate and most significant domain. It is not a closed, inner concept, a psychic spring that adjusts the wheels of reason and will and the senses, and which, therefore, does not really belong to ethics at all, as the term was understood in the Hebraic mind. But justice is all in all ethical, a going out from one man to another, and this psychic "going out," and not the inner harmony, is what matters.

There is in Plato a short dialogue which brings out astonishingly the greatness of this contrast. The title of this dialogue is "Lesser Hippias," and it all revolves around the strange idea that a man who sins intentionally is morally better than the unintentional sinner. Hippias revolts, but Socrates brings up inductive arguments in defense of this paradoxical thesis. A good mathematician, for example, is more capable of deceiving us with a false proof than a weak mathematician is. And it is so in other spiritual pursuits, but also in manifestations of bodily aptitudes. The runner who willfully slows down and the wrestler who slips intentionally are superior to the runner and the wrestler who are overcome in spite of their best efforts. And the singer who utters a false note purposely is better than one who could not help singing falsely. The conclusion then follows necessarily: He who commits a crime willingly is superior to the one who does wrong erringly. And Socrates ends by saying that, although he disagrees with himself, he sees no escape from the conclusion. Commentators struggle with this passage, some thinking that Socrates here is trying to prove his intellectualistic view that a man who sins willingly does not exist.[13] But this entire argumentation is a good illustration of the identification of ethics with psychologism, with the development of the inner powers. In all these talents, bodily as well as mental, the main character is power and ability; and, therefore, designed failures prove greater talent, more dash and flexibility, than those resulting from clumsiness and rigidness.

And from this standpoint of talent, the conclusion is valid also in ethics, and there is no escape. But in the sphere of biblical morality the fallacy is obvious, for the criterion here is not the measure of power and ability, but always the measure of positive attitude to the neighbor. Therefore, evil by design is worse, more immoral, than unintended evil. That tricky mathematician is certainly more gifted than one who is too clumsy to deceive, but from the standpoint of human relations he is a villain. Socrates did not distinguish between talent and morals. And, alas, this failure is still rampant.

Secondly, biblical ethics is not staticism, but activity. When a man does not act, he is not moral. The deity too in the Bible is conceived more as a name of action than as a name of a substance. This is the divine mystery already felt, as we have explained, in the Middle Ages, and this is also the mystery of the human I, the intermittent self, that lives only in action. Hence, the Bible has no concept of Platonic virtues or perfections because these are achievements, finished states of the soul, and in the Bible there is no moral finish. "For there is not a just man upon earth, that doeth good, and sinneth not" (Eccles. 7:20; and cf. 1 Kings 8:46). "The Holy One, blessed be He, deals strictly with those round about him [the righteous] even to a hair's breadth" (*Yebamot* 121b) because the greater the man, the greater the danger of falling. And the chief thing is always the deed. Not to be but to do. The Greeks saw the ground facets of the diamond, and the Bible looked to the restless, colorful fire within. Calm? The Bible is not interested in it. It knows of a zealous God and a consuming fire, and it demands moral zeal also from man, what we called the principle of involvement, the constant wakeful reaction to every crime committed somewhere in the world: hence, the burden of Babylon, the burden of Tyre, the burden of Nineveh. Hebraic justice tears and destroys every web of illusive and appeasing harmony. "Justice, justice, thou shalt pursue" (Deut. 16:20). "Let judgment run down as waters, and righteousness as a mighty stream" (Amos

5:24). "As a burning fire shut up in my bones, and I was weary with forbearing, and I could not stay" (Jer. 20:9). The Greek marmoreal mind is unable to understand the biblical panethical storm, just as the restless mind of the Bible must look with astonishment at the marble faces of the gods: Why are they so calm, the gods? And why this happy smile on their faces? What makes them so happy? Plato says: "And we have no more need to ask for what end a man wishes to be happy, when such is his wish: the answer seems to be ultimate." [14] Why is this the ultimate? Why can we not continue and ask why? And Aristotle remarks: "In evidence of this we have the case of God, who is happy and blessed, but is so on account of no external goods, but on account of himself." [15] And, indeed, all the statutes of the gods are radiant with such happiness. But would artists in ancient Israel, even without the prohibition, have carved such faces? It seems rather that in the Hebrew divinity affliction and suffering would shine forth from its face.

And thirdly, unlike Greek finiteness, we have the ethical infinity of the Bible. Who can really tell where the ethical border lies, where one should cease pursuing justice? In the Talmud, there was developed also the concept of "within the line of the law." And Ben Patura thought: "It is better that both should die than that one should witness the dying of his neighbor." [16] True, there is the advice: "Be not righteous over much; neither make thyself over wise. . . . Be not over much wicked, neither be thou foolish" (Eccles. 7:16-17). But such Hellenic verses are not characteristic of the Bible. Biblical ethics is built upon four foundations: on the conception of God as infinite ethicalness, on the conception of man as a realization and actualization of divine ethicalness, on the idea of Holiness and self-sanctification which is a constant feeling that there is still a higher grade, a constant striving for ascent, essentially for a Nietzschean self-freeing from the limitations of humanity, and on the Messianic idea that God and man pull toward each other from both sides of the infinite, leading to that embrace which will take place at the end of days. And one dynamic word is common to all four concepts: infinity—an ethical boundless romanticism as against the calm harmony of Greece. From this viewpoint, ethics is not, as it is usually defined, a science or kingdom of ends, but a kingdom of endlessness.

And this infinity is not imposed upon man, but comes in response to something deeply hidden within him, the longing to be like God, manifested already in the first chapter of the Bible, in the story of the tree of knowledge, in that of the daughters of man and the sons of

God, and in that of the Tower of Babel—a longing which God does not really condemn but only defers, making use of it until the end of days. Thus this longing wanders in the world, sometimes reaching the highest heights, and sometimes falling into the foul arms of Satan. Tertulian says: *anima naturaliter christiana.* This may be too narrow, but perhaps it may be said that the soul is naturally religious, i.e., infinite. "Also he hath set eternity in their heart" (Eccles. 3:11). For the very concept of end, like all concepts of borders and fences, involves a look beyond, at the other side of the end, and so it automatically moves the end. And on the ethical plane, the very word end is semantically connected with completeness and perfection. And where do we have completeness in life? Who leaves his life as something rounded out and finished? We begin to spin so many threads and leave them all a confused coil, a Rorschach test that stirs in the mind of the beholder unwholesome wonderments. We are perforce in quest of the infinite. But this too disturbs man as something dim, existent and nonexistent, gone as soon as conceived. "Music," says Carlyle, "is a kind of inarticulate unfathomable speech, which leads us to the edge of the Infinite, and lets us for moments gaze into that." [17] Yes, music and ethics too are moments of ethical choice and decision, when the I says: "Thus says the Lord." Carlyle would not hesitate to say: There is something then akin between music and ethics. Thus the sickness of our generation is not Hebraic-biblical but Greek in its origin, the product of finite harmonies which shrank greatly in a greatly expanding cosmos. Despair always comes from a perception of nothingness surrounding us, looking with its dead pale eyes at the little here caught within it.

But the deepest and most fundamental difference is probably—

CLASSIFICATION
OR THE TYRANNY OF THE CONCEPT

Protagoras taught that man, individual man, is the measure of all things, thus introducing sophistic dizziness into epistemology. Came Socrates and created the concept, and concepts, being common to all men, have therefore objective authority; came Plato and created the Idea; came Aristotle and created the Form—all these creations being the same thing, solid cornerstones for the mansion of knowledge. But the trouble is that ontology naturally came and invaded epistemology, completely occupying it. Because, if the general is more fit than the particular to be an object of knowledge, the species more than the

individual, and the genus more than the species, and surely knowledge
is directed to being, to understand the existent, then the more general
tends to be connected with being, more existent, so that the individual, or the living man, comes out of the epistemological process as
deprived of being.

Thus Plato erected his essentialistic philosophy, that all things
are reflections of essences or ideas, and accordingly the principal thing
is not man but the state—to general humanity he never attained [18]—in
which he saw all the essence of man. Hence his ethics is primarily
political, seeking social happiness, the perfect state with its three
classes: rulers, soldiers, and workers. The individual is only a wheel in
the chariot, without demands and claims of his own. This is the
tyranny of logic, already referred to in the previous chapter.

Aristotle explicitly emphasizes the state as a genus or a class, and
the class is more valuable than, and logically prior to, its particulars.
It is the actualization of all the good hidden in man. All the virtues
can develop and become perfected only in it, and to it man is subordi-
nated. He must not even commit suicide, not because it is an escape
from confinement or robbing the gods whose property he is, as Socrates
thought, but because it is apt to harm the state which needs the serv-
ices of every individual.[19] Perhaps also the Stoic idea of *consensus
gentium* carries a conceptualistic element: the group opinion too is a
species or a genus, and therefore the truth, whereas the individual
opinion is confusion.

Thus, the Greeks cared for the group and abandoned the individual, but it is not so with the Hebraic spirit. Here there are no royal
privileges or laws of taxation or maintenance of the state, but there is
the single man. There is the alien, the poor, the orphan, and the
widow. There is the neighbor, the brother, and the friend. "And thou
shalt love thy neighbor as thyself"—says R. Akiba: "This is a great
rule in the Law. Says Ben 'Azzai: 'This is the book of the generations
of man' is a greater rule" (*Sifra* on Lev. 19:18; *Jer. Nedarim* 41c).
"Behold I stand before thee there—the Holy One, blessed be He, said
to Moses: Wherever you find human steps, *there* I am before thee." [20]
The individuality of man is surprisingly emphasized in the mishnah
entitled "How Were the Witnesses Inspired with Awe" in *Sanhedrin*
37a: "For this reason was man created alone, to teach thee that whosoever destroys a single soul of Israel,[21] Scripture imputes to him guilt
as though he had destroyed a complete world; and whosoever preserves
a single soul of Israel, Scripture ascribes to him merit as though he
had preserved a complete world. . . . Again to proclaim the greatness of

the Holy One, blessed be He: For if a man strikes many coins from one mould, they all resemble one another, but the supreme king of kings, the Holy One, blessed be He, fashioned man in the stamp of the first man, and yet not one of them resembles his fellow. Therefore every single person is obliged to say, the world was created for my sake." Here is the whole doctrine of the image of God: something generally human but also singularly individual and valuable.

Thus these two peoples differed from one another in the form they gave to the material life. The Greeks created a logically artificial world, in which all parts are joined and chained together, grouped in species and genera, and the stubborn particularity which refused to be joined they omitted from their universe. And the Hebrews set their minds on the living and particular and tried to join them with threads of justice, mercy, and love. This point of departure perhaps brought about the two previous distinctions, for the concept is by origin and character rational and hence leads to rationalism, whereas the individual is the subject and direct object of morality. Again, the concept is in itself harmony, an abandonment of individuality, watching only for the symmetrical and parallel in individuals, but man, every man, is infinite and cannot be pressed into the circle of the concept, the old definition "a rational animal" scarcely touching the complicated and stormy essence of man. Perhaps we have here also the origin of the division into Greek determinism and biblical free will. In logic every individual is subject to the concept from which and into which he or it enters, just as every part, as Aristotle points out concerning man's relation to the state, is determined by the whole and, therefore, is bound and caused, so that we have a determinism not only intellectualistic-Socratic, but also stemming from the very nature of logic. In the Bible, we have no such vertical order. Every man is infinite and free, first and last, irreducible into a concept. He is all, in all his particularities, an image of God. Even the concept humanity is not an abstraction in the Bible but the totality of human beings as they are, with all their variety and colorfulness, without abstraction, without a loss. The general is the same as the particular, only more thereof, no creation but a multiplication. It is the same word—adam, man.

And again [22] we are confronted with the dichotomy of space and time. The concept is crystallized and finite. It is born of the human mind, rounded out and locked, although sometimes the individual painfully struggles under the sharp blade of the circle, his head on one side and body and legs on the other. It is finished and frozen, already existing in all its fulness, and consequently partakes of the nature of space. The percept, on the other hand, alive and ever-changing, with multitudes of living impressions showering constantly from it—the percept is time and becoming. It is still a flow, a constant flux. The conceptual names, which man gives to percepts, give him orientation among the objects—it is so safe and easy to walk in a world of space —but they reduce and squeeze the things they name. They take away from them the vitality of time, as well as the terror of the abysmal nothingness of time. It follows then that the Greeks were captivated by space. And from space, they came under the dominance of matter, which manifested itself at the very beginning of their thinking, in their quest of primordial matter, being unable to posit being without matter. The Bible, on the other hand, starts off with the metaphysical notion "In the beginning," i.e., time without matter, or—perhaps even more—time without time, nought, one of the most fruitful notions in speculation, paralleling the notion of zero in mathematics. The Hebrews were always fascinated by time, that moving verse which, like a ribbon, endeavors to express something and never reaches the end of the sentence, the revelation of all its intent. Hence time is called in Hebrew 'olam, unknown, "from eternity to eternity," from mystery to mystery. Judaism then is nearer to Heraclitus, to the philosophy of becoming, and Hellenism—to Parmenides, to staticism. And all staticism is finality, completeness, limitedness, paganism. Greek ethics is carved out of marble esthetics, but Judaism is all music, all time that moves restlessly to a Messianic rendezvous with eternity.

So the Bible and Hellenism diverge; and one should not seek a harmonization or a reconciliation between them, as they tried to do in the Middle Ages. We should let them play out their contrasting parts in all their fulness and sharpness, thereby generating a tension, in mind and soul, which will strengthen the spiritual progress of humanity. Contradiction, and not harmonization, is the fertilizing element.

‹ 11 ›

ETHICS AND RELIGION

Ethics and religion in their joint
presence in the Bible create a high seriousness, which in order to understand we must examine their mutual relationships from three
standpoints: borders, experience, and direction.

BORDERS

By and large, there is no necessary connection between these two
manifestations of the human spirit, and every feeling in favor of such
a connection is due to the Hebraic root in general culture, as non-
ethical religions have not been lacking. The Greek religion was
primarily a cult of natural forces, and its beautiful gods did not particularly distinguish themselves on the plane of morality. The same
was true of the Scandinavian and Germanic myths. On the other
hand, ethics was not always dependent upon religion or metaphyhics.
Plato, it is true, urged his disciples to strive to resemble God who is
the good, but he did not develop this resemblance and did not form
his deity from an essentially religious-providential viewpoint. And Aristotle saw no relation at all between human conduct and metaphysics,
because in his opinion such conduct springs entirely from our rational
nature. Among the Greeks, therefore, religion and ethics were unconnected.[1] Even where they do dwell together, there is still the question: which is conceived as primary, and which as secondary? Who is

the landowner, and who the occupant? Leibnitz expressed his view that ethics is logically prior to theology. Kant stressed the idea that the existence of God is an ethical postulate to guarantee the ultimate triumph of the good. Feuerbach defined religion as a deification of human attributes. God is good means: the good is God; God is just means: justice is God; God is the glorification of the human heart. And Carlyle pointed to the etymological and semantic affinity between "worship" and "worthship." From all these opinions one gathers that the road is from ethics to religion. But there were some who thought otherwise. Arabic orthodoxy of the school of al-Ash'ari in the Middle Ages maintained not that God commanded the good because it is intrinsically good, but that the good is good because God commanded it; and if He had commanded the opposite, the opposite would have been good. Such also in Christian scholastics was the stand of positive theology as taught by Duns Scotus. And here we must join, through a leap of times and worlds, the view of Nietzsche that the disappearance of the God-concept deprives the concepts of equality and justice of all justification, and the utterance of Dostoevsky that "without the existence of God everything is permissible." [2] From all the discussions in the previous chapters, we must conclude that the biblical spirit would favor neither the view of Leibnitz nor that of Dostoevsky. Ethics is not prior to religion, nor posterior to it; it is religion, since ethics, absolute and abstract, is itself conceived as the deity.

Note that even with Kant religion is external to ethics. It is a guarantee or a justification, but outside. Hence, religious ethics, i.e., a system of acts intended to be a fulfillment of commands, is heteronomous and, therefore, not ethics at all. But in the Bible there is no relation of priority between ethics and religion, but an identification without any residue, without there possibly being any residue. This means that biblical Judaism is neither an ethical religion, nor a religious ethics, but a religio-ethics, a theoethics. "Is not this the fast that I have chosen? . . . Is it not to *deal thy bread* to the hungry, and that thou bring the poor that are cast out, to thy house" (Isa. 58:6-7). The fast is bread to the poor. The whole fierce and irreconcilable fight of the prophets in behalf of justice and righteousness and against the stress on cult—and the cult was surely central in the religious consciousness of antiquity—can be grasped only on the basis of this identification, that good deeds are the real cult. And all this flows from our fundamental view that God is conceived in the Bible only in ethical terms, as an essence which is only infinite ethicalness, as a value which is a being, so that ethics is in itself cult, *imitatio dei*, or perhaps even something deeper, full of mystery and pregnant with consequences in religious history, a *participation in divinity*, or—in talmudic terms—causing the Divine Presence to dwell.

Nor are there any dogmas outside of deeds, and this is in opposition to Luther who held that man attains salvation only by faith, *sola fide* —a view which he did not create but which has deep roots in the Gospel: "I am the way, the truth, and the life: no man cometh unto the Father, but by me" (John 14:6. Comp. Heb. 10:20). And Moses Mendelssohn saw rightly when he denied in his *Jerusalem*, part two, the existence of dogmas in Judaism, basing all on deeds. But one must make it clear: there are dogmas; however, they do not stand outside, but inside, of the deeds, as we shall soon see, and one cannot sever and isolate them. This ethical-religious immanence is similar to the immanence of Ideas which Aristotle stressed in opposition to Plato. This is the tendency of Glory in the ethics of Judaism.

EXPERIENCE

Psychologically, too, ethics is man's reach and touch of upper worlds, for in the moment of decision he becomes, as we said, an I-*Anoki*, i.e., his I joins the I of all being, the Infinite Ethicalness, so that the voice within him calling to do or to forbear is conceived with majestic sovereignty as the voice of the Almighty. Else what indeed is the ultimate truth of the prophets' "Thus said the Lord"? And how do we account for their imperiousness and readiness for self-sacrifice? It was a genuine experience, a psychological-metaphysical fact; the soul's voice was conceived, because of its absolute authoritativeness, as a divine voice. And ethics as experience becomes, therefore, identical with religion.

The same conclusion is reached when we look at the ethical material, the social relation, the love of the neighbor. What is this relation? I love the thou not as thou, nor as he, but as I, as a subject, i.e., as a personality. Toward an object there can be no love, and in general there is no personal contact with an object. How can I hear the voice of your cry, *feel* the voice of your cry, when you remain you, when your I does not turn through a miracle or soul-alchemy into my I? What else does hearing and feeling a human cry mean? For every "you" closes, and only the I opens. But your I awakes only at the sound from above: Where art thou? And in the name of that sound it decides, takes on obligations, and makes a step. Hence, the I in you is always both a psychological and a metaphysical event, I-*Anoki*. The finger that points to one's own heart also points to the heavens above. The love of the neighbor and the love of God are therefore the same thing, and ethics is again religion.

And also, from above downward, religion is not a mask for ethics; it is ethics itself. On the one hand, moral legislation by the I-*Anoki* is impossible except in the name of *Anoki*, who alone imparts eternal and universal authority to the moral choice of man and gives new meaning to Kant's rule: Act so that the maxim of thy conduct may become a universal law—which means that the maxim of thy conduct *becomes* and is a universal law; but, on the other hand, the decision is also human-individualistic; it is entirely my own. Biblical man is not like Kafka's heroes receiving commands they do not understand, not knowing from whence and from whom they come. The commands which he, the ethical man, receives are signed with his own stamp and his own initials: "And in his law doth he meditate day and night" (Ps. 1:2); the law becomes his own. Man does not discover the categorical imperative in a moral situation; he creates it by his I-*Anoki*, or, more correctly, he discovers and creates at the same time. This is the peculiarity of the divine command, that it claims no possession or ownership. It lets man feel that the command is his own. It tells him: It is your command, that of your own heart. The voice is both external and internal, the voice of I-*Anoki*. Man hears his own voice through the thunder of God, and one voice does not subdue the other. This also is the meaning of the talmudical dictum: "Every single word that went forth from the omnipotent was split up into seventy languages" (*Shabbat* 88a), and, therefore, "No two prophets prophesy in the same style" (*Sanhedrin* 89a). Thus religion and ethics in the Bible are entirely coincident with each other. Ethics is personal and metaphysical at the same time.

DIRECTION

Not only from the standpoint of revelation but also from that of redemption, not only psychologically but also historiosophically, does biblical ethics assume religious-metaphysical dimensions. Man's career does not begin with his birth, nor does it end with his end. Else each man could rightly ask: With all the good qualities in me, what's my meaning? What sense do I make? Why and wherefore did I come into the world? What am I here to improve? What can I improve? And if there is any purpose to my life, what relation does it bear to the life-purposes of others? Are there billions of purposes? Does not one purpose collide with others like boats upon a crowded lake on a summer day? Either it is all a chaos of chance or there is a chaos of purposes. Biblical ethics sees the whole march of human history as *one* arrow shot from one bow, like a mathematical vector, like a line with direction. It sees divinity as Infinite Ethicalness seeking to be invested with existence through human deeds. For what is ethicalness without deeds, without man? Therefore, creation is no divine caprice, or a demonstration of demiurgic power, but a divine-ontic need, a moral necessity. It implies a mutual want between God and man: "My soul thirsteth for thee, my flesh longeth for thee" (Ps. 63:1). And the longing of God for man, since it is divine, is even greater and deeper than the longing of man for God. This is why naked divinity knocks on all the windows of the world, on all human hearts: Admit me, clothe me! Always "understand and know me"—sixty times "and they shall know that I am the Lord" in the Book of Ezekiel alone! But how? He is so infinite, and how can we clothe with human deeds His infinite nakedness? No, but there are additions and augmentations: man to man is added. Everyone is a step on the Messianic road toward the realization of the Divine Ethicalness. Everyone is a role in a divine drama which began "in the beginning" and will end "in the end of days." And only our great thinkers of the Middle Ages, who were captivated by Greek wisdom, arrived at the thought that God is without dependence or change or history or metahistory—a calm and icy sea. Go skate on its ice!

So there, nevertheless, develops out of the concept of infinite morality a sort of doctrinal theology, but it is all embodied and expressed, as stated, in the moral deeds themselves, whose bonds it never breaks to become a kingdom by itself. These doctrines are three: first, "In the beginning he created," creation. Infinite morality created the world, for morality always creates, through its zeal and flame, through its urge to be clothed; and, if infinite, its creations will be worlds. We may say, therefore, that being is both beginningless and temporal: beginningless from the standpoint of the creator, for He always creates, and from its own standpoint—temporal. The eternal event, when it descends, begins to float in time. This is how Aristotle and the medieval thinkers can be reconciled with each other. The concept, "in the beginning," carries within itself the stimulating contradiction of both sides: from the standpoint of what comes after, it is time; but from the standpoint of what preceded, it is outside of time, it comes after no-time, that is, after eternity. Hence, it is an eternal beginning. The second doctrine is revelation and providence.

At every step the moral bush burns, and in every strike of the heart with self-reproof God reveals Himself, the *Anoki*, and inquires and demands; and in every historical event there strikes, sometimes too deep for hearing, what we called the law of moral causality. And revelation, too, is a creation, the creation of a human personality, the awakening of the I from its slumber at each scepter-touch of the *Anoki*. The Bible knows no other kind of I. Third, there is Messianic redemption, the heart of all Hebrew theology or theoethics, the primary urge of the whole historic unfoldment and its goal, the redemption of the world and man, which is also the redemption of God Himself returning from time, sated with concretization and realization, while behind Him the elliptic rent in eternity is made whole again and healed.

And again we return to the nature of the ethical experience itself. It may be argued: That Messianic encounter is to take place at the end of days and is therefore a *fata morgana*, always vanishing and retreating. How then can we build a philosophy of the superhuman struggle of human history on an illusion? No, it is not an illusion. The essence of the concept of the "end of days" is that of a border and a fence; and a fence is not an absence of belonging to either side, something neither of this side nor of the other, that is to say, a fiction, but quite to the contrary, something of either flank, a partnership of sides. The same is true of the concept of the "end of days." It is a meeting and a juncture of this side and that side, of time and eternity together, for every part of an infinite *participates* in the infinite, becomes itself therefore infinite, itself Messianic. Hence, the ethical life always constitutes a mystery of yes and no, of already and not yet, of the exultation of identification and arrival and of the sorrow of distance unto despair. This means that in ethics as in religion there is the vibration—endlessly and relentlessly—of Holiness and Glory.

Kierkegaard distinguishes between ethical existence and religious existence, the first being a struggle and a triumph and the second—suffering. From the foregoing, it follows that they are the same, that there is in both triumph and suffering simultaneously, Glory and Holiness. And the oscillating rhythm between the two extremes is the constantly refreshing urge, the endless dynamics, the protection and shield against all moral Philistinism and self-satisfaction. It is the three steps forward and three steps backward before the Hebrew Eighteen Benedictions. It is the dance in the entire life of the spirit.

Now come and see, dear reader. Our generation stands thoroughly shattered with fear of annihilation, with fear of the *possibility* of annihilation. The ground has slipped from beneath us, and there is no place to run. There is no refuge, for we took care of the situation in due time and set fire to all refuges. We scratched and drew out every metaphysical vein from our spirit, and there is no secret and no mystery. We knocked the door closed against every theorem which does not bring upon the platter an immediate Q.E.D. . . . What is the problem of man in our time? It is essentially the problem of the amoral man, the unconnected man whose I-*Anoki* has broken apart, so that, having lost his metaphysical *Anoki*, the remaining piece of the I naturally rots, and he struggles to shake himself free from this stub too, out of a morality of irresponsibility, of detachment and emptiness. He finds no subject above or below with whom to walk and converse. All turns into an object under his thought. All stands opposite to him as mute matter, scientific and mute, like some fat little worm curling upon itself and feigning dead when a cat approaches to smell its being. . . . And some complain that the young generation ceased to feel itself at home in any group, in society, in the world, that it feels alone and abandoned. How else can it feel, without the metaphysical link which alone connects, across the frightening gulf, one man with another, or with his surroundings, and which alone is the secret of the feeling of at-homeness,[3] reminiscent of "and thou givest life to them all" (Neh. 9:6)? And morality denotes maturity. "The imagination of man's heart is evil from his youth" (Gen. 8:21). Man remains a youth, irresponsible in spite of all his technological progress, as long as he does not bend his neck under the yoke of the ethical kingdom.

Stronger and clearer than ever is the biblical voice calling to our generation.

APPENDIX

EXPANDING MATTER

In the Amoraic period, the idea was rife that the world in its beginning, in its entirety or in its parts, the sea, the heavens, and the earth, kept on expanding until God rebuked it or said to it, enough! (Hebrew *dai*, whence the name of God *Shaddai*). See, for example, Rab and Resh Lakish in *Ḥagigah* 12a, and R. Yiẓḥak in *Gen. Rabba* 5:7; 46:2. It seems that this myth derives from several sources. First, the Pythagorean belief in the two elements of creation, the *limited* and the *unlimited*, or fire and darkness. Second, the gnostic idea that the last aeon, named Sophia, desired to break through to her first father, "ever stretching herself forward," until Horos (border) restored her to her place. Sophia is also called earth. See Irenaeus, *Against Heresies*, I, 2, 1-3; 5, 3. But the motivation for this stretching, in the talmudic version, is not gnostic, but is —and here is the third source—neoplatonic in that it regards matter as a demonic, anarchic element.

ESCHATOLOGICAL TERMS

In Chapter 5, note 30, and in other places in this work, we cited various terms for *'olam ha-ba*, or the world to come. The abundance of such terms is surprising. It may be that in the absence of any explicit eschatological statement in the Bible, the Rabbis looked for hints in various biblical expressions. Here are more such terms.

1. *Ereẓ*, land or earth. Thus, *Ḥagigah* 15a: "if the righteous person is privileged, he takes his portion and the other man's portion . . . as it is said, therefore in their *land* they shall possess the double" (Isa. 61:7). See also *Sanhedrin* 90a: "all Israel have a share in the world to come, as it is said, your people shall all be righteous; they shall possess the *land* forever" (Isa. 60:21).

2. *Tob*, good. Thus *Abot* 4:1: "Happy shall you be and it shall *be well* with you (Ps. 128:2), happy shall you be in this world; and it shall *be well* with you in the world to come." *Berakot* 4a: "Had I not believed to see the *goodness* of the Lord in the land of life (Ps. 27:13), David said before God, Lord of the universe, I am sure that thou givest a good reward to the righteous, but I do not know whether I have a portion among them." *Ḳiddushin* 39b: "In order that it shall *be well* with thee, in the world to come which is all good." See also comment in *Jer. Hagigah* 77c and *Debarim Rabba* 7:10 on Ps. 31:20: "How great is thy *goodness* which has laid up for them that fear thee." See also Saadia, *Emunot we-deot*, IX, 3: "The seventh general division consists of passages in which man's reward is called *good*." It should be remarked, however, that this eschatological interpretation of Ps. 31:20 leans also on the expression "thou hast laid up" (*zafanta*), as the comment in *Debarim Rabba* 9:3 shows. Compare expression of King Monabaz in *Baba Batra* 11a: "My fathers stored up below and I am storing above." Similarly, in the Apocrypha. See references in Charles, *op. cit.*, II, 311 n. 5, to which add 2 Baruch 84:6; Sirach 3:4; I Tim. 6:19.

3. *Yom*, day. Thus *Ḥagigah* 12b: "the world to come which is like unto *day*." *Shabbat* 118a: "*day* stands for the Messianic pains, the punishment of hell, and the war of Gog and Magog." *Zebaḥim* 118b: "All the *day*—this refers to Messianic days." *Gen. Rabba* 91:13: "all the days—this is the world to come which is all *day*." II *Baruch* 49:2: "in what shape will those live who live in Thy *day*?" Similarly *Shir ha-Shirim Rabba* 7:7: "the day of God." See also

Saadia, *op. cit.*, "the sixth general division . . . concerning a *day* reserved by God for retribution."

4. Spinoza and Judah Hallevi. In chapter 1, page 10, we cited Spinoza's statement: "this love or blessedness is called Glory in the sacred writings, and not without reason" (Ethics, V, Prop. 36, Schol.). Scholars are in search of the verse which seems to identify love or blessedness with Glory. It seems however that Spinoza here draws from Hebrew philosophical literature, particularly from the writings of Judah Hallevi, famous poet and thinker of the Twelfth Century. In his Kuzari 11, 50, this author, discussing the divine light, frequently called Glory (Hebrew: *kavod*) by Saadia Gaon and by Judah Hallevi himself, which descends upon those who are endowed with "a peculiar essence," states that it is called Love, or, in the language of Buxtorf's version: *et hoc vocatur amor dei*. Indeed Hallevi makes his protagonist in this dialogue apply to this love-relationship the phrase from Isaiah: "O Israel, thou on whom I will be glorified," to which the Khazar-king replies: *haec est gloria magna*. Similarly in Kuzari 111, 17: "Whenever some few, or a whole community, are sufficiently pure, the divine light rests on them and guides in an incomprehensible and miraculous manner which is quite outside the ordinary course of the natural world. This is called Love and Joy," or as in the Latin version: *vocaturque id a nobis Amor* (Dei) *et Laetitia* (ex eo orta). Similarly Albo, *Ikkarim* (ed. Husik), 111, 347: "Hence the Bible calls this love a peculiar essence."

5. *Kol*, all. The Valentinian gnostics call the Messiah, as well as the aeons, *pan*, all. See F. Sagnard, *La Gnose Valentinienne*, pp. 274, 425. This may have had an influence on the talmudic usage of the term. Thus, *Berakot* 12b: "and the sages say, the days of thy life are this world, '*all*' adds the days of Messiah." *Baba Batra* 17a: "there were three who were given in this world a taste of the world to come: Abraham, Isaac, and Jacob; Abraham, as it is written, *with all*; Isaac, as it is written, *from all*; and Jacob, as it is written, *all*."

6. *Zedek*, righteousness. Thus, *Makkot* 23b: "R. Hananiah ben 'Akashiah says, God desired to make Israel worthy, wherefore He gave them abundantly Torah and commandments, as it is said, it pleased the Lord for the sake of His *righteousness* to magnify the Torah and glorify it." Here the term "righteousness" seems to mean eschatological reward. Saadia too (*op. cit.*, III chapter 1, end) thus interprets it: "to increase our reward and happiness, as it is said, it pleased the Lord for the sake of his *righteousness*," etc. Compare, however, Wilhelm Bacher, in his *Die Agada der Tannaiten*, II, 376, who thinks that the reading of the sage in the Bible was *zadqo*, "To make Israel righteous." See also I En. 32:3; 77:3; Books of Adam and Eve, 25:3, where we read about the *garden of righteousness*, to which the righteous go after they die, and which is also called *the garden of the righteous* (I En. 1:60; 8:23; 70:3) and also *the garden of life* (I En. 61:12). Similarly in *Hagigah* 12a: " 'Arabot (a sky) in which there is righteousness . . . and the souls of the righteous." The difference is that in the Apocrypha, as also in II Cor. 12:2, 4, the garden is in the third heaven (see Apocalypsis Mosis 40:2; II Enoch, chapters 8-9); but in the Talmud it is in the seventh heaven.

Thus we see how eschatological terms and phrases, that came into use after the Bible and appear suddenly in the Mishnah and Gemara, become clarified in the light of the intervening apocryphal literature.

NOTES

1. See W. R. Harper, *Amos and Hosea*, International Critical Commentary (New York, 1905), XC, 1 ff.

2. See John Skinner, *The Book of Genesis*, International Critical Commentary (New York, 1910), pp. 7, 43, 47.

3. This term, as referring to God, is frequent in the Zohar. See, for example, II, 288b: "And because of this the Holy Ancient One is called *'ain*, Nought." See also *ibid.*, 290a; 43a. Cf. Reuben Margoliyyot, *Nizozei Zohar* on *Zohar* II, 43a, citing *Midrash Tanhumah*, *Emor* 15, where this term is used in the sense of speech or reason. Moses Cordovero in "Definition of Terms," chap. 1, *Pardes Rimmonim*, identifies this term with the Crown (*Keter*) because this *sefirah* is above comprehension. But this term already occurs in the writings of the later Neoplatonists who conceived the Supreme Being as superessential, and therefore called Him μὴ ὄν, or *nihil*, and in this respect they were influenced by Buddhism. Thus, Dionysius speaks of "the absolute No-thing which is above all existence," and Scotus Erigena explains: *Deus propter excellentiam non inmerito nihil vocatur.* See W. R. Inge, *Christian Mysticism* (Meridian Books), pp. 106, 126, 134, 136 n. 1.

4. See Israel Efros, "Some Aspects of Yehudah Halevi's Mysticism," *American Academy for Jewish Research*, XI (New York, 1941), 39-40.

5. Spinoza, *Ethics*, V, Prop. 36, Schol. Spinoza is here guided by Jewish medieval thinkers, particularly by Judah Halevi, in his *Kuzari* II, 50-52 as translated by the younger Buxtorf: *et hoc vocatur amor dei . . . haec est gloria magna.*

6. See I Sam. 4:22; Num. 24:22; Exod. 33:18; 34:5-7. Exod. 14:18 uses for glory through miracles the expression בהכבדי בפרעה and similarly Ezek. 39:13

יום הכבדי

7. For example, see Isa. 59:10.

8. For example, see Ezek. 1:28.

9. Exod. 16:7, 10; 24:17; 40:34-35; Lev. 9:6; Num. 14:10; 16:19; I Kings 8:11. See also Exod. 29:43.

10. See Saadia Gaon, *Emunot we-De'ot* (Josephof, 1885), II, 10, and his *Commentary on Sefer Yesirah*, ed. Lambert, p. 94; and also Maimonides, *Moreh Nebukim*, I, 5, 10, 18, 19, 21.

11. Ps. 19:20. See also Ps. 24:10; 29:3, 9.

12. As to the manner of counting these thirteen attributes, see Ibn Ezra on Exod. 34:6, and Rabbenu Tam in the "Tosafot" on *Rosh ha-Shanah* 17b.

13. The LXX reading is ויהי להם למושיע בכל צרתם, לא ציר ומלאך, פניו הושיעם

14. See *Kitāb ma'āni al-nafs*, ed. I. Goldziher, p. 37, and my above-mentioned "Some Aspects of Yehudah Halevi's Mysticism," pp. 38-39.

15. The expression כבוד ה' (Isa. 35:2) and its entire section are generally regarded as belonging to Deutero-Isaiah.

16. See Isa. 5:16 ויגבה ה' צבאות במשפט והאל הקדוש נקדש בצדקה where ה' צבאות is parallel with האל הקדוש and ויגבה with נקדש.

17. In Isa. 30:18, the idea is that He will hold back His mercy. Isa. 14:1 is generally taken to be by a later prophet.

18. See Meir Ish-Shalom היכן הוא הארון in *Hashiloah* XIII, 511-49, and Neumark's תולדות העיקרים בישראל I (Odessa, 1913), 49.

19. See I Sam. 4:21-22 גלה כבוד מישראל כי נלקח ארון אלהים.

20. Jer. 3:16-17; 7:4.

21. בעת ההיא יקראו אל תנבל כסא כבודך (Jer. 14:21). See also Jer. 3:16-17: כסא כבוד מרום מראשון and Jer. 17:12: לירושלים כסא ה׳.
22. See Jer. 14:9, and compare Deut. 7:21; 9:3; 23:15.
23. Hugo Gressman, Der Ursprung der Israelitisch-Jüdischen Eschatologie (Göttingen, 1905), p. 202; John M. P. Smith, Book of Malachi, International Critical Commentary (New York, 1912), XXV, 63.
24. The expression in Isa. 12:6 כי גדול בקרבך קדוש ישראל is generally regarded as a postexilic psalm.
25. Ezek. 20:39; 36:20; 21:22; 39:7, 25; 44:7-8. This expression is also a favorite of Leviticus. For the parallelism of shem (name) with kavod, see Isa. 43:7; 59:19.
26. Ezek. 1:26-28. The usual interpretation is that the נגה encompasses the whole appearance of the Man on the Throne, but the Targum's rendering seems to be correct.
27. See Ezek. 39:21, and compare Isa. 66:19. See also Ps. 97:6; I Chron. 16:24.
28. Isa. 40:5; 58:8; 59:19; 60:1; 66:19.
29. As for Isa. 63:9, the LXX seems to have the correct reading, for which see n. 13 above.
30. See Isa. 42:19; 44:26.
31. For the term zaddiq, see Isa. 41:26; 45:21; 49:24. As for zedeq and zedaqah, see particularly Isa. 41:2, 10; 42:6; 45:8, 13, 23; 51:5-9; 59:17; 61:10, 11; 62:2; 63:1. In some of these references the term is parallel to yeshu'ah.
32. See Isa. 45:15.
33. Isa. 54:10; 55:3; 59:21; 61:8.
34. ברית עם Isa. 42:6; 49:8. Similarly in Isa. 42:5 (see Karl Marti, Das Buch Jesaja [Tübingen: J.C.B. Mohr, 1900], ad loc.) and in Exod. 33:16, 'am means mankind.
35. See Isa. 42:6; 49:6.
36. עבד ה׳ Isa. 52:13-53:12.
37. Compare Prov. 3:12.

CHAPTER 2

1. See Skinner, op. cit., pp. 206, 287; A. H. McNeile, The Book of Exodus. (London, 1908), p. 144.
2. Zech. 14:5; Ps. 89:6; Job, 5:1; 15:15.
3. "Behold I was shapen in iniquity; and in sin did my mother conceive me" (Ps. 51:7). Compare Job 15:14: "What is man that he should be clean? and he who is born of a woman, that he should be righteous?"
4. Ps. 10:4-6; 18:28; 101:5.
5. Ps. 19:10; 34:12; 111:10.
6. Ps. 24:8. Similarly, for God's self-manifestation in history, Ps. 57:6, 12; 66:2; 96:3; 97:6; 102:16; 108:6; 138:5; 145:11, 12.
7. Ps. 37:25. See also, for this naive optimism, Ps. chap. 1; 34:8, 11; 58:12; 73:1; 145:20; 146:8.
8. Ps. 92:8-16. See also 53:2; 94:7.
9. Prov. 13:9; 20:20; 24:20. See also Job 18:5-6; 21:17.
10. See our later discussion of the term "wonder" in chap. 4, beginning with section entitled "Eschatology."
11. See Crawford H. Toy, The Book of Proverbs, International Critical Commentary (New York, 1899), on Prov. 30:6.

CHAPTER 3

1. Hag. 1:13.

2. See R. H. Charles, *Apocrypha and Pseudepigrapha* (Oxford: Clarendon Press, 1913), II, introduction, pp. viii, 9; and his *Religious Development between Old and New Testament*, pp. 38-41. Charles' edition of the Apocrypha is here used, unless otherwise stated, as a basis of reference.

3. The word "Torah" is frequently employed by the prophets in the sense of instruction, and not technically as law. But see Jer. 9:12; 26:4; 32:23; 44:10, 23; Ezek. 22:26; 44:24; Hos. 4:6; 8:1; Amos 2:4; Hag. 2:1; and Harper's notes in his *Amos and Hosea*, pp. 45-46, 255, 309.

4. Wisd. 7:27.

5. Wisd. 1:7; 7:22, 27; 8:1, 5.

6. See J. A. F. Gregg, *Wisdom*, introduction, xxxiv.

7. See W. J. Deane, *Book of Wisdom*, 1:3 and also Gregg, *op. cit.*, ad loc.

8. Wisd. 2:12.

9. Wisd. 8:7.

10. Wisd. 7:11.

11. Wisd. 8:10.

12. Thus Gregg, *Wisdom*, 8:13 n.

13. Wisd. 7:16-22.

14. See n. 33, below.

15. Thus Box and Oesterley in their introduction to Sira in Charles' *Apocrypha*, I, 284; Oesterley, *Ecclesiasticus*, introduction, xxvi. See also the latter's introduction to I Macc. in Charles' *Apocrypha*, I, 59.

16. Thus Oesterley, *Ecclesiasticus*, on 3:22.

17. 1 En. 9:6; 10:7; 16:3; 17:3; 65:6, 11.

18. See Dan. 8:26: ואתה סתם החזון; 12:4; 1 En. 68:6; 89:1; 106:9-107:1; Asmp. M. 1:13, 16; 10:1; 11:1; 2 En. proem B; 24:3; 3 Bar. 1:6; 2:5; 4 Ezra 12:37.

19. Already in Tob. 12:12, 15: and see Test. Levi 3:7; 3 Bar. chaps. 11, 12.

20. See Bk. Jub. 1:27, where the author may not refer to the Pentateuch, but nevertheless conceives of revelation as indirect. See Charles' note ad loc. and the introduction in his *Apocrypha*, II, 9.

21. See Henry J. Wicks, *The Doctrine of God*, p. 44; Bk. Jub. 16:1; 12:22; 14:20.

22. Test. Dan 6:2.

23. See Test. Levi 3:7 n.; 3 Bar. chaps. 11, 12.

24. 1 En. 9:3.

25. Similarly, Asmp. M. 32:2.

26. See Charles, *Book of Jubilees*, pp. 10-12, and *Apocrypha*, II, 13, who cites also the view of Philo in *Leg. Allegor.* I, 2, that the creation of the angels was finished on the seventh day. This is rather a strange view for Philo.

27. Bk. Jub. 2:18; 15:27.

28. See Charles' notes on 2 Bar. 13:3; 59:5-11.

29. A repudiation of the Hokmah-view may perhaps be discerned in the pessimistic lines in 1 En. 42:1-2 that Wisdom came to make her dwelling place among the children of men and found no dwelling place; then Wisdom returned to her place and took her seat among the angels."

30. Commentators note the symbolic decline of value in the vision of the four metals in Dan. 2 and the progressive fierceness of the four beasts in Dan. 7. For the deterioration of man, see Bk. Jub. 22; and for the feeling of world-senescence and the growth of evil, see 4 Ezra 4:27, 33; 5:50-55; 14:10, 16-17; and 2 Bar. 85:10.

31. The End is conditioned not only by the number, which historiosophy tries to determine, of empires or world-ages, but also by the fixed number, known only to God, of souls to be born. See 2 Bar. 23:4-5. According to 1 En. 47:4 and 4 Ezra 4:36-43, there is a fixed number only of righteous souls. Cf. Yeb. 62a, 63b, 'Ab Zarah 5a, Niddah 13b, which agree with the former view.

32. W. O. E. Oesterley, The Books of the Apocrypha, p. 102.

33. ἡ ἐλπίς. In Wisd. 3:4, 18; 5:14 (cf. however note ad loc.); 15:10, it means immortality. In 2 Macc. 7:14, it means resurrection. Similarly in Test. Judah 26:1; En. 40:9; 104:4; 2 Bar. 57:2 (Ceriani, p. 153, ܗܒܪ ܓܠܝܬܐ, spes mundi); 78:6 (ܗܒܪ ܓܠܝܬܐ ܐܡܠܟܡ, spem aeternam, Ceriani, p. 169); 4 Ezra 7:119: perennis spes. The Syriac quotations from 2 Bar. are according to the text of Ceriani in Monumenta Sacra et Profana, Tom. V. The quotation from 4 Ezra is according to the Latin text of Robert L. Bensly, The Fourth Book of Ezra (Cambridge, 1895). This "hope," whether in the sense of immortality or the reward in the Hereafter is also called "mystery" or "secret" in 1 En. 38:3; 58:5; Wisd. 2:22 (cf. also 2 Bar. 81:4), and is included in the פלאות into which Sir. 3:21 forbids inquiry, though a hint thereof is given in, and constitutes the meaning of, the previous words ולעגוים יגלה סודו. This, I think, may be the meaning also in the Megillat Hodayot 3:21. ואדעה כי יש מקורה לאשר יצרתה מעפר לסוד עולם (Sukenik's first report on the Megillot Genuzot p. 31, second report p. 38, published by Mosad Bialik).

34. 1 En. 104:4, 6; 2 Bar. 51:5, 10, 12. Cf. 4 Ezra 7:97, 125.

35. 1 En. 39:9; 2 Bar. 51:3 (Ceriani, p. 145 ܐܡܚܫܒܬܐ), 16 (Ceriani, p. 147 ܒܪ ܐܡܚܫܒܢܘ, where Ryssel emends ܒܐܡܚܫܒܢܘ. See note in M. Kmosko, "Liber Apocalypseos Baruch," in Patrologia Syriaca, Tom. I); 54:15 (Ceriani, p. 150 ܓܠܝܬܐ (ܐܡܒܠ̈ܝܬܐ) ; 66:7; 4 Ezra 8:51; 3 Bar. 16:4 n.; Ap. Abraham 30. Cf. Zad. Frag. 5:6.

36. 2 En. 22:8; 56:2; Test. Benj. 4:1; Test. Levi 18:6(ἐκ τοῦ ναοῦ τῆς δόξης).

37. 2 En. 22:7, 10. Similarly, the talmudic term מכובדים for angels in Ber. 60b and the terms כבודים and נכברים in Medieval Jewish philosophy, for the references of which see Goldziher, in his introduction to his edition of Pseudo-Bahya's Kitab ma'ani al-nafs, p. 37. However, Goldziher's view that the Jewish philosophers borrowed those terms from the Koran rather than from the Talmud is unnecessary as both the Arabic and the Hebrew terms probably stem independently from apocalyptic literature. See also my "Some Aspects of Yehudah Halevi's Mysticism," in the Proceedings of the American Academy for Jewish Research, XI (1941), p. 39.

38. 4 Ezra 7:112, 122.

39. Test. Levi 3:4 (μεγάλη δόξα); 1 En. 14:20 (ἡ δόξα ἡ μεγάλη); 102:3.

40. 2 Bar. 51:13 (Ceriani, p. 145 ܢܫܒܚܘܢ); 54:21 (p. 150 ܐܬܠ ܠܡܫܒܚܘܬܗ ܢܫܒܚܘܢ); 66:6 (p. 159 ܢܫܒܚܘܢ ܠܗ ܣܓܝܐ); 4 Ezra 8:49: ut plurimum glorificeris. These passages are linguistically interesting. One wonders what the Hebrew original was. In classical style it might be ינחל כבוד. But all these versions show that, instead of a phrase, one word was used, perhaps יתכבד, and a pi'el-form for the active. However, such a usage with an eschatological meaning in Hebrew literature is to me unknown.

CHAPTER 4

1. So translated by Millar Burrows in his Dead Sea Scrolls (New York, 1955), 381. But perhaps the meaning is "chosen for will or for divine pleasure." Thanksgiving Psalms 15:16.

2. See Josephus, *Wars* 2, 8, 12, and also his account of Menahem the Essene in *Antiquities* 5, 10, 15.

3. *Habakkuk Commentary* 2:7-10 and almost verbatim in *Damascus Document* 1:12-13.

4. The term *midrash Torah* also occurs in a Baraita, in *Kiddushin* 49b.

5. See *Manual of Discipline* 9:11-15, and also 8:1. See also *Damascus Document* 7:7; 8:2; 9:20; and hence also in 2:2; and see also 6:7; 8:16.

6. See Charles, *Apocrypha*, II, 789-91.

7. On the one hand, see *Hagigah* 10b; *B. Kam.* 2b; *Nidd.* 23a. See also *Jer. Hallah*, 57b above: "Does one learn from post-Mosaic Scriptures?" See also *Bereshit Rabba* 7: "Wilt thou condemn me to lashes on an inference from a post-Mosaic book?" On the other hand, we find in *Rosh ha-Shanah* 19a: "R. Ashi said, 'Gedaliah ben Ahikam belongs to post-Mosaic Scriptures and post-Mosaic Scriptures are as authoritative as the Torah.'"

8. Jacob Licht, *Megillat ha-Hodayot* (Jerusalem, 1956), p. 113.

9. ידעים (*Thanksgiving Psalms* (11:14). Hence perhaps also in fragment 10, line 6: דעים [..*.]ואנחנו ביחד נועדנו ועם should read ועם ידעים that is, "with the knowers" or "the spirits of Knowledge." Perhaps the term is the plural of the abstract noun יידע. A personification of knowledge is also found in the *Damascus Document* 2:2-3 אל אהב דעת חכמה ותושיה הציב לפניו ערמה ודעת הם ישרתוהו "God loveth knowledge and wisdom, and counsel He hath set before Him; Prudence and Knowledge minister unto Him." Incidentally, the sect is also called אנשי דעות, "men of knowledge," in *Damascus Document* 9:44. The spheres and aeons themselves were also called "gnoses." See François Sagnard, *La Gnose Valentinienne* (Paris, 1947), pp. 276, 408, 540.

10. See *Manual of Discipline* 4:6, 10:24.

11. *Thanksgiving Psalms* 1:21; 2:13; 4:28; 7:26; 12:11; *Manual of Discipline* 11:3, 5. See also chapter 2 above for our discussion of the term פלא "wonder."

12. *Manual of Discipline* 3:23. It is also called goral, "destiny." See *Milḥemet Bnei Or* ed. Yigael Yadin (Jerusalem, 1955), 254 n.

13. *Manual of Discipline* 8:12-15; 9:17; *Damascus Document* 5:3.

14. Thus in many places, e.g., *Habakkuk Commentary* 7:7-8, 13-14; *Manual of Discipline* 4:18. See also quotations under the word raz given by Yadin in his Introduction to *Milhemet Bnei Or*, p. 241. It is an eschatological term used also in talmudic literature. See *Baba Mezi'a* 85b: מאן גליא רזיא בעלמא "Who revealed the secrets in the world," referring to resurrection. See also *Sanhedrin* 94a: רזי לי רזי לי "the secret is mine," referring to the proposal of the genius of the world to make King Hezekiah the Messiah. See also chapter 3, above, for a discussion of the term סוד "secret," in the Apocrypha.

15. *Damascus Document* 9:40; 15:5; 18:8.

16. See Charles, *op. cit.*, p. 795.

17. See e.g., *Damascus Document* 1:6; 8:3.

18. See A. Dupont-Sommer, *Dead Sea Scrolls, a Preliminary Survey* (Oxford, 1952), pp. 90-91, 99; *The Jewish Sect of Qumran and the Essenes* (London, 1954), pp. 32-37, 54-55, 147-66; Charles T. Fritsch, *The Qumran Community* (New York, 1956), pp. 81-82, 110, 119, 121; J. M. Grintz' article in *Sinai*, XXXII (Jerusalem, 1952), 11-43. I. L. Teicher even proposed that the teacher of righteousness is Jesus, the evil priest is Paul, and the sect is that of the Ebionites. See his articles in the *Journal of Jewish Studies*, II (1951), 69-99, 115-43.

19. J. M. Allegro, *Further Light on the History of the Qumran Sect*, JBS, LXXV (June, 1956), Part II, pp. 94-95.

20. A. Dupont-Sommer, *The Jewish Sect of Qumran and the Essenes* (London, 1954), pp. 33-35.

21. J. M. Grintz, *op. cit.*, p. 28, seeks to explain the verse in the Damascus Document 5:4: וביד בחירו יתן אל את משפט כל הגויים in the spirit of the Book of Enoch, that the chosen one is a heavenly Messiah. But it seems that בחירו stands for בחיריו in keeping with ובתוכחתם . Similarly מצותו stands for מצותיו

22. See D. Barthélemy and J. T. Milik, *Qumran Cave* (Oxford, 1955), I, 110-11. See also the phrase כהנותא רבה מן מלכותא "priesthood is greater than kinghood," cited by Grintz, *op. cit.*, p. 32, n. 52a.

23. *Manual of Discipline*, 4:18-20.

24. *Milḥemet Bnei Or*, 258, 332, 356. See also *Manual of Discipline*, 4:8.

25. See chapter 3 above, notes 33-40.

26. This differs from the translation of Burrows, *op. cit.*

27. This differs from the translation of Dupont-Sommer, *The Jewish Sect of Qumran and the Essenes*, p. 144.

25. It seems that the sages of the Talmud also took the word *kavod*, or glory, in this sense, in their explanation of the verses "his horn shall be exalted with glory" (Ps. 112:9), i.e., *in* glory, in the world to come, and "the glory of the Lord shall be thy rereward" (Isa. 58:8). See *Baba Batra* 10b, 11a.

29. See *Thanksgiving Psalms* 6:34; 11:13, 14; *Manual of Discipline* 4:7, 25; 11:8, 16; *Damascus Document* 11:13. The Essenes too seem to have believed in bodily resurrection, which does not contradict the statement of Josephus that they maintained immortality. See Dupont-Sommer, *op. cit.*, p. 8, n. 12; Burrows, *op. cit.*, p. 270.

30. See *Damascus Document* 9:11-12: "The King is the congregation," where the intention is to transfer authority from the king to the community. See also n. 19 above. The point is not, as Charles thought, against the Davidic Messiah, but against the ruling aristocracy in Jerusalem.

31. Philo also, according to a quotation in Eusebius' *Praeparatio Evangelica* 8:11, emphasizes that membership in the Essene order does not depend on racial origin, but on free will.

CHAPTER 5

1. See *Hagigah* 12a; *Bereshit Rabba* 1:21: ת״ר ב״ש אומרים שמים נבראו תחלה ואחר כך נבראת הארץ שנאמר בראשית ברא אלהים את השמים ואת הארץ, וב״ה אומרים ארץ נבראת תחלה ואחר כך שמים שנאמר ביום עשות ה׳ אלהים ארץ ושמים See also *Tamid* 32a, where we read that Alexander of Macedonia addressed this question to "the sages of the South," and they answered like the school of Shammai. See David Neumark, *Toledot ha-Pilosotiyyah be-Israel* (New York, 1921), I, p. 58. See also n. 5 below.

2. See Philo, *De Opificio Mundi*, 27. On the priority of thought, see there 16, 19, 24.

3. *Bereshit Rabba*, 12:14.

4. See Harry A. Wolfson, *Philo*, (Cambridge: Harvard University Press, 1947), I, p. 237.

5. *Hagigah* 14b. More stories told there about R. Johanan ben Zakkai indicate the reverence he paid to esoteric study. See also *Mekilta* on Exod. 15:11: "When a man builds, he builds the lower before the higher story. But the Holy One, blessed be He, built the upper before the lower story, as it is said, In the beginning God created the heaven and the earth"—which follows the school of

Shammai. This anonymous *Mekilta* may belong to the school of R. Akiba, about whom more anon.

6. *Sifra* on Deut. 11:22. See Philo, *De Cherubim* 35, 127, where he calls the Logos the vessel with which the world was created.

7. See *Jer. Berakot* 14b. The proof is from the extra word *et*.

8. *Bereshit Rabba* 12:11: ר׳ אליעזר אומר כל מה שיש בשמים

בריאתו מן השמים, כל מה שיש בארץ בריאתו מן הארץ... ר׳ יהושע אומר כל מה שיש בשמים ובארץ אין ברייתו אלא מן השמים ומייתי ליה מהכא כי לשלג יאמר הוא ארץ.

Thus also in *Jer. Hagigah*, beginning of chapter 2, 77a: דרש ר׳ יודה בן פזי

בתחילה היה העולם מ י ם ב מ י ם , מאי טעמא ורוח אלהים מרחפת על פני המים, חזר ועשאו שלג... חזר ועשאו ארץ, כי לשלג יאמר הוא ארץ.

Similarly in *Yoma* 54b: תניא ר׳ אליעזר הגדול אומר וכו׳. But in the expression מ י ם ב מ י ם (also in *Bereshit Rabba* 5:2; and compare *Kohelet Rabba* 3:18), there is no reference to the upper waters as a creative element. See further our discussion on the cosmogonic teachings of Ben Zoma and the reaction that ensued.

9. *Yoma* 54b. ר״א אומר עולם מאמצעתו נברא שנאמר

בצקת עפר למוצק ורגבים ידובקו, ר״י אומר עולם מן הצדדין נברא שנאמר כי לשלג יאמר הוא ארץ.

Compare, however Rashi's explanation.

10. *Bereshit Rabba* 13:9: מהיכן הארץ שותה? ר״א אומר ממימי

אוקינוס... ר״י אומר מן העליונים... והעננים מתגברין מן הארץ ועד הרקיע ומקבלין אותן כמפי הנוד ואין טיפה אחת נוגעת בחברתה.

A different formulation of this idea is found in *Ta'anit* 9b.

11. The sources are as follows: See *Baba Batra* 25a: תניא ר״א אומר עולם

לאכסדרה הוא דומה ורוח צפונית אינה מסובבת וכיון שהגיעה חמה אצל קרן מערבית צפונית נכפפת ועולה למעלה מן הרקיע, ור״י אומר לקובה הוא דומה ורוח צפונית מסובבת וכיון שהחמה מגעת לקרן מערבית צפונית מקפת וחוזרת אחורי הכפה.

In *Bereshit Rabba* 6:13, we read:

כיצד גלגל חמה ולבנה שקועים ברקיע? ר׳ יהודה בר אלאעי ורבנן. רבנן אמרין מאחורי הכיפה ולמטה ור׳ יהודה בר אלאעי אומר מאחורי הכיפה ולמעלה.

In *Pesahim* 94b we read: חכמי ישראל אומרים ביום חמה מהלכת

למטה מן הרקיע ובלילה למעלה מן הרקיע וחכמי אומות העולם אומרים ביום חמה מהלכת למטה מן הרקיע ובלילה למטה מן הרקיע.

See also *Ha-Maggid* (Lyck, 1861), V, 98, 206. As for Anaxagoras, see John Burnet, *Early Greek Philosophy* (London: A. & C. Black, 930), pp. 76, 77, 108. As for Severianus and other patristic writers, see J. L. E. Dreyer, *A History of Astronomy* (New York: Dover Publications, 1953), pp. 211, 212.

12. See *Bereshit Rabba* 25:2: ר״א אומר לא ישבתו מכאן שלא שבתו.

See also *ibid.*, 33:10; 34:15. ור״י אומר לא ישבתו מכאן ששבתו.

13. *Sifra* on Lev. 23:43: ר״א אומר כי בסוכות הושבתי את בני

ישראל בסוכות ממש, ור״ע אומר ענני כבוד היו.

14. *Bereshit Rabba* 78:1.

15. See Wilhelm Bacher, *Die Agada der Tannaiten* (Strassburg, 1903), I, 148, nn. 4, 5.

16. See Bacher, *op. cit.*, p. 178. For Plato, see the beginning of his *Timaeus*. See also Theodor Gomperz, *Greek Thinkers* (London: J. Murray, 1914), II, 209. For Anaximenes, see Burnet, *op. cit.*, p. 74.

17. *Hagigah* 14a: אחד לדין ואחד לצדקה דברי ר׳ עקיבא. אמר לו

ר״א בן עזריה עקיבא מה לך אצל הגדה כלך מדברותיך ולך אצל נגעים ואהלות אלא אחד לכסא ואחד לשרפרף... שנאמר השמים כסאי והארץ הדום רגלי.

18. *Hagigah* 14b: הירצה לפני

19. See *Hagigah* 12b: את הארץ למה לי ? להקדים שמים לארץ
20. כלי חמדה See *Abot* 3:14.
21. See *Mekilta de Rabbi Ishmael*, ed. Jacob Z. Lauterbach (Philadelphia: J.P.S., 1949), II, 275 (*Bahodesh* 9); and also 224 (*Bahodesh* 4).
22. See *Shir ha-Shirim Rabba* 1:55: ר״א אומר עד שהמלך מלכי המלכים
הקב״ה במסבו ברקיע כבר היה הר סיני מתמר באור... ר״ע אומר עד שהמלך מלכי המלכים
הקב״ה במסבו ברקיע כבר וישכן כבוד ה׳ על הר סיני.
23. See *Mekilta* II, 266 (*Bahodesh* 9): וכל העם רואים את
הקולות ואת הלפידים — רואין הנראה ושומעין הנשמע דברי ר׳ ישמעאל. ר׳ **עקיבא**
אומר רואין ושומעין הנראה, ואין דבר שלא יצא מפי הגבורה ונחצב על הלוחות **שנאמר**
קול ה׳ חוצב להבות אש.
24. *Mekilta* I, 15 (*Pisha* 2): החודש הזה לכם — ר׳ ישמעאל
אמר משה הראה את החודש לישראל... ר׳ עקיבא אמר זה אחד משלושה דברים שנתקשה
משה והראהו המקום את כלן באצבע.
25. *Yoma* 75b: לחם אבירים אכל איש — לחם שמלאכי השרת
אוכלין אותו, דברי ר״ע. כשנאמרו הדברים לפני ר׳ ישמעאל אמר להם צאו ואמרו לו
לעקיבא, עקיבא טעית, וכי מלה״ש אוכלין לחם ?
26. *Shoher Tob* on Ps. 104:12: עליהם עוף השמים ישכון — ר״ע אומר
אלו מלה״ש. אמר לו ר׳ ישמעאל כלה מדברותיך ולך אצל נגעים ואהלות. זהו עוף ששוכן
על האילנות שקילוסו של הקב״ה מהם.
27. *Mekilta* I, 13 (*Pisha* 1).
28. *Bereshit Rabba* 34:20: כל מי שהוא שופך דמים מעלים עליו
כאלו הוא ממעט את הדמות
29. See Bacher, *op. cit.*, I, 319, n. 1, who regards the version in *Bereshit Rabba* 21:5 as more authoritative. To me it seems that the text in *Shir ha-Shirim Rabba* is nearer to the spirit of R. Akiba.
30.   הנני עומד לפניך שם וגי׳ אמר לו המקום
כל מקום שאתה מוצא רושם רגלי אדם שם אני לפניך
And see R. Johanan in *Sanhedrin* 86a: סתם מתניתין ר׳ מאיר... וכולהו
אליבא דר״ע
Concerning the principle סתם מכילתא ר״ע see Lauterbach in his introduction to the *Mekilta de-Rabbi Ishmael*, ibid., n. 21.

30ª. See n. 13 above. This is also seen in R. Akiba's proof about the power of charity from Ps. 112:9: "His righteousness endureth forever, his horn shall be exalted with glory," which he took to mean in glory, i.e., the world to come (*Lev. Rabba* 34:16). See chapter 3, n. 35 above. On this basis, one can explain the expression in the prayer תכנת שבת: "They that find delight in it shall inherit glory for everlasting, they that taste in it are worthy of life." The word "glory" in this passage means the world to come, as we have shown. Also the word "life" in this passage means the world to come, as in talmudic literature. Thus the Rabbis in *Berakot* 4a explain the verse in Ps. 27:13: "Had I not believed to see the goodness of the Lord in the land of *life*" as referring to the Hereafter. See also *Abot de-Rabbi Natan*, ed. Solomon Schechlter, version B (London: D. Nutt, 1887), chapter 43, p. 122.   העולם הבא
נקרא חיים שנאמר אתהלך לפני ה׳ בארצות החיים
31. *Shabbat* 153a, *Abot* 3:20; and compare Rev. 19:9.
32. *Hagigah* 14b.
33. *Bereshit Rabba* 5:2.
34. About R. Akiba see n. 23 above; and about R. Joshua ben Hanina, see n. 15 above.
35. See *Tosefta Hagigah* 2:5: מעשה ב״ר יהושע שהיה מהלך
באיסטרטא ובן זומא בא כנגדו ולא שאל לו בשלומו. אמר לו מאין ולאן בן זומא ?

אמר לו מסתכל הייתי במעשה בראשית ואין בין מים עליונים למים התחתונים אפילו טפח
שנאמר ורוח אלהים מרחפת על פני המים ונאמר כנשר יעיר קנו על גוזליו ירחף.
מה נשר זה טס על גבי קנו נוגע ואינו נוגע כך אין בין מים עליונים למים התחתונים
אפילו טפח. באותה שעה אמר להן ר' יהושע לתלמידיו כבר בן זומא מבחוץ. לא היו
ימים מועטים עד שנסתלק.

Other versions of this story are in *Hagigah* 15b; *Jer. Hagigah* 77a; *Bereshit Rabba* 2:6.

36. *Bereshit Rabba* 13:14:   א״ר לוי המים העליונים זכרים והתחתונים
נקבות והן אומרים אלו לאלו קבלו אותנו. אתם בריותיו של הקב״ה ואנו שלוחיו. מיד
הם מקבלים אותן.

See also Louis Ginzberg, *The Legends of the Jews* (Philadelphia: J.P.S., 1909-25), V, 182, n. 39.

37. See Hans Leisegang, *Die Gnosis* (Leipzig: Kroner, 1924), 74.

38. *Bereshit Rabba* 4:7:   ויעש אלהים את הרקיע — זה אחד מן
המקראות, שהרעיש בן זומא את העולם. ויעש אתמהא ! והלא במאמר הן נבראו
שנאמר בדבר ה' שמים נעשו וברוח פיו כל צבאם.

See also Bacher, *op. cit.*, I, 423, n. 3.

39. See Gustav Krüger, *Die Apologien Justins des Märtyrers* (Tübingen, 1915), chapter 60. For an English translation, see Thomas B. Falls, *St. Justyn Martyr* (New York: Christian Heritage, Inc., 1948), pp. 97-99. (In the series: Fathers of the Church.)

40. הקב״ה מקומו של עולם ואין העולם מקומו   For the various versions of this dictum, see Bacher, *op. cit.*, II, 185, nn. 1, 2.

41. See Leisegang, *op. cit.*, p. 70.

42. *Bereshit Rabba* 46:2:   אני אל שדי — אני הוא שאין העולם כדאי לאלהות

43. *Sifra* on Num. 12:8:   לא זה לבד שאין מלה״ש רואים את
השכינה אלא אף שאינן שומעין ואינן יודעין היכן שכינה

44. *Bereshit Rabba* 4:3.

45. See Wolfson, *Philo*, I, 236.

46. *Sukkah* 5a: מעולם לא ירדה שכינה למטה ולא עלו משה ואליהו למרום
In *Mekilta*, II, 224 (*Bahodesh* 4):   ולא ירד הכבוד למטה.

47. About R. Jose, see Sifra on Num. 12:3, 7. About R. Joshua ben Korḥah, see *Bereshit Rabba* 55:6. About Rabbi, see *Mekilta*, II, 226 (*Bahodesh* 4).

48. It should be noted that it was probably the forestalling of the Pauline idea of Jesus as co-creator (see particularly Col. 1:16f), that the Tannaim gave as reason for the deferment of the creation of man till all else was done. Thus *Sanhedrin* 38a:

ת״ר אדם נברא בע״ש, ומפני מה ? שלא יהו צדוקים אומרים שותף היה לו
להקב״ה במעשה בראשית.

49. See references above, n. 21.

50. *Bereshit Rabba* 4:3. R. Simon and R. Eleazar also accept the idea of the upper waters, but apparently not as a metaphysical entity. See *Abot de-Rabbi Natan* 33, end, where they both maintain that the upper and lower waters tossed the Egyptians. See also *Mekilta* on Exod. 14:21; 15:11.

51. See passages collected by Bacher, *op. cit.*, II, 60. See also *Jer. Hagigah* 73:3:   זה הקב״ה שהוא טוב   "This refers to God, who is good." All this is aimed against the gnostics who believe that the Jewish God is a God of justice, not of mercy, that He is right, but not good.

52. *Bereshit Rabba* 1:21.

53. See Bacher, *op. cit.*, II, 222, n. 1.

54. *Tanhuma* (Buber), *Bereshit* 5.

55. *Mekilta*, I, 16 (*Pisha* 2): נדבר עמו ביום עם חשכה. And see Bacher, *op. cit.*, II, 280, n. 6.

56. *Bereshit Rabba* 12:14: תמיה אני איך נחלקו אבות העולם ב״ש וב״ה על בריית שמים וארץ. אלא מחשבה בין ביום ובין בלילה ומעשה עם דמדומי חמה.

57. *Bereshit Rabba* 1:21.

58. *Bereshit Rabba* 55:9. Similarly, *Tanhauma*, *Pikkudei* 2: ארשב״י זאת אומרת שההיכל שלמטה מכוון כנגד היכל שלמעלה See also *Tanhuma*, *Mishpatim* 1; *Pikkudei* 1. Compare *Mekilta* on Exod. 15:7: מכון לשבתך זה אחד (מן הדברים שהוא כנגד של מעלה) שכסא של מטה הוא מכוון כנגד כסא של מעלה.

59. See *Tanhuma*, *Vayaqhei* 7.

60. *Sifre*, Num. 8b; *Menahot* 98b; and see *Megillah* 21b. See also Saadia, *Emunot we-De'ot* (Josephof, 1885), p. 46: כל דבר חשוב שמור באמצע

61. *Shir ha-Shirim Rabba* 1:13: שהיה הדיבור יוצא מימינו של הקב״ה לשמאלן של ישראל וחוזר ועוקף את מחנה ישראל... מימינן של ישראל לשמאלו של הקב״ה והקב״ה מקבלו על ימינו וחוקקו על הלוח.

62. *Sanhedrin* 102a; *Jer. Makkot* 31d; *Tosefta Ta'anit* 49.

63. *Menahot* 29b.

64. *Sukkah* 52a.

65. *Abot de-Rabbi Natan* 16:3. See also Rabbi in *Sanhedrin* 91b.

66. *Berakot* 16b; *Shabbat* 30b: רבי בתר צלותיה אמר הכי יהי רצון מלפניך ה' אלהינו ואלהי אבותינו שתצילנו מעזי פנים... מיצר הרע... ומשטן המשחית.

67. *Abot* 4:21.

68. *Abot de-Rabbi Natan* 28:5.

69. *Mekilta*, III, 198 (*Shabta* 1).

70. *Nazir* 22a.

71. *Sifra* on Deut. 32:1. See also *Hagigah* 12b: ר״א בן שמוע אומר על עמוד אחד וצדיק שמו

72. *Sifra* on Deut. 11:21.

CHAPTER 6

1. See *Makkot* 11b, 23b; *Baba Mezi'a* 86a. See also *Bereshit Rabba* 49:6: אין יום ויום שאין הקב״ה מחדש הלכה בב״ד של מעלה.

2. On Philo, see his *De Somniis*, I, 63f. On R. Jose ben Halafta, see *Tanhuma*, *Ki Tisa* 27.

3. *Shoher Tob* 19:2. Also R. Johanan, R. Jonathan, R. Huna in the name of Rab, R. Abbahu in the name of R. Johanan, and others—in *Jer. Berakot*, beginning of chapter 9.

4. See *Sifra*, ed. I. H. Weiss (Vienna, 1862), on Lev. 2:12: הכבוד הזה שנאמר בו את השמים אני מלא, ראה חיבתן של ישראל להיכן גרמה לכבוד הזה כביכול דחק להיות מדבר מעל הכפורת מבין שני הכרובים.

5. *Tanhuma*, *Ki Tisa* 27: כביכול גבהותו של עולם הרכין עצמו שנאמר וירד ה' בענן

6. See also *Shoher Tob* 22: ר' שמואל בשם ר״ח אמר: על כל תהלה ותהלה שישראל מקלסין, אתה למעלה מן הקלוס שנאמר ומרומם על כל ברכה ותהלה.
"Said R. Samuel in the name of R. Haninah: Despite every song of praise which

Israel offers, you are higher than any praise, for it is said, and exalted above all blessing and praise.'

7. *Jer. Ta'anit* 65b: אהבה זו שכינה

8. *Shir ha-Shirim Rabba* 3:15: חביבים ישראל שנקראו בנים למקום

9. *Berakot* 35b, *Sanhedrin* 102a, and compare the expression "our father in heaven" אבינו שבשמים in *Sotah* 49b, and R. Akiba's expression in *Abot* 3:18: "Beloved our Israel, for they were called the children of God."

חביבים ישראל שנקראו בנים למקום

10. *Shir ha-Shirim Rabba* 6:6; and compare R. Akiba in *Mekilta* on Exod. 15:2.

11. See Philo, *De Mutatione Nominum* 12; *Questiones et Solutiones in Exodum*, II, 13. On the "Word" in the sense of Logos, see also Asmp. M. 8:5; 11:16.

12. See Philo, *Legum Allegoria*, III, 31, 96, quoted by Wolfson, op. cit., II, 83, n. 45. See also E. E. Goodenough, *By Light, Light* (New Haven: Yale University Press, 1935), p. 41, where it is quoted that Philo called the powers "beaming shadows."

13. *Bereshit Rabba* 82:2: איקונין של יעקב שחקוקה בכסא הכבוד Compare *Hullin* 91b: דיוקנו של מעלה. "Jacob's image on high."

14. *Aggadot Bereshit* (Buber), chapter 79, beginning.

15. *Shemot Rabba* 52:1. Compare Philo's view (see Goodenough, op. cit., p. 113) that just as the Ark symbolized the upper world, so the Tabernacle and the curtain in all its colors symbolized the lower world. See *Bamidbar Rabba* 12:16: המשכן שהוא שקול כנגד העולם "the tabernacle which corresponds to the world." Similarly *Tanhuma, Pikkudei* 2:

ומקום משכן כבודך בשביל ששקול כנגד בריאת העולם

16. See Bacher, op. cit., I, 183 n. 4; and my essay "Rab Hai Gaon" in *Hashiloah*, XXX (Odessa, 1914), 434.

17. *Shabbat* 88b: חמדה גנוזה and compare *Zebahim* 116a:

ר׳ אלעזר המודעי אומר : ח מ ד ה טובה יש לו בברכת גנזיו שהיתה גנוזה אצלו תתקע״ד דורות קודם שנברא העולם.

Compare also *Jer. Ta'anit* 65a: אמר ר׳ חייא ברבא... כ ל י א ח ד ש ל

ח מ ד ה שהיה לנו גרמו עוונותינו שיתבזה

See also R. Simon ha-Hasid in *Hagigah* 13b, and R. Abbahu in the name of R. Jose ben Haninah in *Shemot Rabba* 30:6

18. *Bereshit Rabba* 1:2: היה הקב״ה מביט בתורה ובורא את העולם Similarly R. Judah bar Il'ai in *Tanhuma* (Buber), *Bereshit* 5. As to its origin in Philo, see Bacher, op. cit., I, 107, n. 2.

19. See Kathleen Freeman, *Pre-Socratic Philosophers* (Oxford: B. Blackwell, 1949), p. 231.

20. Quoted by Nahman Krochmal in *Moreh Nebukei ha-Zeman*, ed. Simon Rawidowicz (Waltham, Mass., 1961), "gate" 15, p. 264.

21. This threefold division of man corresponds to the gnostic idea of the Valentinian school that man may be divided into three groups: the hylic, the psychic, and the pneumatic, and also to the threefold division of the soul according to Plato. Note that the *nefesh* is here higher than the *neshamah*. On the other hand, see, for example, Abraham ibn Ezra on Exod. 23:25, where the order of ascent is *nefesh, ruah,* and *neshamah*. Compare also, on these names, *Bereshit Rabba* 14:13, where these three terms, as against 14:10, are regarded as identical.

22. *Vayyikra Rabba* 32:2; *Kohelet Rabba* 10:23; and compare R. Aha in *Pesikta Rabbati* 8, beginning. See also n. 24 below.

23. For example, as in the case of Phinehas in *Sanhedrin* 82a; in the case of Micah, *ibid.*, 103b; and in the case of R. Akiba in *Hagigah* 16a.

24. *Vayyikra Rabba* 31:1: כשם שהתחתונים צריכין צדקה אלו

מאלו כך העליונים צריכין צדקה אלו מאלו.

Compare *ibid.*, 26:8: הקב״ה אמר למלאך והמלאך לכרוב, א״ל

גזר עלי הקב״ה ואני אין לי רשות ליכנס במחיצתך אלא עמי עשה צדקה ותן לי שני

גחלים משלך.

"God said to the angel, and the angel said to the cherub. The angel said to the cherub: The Holy One, blessed be He, has decreed that I should do it, but I have no right to enter your division; do it then for me as an act of charity, and give me two coals of fire." So also in *Tanhuma, Emor,* 3.

25. *Midrash Shir ha-Shirim*, ed. Lazar Grünhut (Jerusalem, 1897), 3:7, quoted by Bacher, *op. cit.*, III, 296. Compare *Shir ha-Shirim Rabba* 3:14:

תני עד שלא יחטא האדם וכו׳.

26. See *Berakot* 16b, 60b; *Jer. Berakot* 7d end (chapter 4, *halakah* 2); *Temurah* 16b.

27. Bacher, *op. cit.*, III, 105.

28. Similarly *Bereshit Rabba* 45:10: א״ר חייא ציפרנן של אבות

ולא כריסן של בנים.

"Rather a fingernail of the fathers than the belly of the sons."

29. See *Aggadot Bereshit* (Buber), chapter 57: א״ר ברכיה אמר הקב״ה

אעפ״י שאני בראתי את העולם ואני טוענו. אלא בשעה שיש צדיקים למטה כאלו הן

טוענים את העולם. כך — ומתחת זרועות עולם.

See also *Tanhuma* (Buber), *Vayyishlah* 10: א״ר ברכיה הכהן מהו ויקם לך ?

אמר הקב״ה לצדיק אני אומר דבר ואתה אומר דבר, כביכול אני מבטל את שלי ואקיים לך.

and *Shabbat* 63a: אמר ר׳ אמי ואיתימא ר׳ חנינא אפילו הקב״ה

גוזר גזירה הוא מבטלה .

30. R. Alexander and R. Berechiah in *Bereshit Rabba* 49:7, and R. Manni in *Jer. Abodah Zarah* 40c. Compare R. Judah in *Hullin* 92a. The number is gnostic, inspired by the conception of thirty spheres or aeons in the Pleroma or the Fullness. R. Johanan and R. Hannin interpret in *Bereshit Rabba* 98:14 the expression "thirty pieces of silver" to mean the thirty commandments (which Messiah will give the nations of the world), whereas Rab interprets them to be thirty mighty men, i.e., zaddiqim. See also *Jer. Abodah Zarah* 40c.

31. See also *Hagigah* 12b: ר״א בן שמוע אומר על עמוד אחד

וצדיק שמו שנאמר וצדיק יסוד עולם

R. Johanan, furthermore, regards the righteous as higher than angels. See *Sanhedrin* 93a: א״ר יוחנן גדולים צדיקים יותר ממלאכי השרת Similarly other Amoraim in *Tanhuma, Vayyishlah* 2; *Vayyikra* 1.

32. On the other hand, see Targum Jonathan on Gen. 5:24. About R. Abbahu's Greek learning, see Saul Lieberman, *Greek in Jewish Palestine.* (New York: Jewish Theological Seminary of America, 1942), p. 21 ff.

33. See also A. Aha in *Debarim Rabba* 2:24: אין לו לא אח ולא בן אלא שמע

ישראל ה׳ אלהינו ה׳ אחד.

CHAPTER 7

1. See Th. C. Vriezen, *An Outline of Old Testament Theology* (Oxford, 1958), pp. 317-18.

2. See Joseph Klansner, *Yahadut we-Enoshiyyut'* (Tel-Aviv: Massadah, 1941), pp. 136-48; *Historiyyah Isreelit*, I, 1, chap. 2; and David Neumark's essays

"Musar ha-Yahadut" vol. 6 (Berlin, 1899), and "Hashkafat ha-Hayyim we-Hash-kafat ha-'Olam" in *Hashiloah*, vol. 11 (Krakau, 1903).

3. Hence God is not *hasekel ha-ne'elam mi-kol ra'yon*, the secret mind, but the secret ethicalness, or the secret good, that is concealed from all thought. This is the biblical approach and starting point. It is therefore regrettable that the Jewish philosophers in the Middle Ages, like their brethren, the Arabs and Christians, surrendered to Greek intellectualism by accepting God as reason and failed to continue to develop all the philosophical problems and implications of the original Hebraic approach, the mystical union of value-being, and thus missed perhaps making a more salient contribution to human thought.

4. On the Greek background of this problem as discussed in *Jewish Philosophy of the Middle Ages*, see my Hebrew essay on "The Approach of Reason to Morals according to Saadia and Maimonides" in *Tarbiz* (Jerusalem, 1959), XXVIII, 325-29.

5. Jean-Paul Sartre, *L'Etre et le Néant* (Paris: Gallinard, 1943), 653.

6. Concerning the negation of endaemonism or pleasure as a moral incentive, cf. the talmudic principle *misvot lav leanot nittnu*, "the commandments were not given for the sake of pleasure" (*Rosh ha-Shanah* 28a). The autonomic principle is formulated in the doctrine of Antigonos of Soko: "Be not like servants that serve the master for the sake of reward, but be like servants that serve the master not for the sake of reward" (*Abot* 1:3), and is concentrated in the concept of "Torah for its own sake" (*Sanhedrin* 99b), and in the angry dictum of Raba: "He who acts not for its own sake—it would be better for him not to have been created" (*Berakot* 17a), and even in the pedagogic modification of Rab: "Through acting not for its own sake one is led to acting for its own sake" (*Pesahim* 50b). See also *Tosafot, ad loc.*, explaining an apparently contradictory statement by Rab himself. The same pedagogic principle is ascribed to R. Huna in the introduction to *Ekah Rabbat*: 2. Spinoza clearly formulated this principle in his *Ethics* IV, 18 note: "Virtue is to be desired for its own sake nor is there anything more excellent or more useful to us than virtue, for the sake of which virtue ought to be desired." On the other hand, religious heteronomy, making obedience a moral sanction, is reflected in R. Hanina's rule: "He who is commanded and acts is greater than he who is not commanded and acts" (*Qiddushin* 31a)—a rule that opens a gap between religion and ethics and deviates from our conception of the prophetic attitude which is inclined to view them as identical. See the last chapter in this work, entitled "Ethics and Religion."

7. See Vriezen, *op. cit.*, 316-17.

8. One should note verses like Gen. 39:9: "and how then can I do this great wickedness and sin against God," the inference being that wickedness is intrinsic and *therefore* a sin; and Gen. 13:13: "Now the men of Sodom were wicked and sinners against the Lord exceedingly;" and Num. 5:6: "When a man or woman shall commit any of the sins of man to do tresspass against the Lord" (and compare Lev. 5:21).

CHAPTER 8

1. *Sifra* on Lev. 19:18; *Jer. Nedarim* 41:3; *Bereshit Rabba* 24:8.

2. *Abot* 3:14. Comp. R. Akiba's expression: "as if he diminishes the image" in *Bereshit Rabba* 34:20. See also *Ekah Rabbat* on Lam. 1:35: "When the Israelites do the will of God, they add strength to the power above . . . and when they do not do the will of God, they weaken the great strength above."

3. Such exaltation of the poor we find particularly in Proverbs. "He that oppresseth the poor reproacheth his Maker: but he that honoreth him hath mercy on the poor" (Prov. 14:31). "Who so mocketh the poor reproacheth

his Maker" (Prov. 17:5). "He that hath pity upon the poor lendeth unto the Lord" (Prov. 19:17). "Remove not the old landmark; and enter not into the fields of the fatherless; for their redeemer is mighty; he shall plead their cause with thee" (Prov. 23:10-11). Comp. Zech. 9:9: "Behold thy King cometh unto thee: he is just and having salvation; lowly ['ani usually means poor] and riding upon an ass." Hence we read in Sifra on the verse, "And when ye reap the harvest of your land, thou shalt not make clean riddance of the corners of thy field when thou reapest, neither shalt thou gather any gleaning of thy harvest" (Lev. 23:22), that R. Ebdimos, son of R. José says: "Why does the Bible include these laws in the middle of the laws about the holidays: Passover and Pentecost on one side and the Beginning of the Year and the Day of Atonement on the other? In order to teach us that he who fulfills the laws about the gleanings, forgotten sheaves, the corner and the tithe for the poor is accounted as if the Temple stood and he offered his sacrifices in it." See also Rashi ad loc.

4. See also Aristotle, Nicomachean Ethics VIII, 11, 1161b: "There can be no friendship, nor justice, towards inanimate things; indeed not even towards a horse or an ox, nor yet towards a slave as slave. For master and slave have nothing in common: a slave is a living tool, just as a tool is an inanimate slave. Therefore there can be no friendship with a slave as slave, though there can be as human beings." Such a concept of a slave could not occur to the biblical mind even abstractly, theoretically, because practically he is also a human being.

5. Cf. Exod. 21:21: "For he is his money"; but the preceding verse, that if the servant dies under the master's hand, the master shall be surely punished, proves the servant's legal status as man, and that therefore the meaning of verse 22 must be taken differently, as indeed the commentaries do. See, e.g., S. R. Driver, The Book of Exodus (Cambridge: University Press, 1953), ad loc., and U. Cassuto, The Book of Exodus (Jerusalem: Hebrew University, 1953), ad loc.

6. See also the solemn oath of Job: "If I did despise the cause of my manservant or of my maidservant, when they contended with me . . . did not he that made me in the womb make him? And did not one fashion us in the womb?" (Job 31:13-15).

7. Comp. Plotinus who maintains that the higher cares for the lower and embellishes it. See his Enneads IV, 8, 8.

8. "The fool hath said in his heart, there is no God" (Ps. 14:1). "And they say, How doth God know? and is there knowledge in the Most High?" (Ps. 73:11). Comp. Job 14:9; 21:14-15; 22:12-14; Mal. 3:14-15. Perhaps divine providence is already maintained in the name by which Hagar called God: El roi (a God of seeing), and in the name by which she called the well Beer-lahai-roi (the well of the Living God who seeth me) in Gen. 16:13-14.

9. See supra I, chap. 1.

10. A cabalistic term for the infinite. For the origin of this term, see supra I, chap. 1, n. 5.

11. For similarities to the doctrine of the mean in the Bible and in the Talmud, see Joseph I. Gorfinkle's edition of Maimonides' Eight Chapters (New York, 1912), p. 54. At any rate, the verse, "Be not righteous over much; neither make thyself over wise" (Eccles. 7:16) is not characteristic of the Bible. Philo too praises the "royal road," i.e., the mean, and condemns extremism. See his On the Unchangeableness of God (Quod Deus Sit Immutabilis), in the Loeb Classical Library, vol. 3 (London: William Heinemann Ltd., N. Y.: G. P. Putnam's Sons, 1930), §§ 162-65, pp. 91-93, and also n. on p. 489.

12. Concerning the prophets negative attitude to sacrifices as an alternative to morality, see I Sam. 15:22; Isa. 1:11-14; 43:23; 58:9-10; Jer. 6:20; 7:22-23 (but comp. 33:18, 22, 24); Hos. 6:6; Amos 4:4-5; 5:22; Mic. 6:6-8; Prov. 21:3. On the other hand, Ezekiel, Joel (1:9, 13), and Malachi stress the importance

of sacrifices. Ezekiel was himself a priest, and the other two—if Joel is post-exilic, as is now generally assumed by scholars—lived under the priestly influence which was strengthened during the Second Commonwealth. See *infra* nn. 23 and 24 in this chapter.

13. See *infra*, end of chapter 10.

14. Exod. 34:6-7. As to how to arrive at this number see Abraham ibn Ezra on Exod. 34:1, and Rabbenu Tam, in *Tosafot* on *Rosh ha-Shanah* 17:1.

15. It seems that the Bible in general did not favor the excessive development of the sense of private ownership: "The land shall not be sold for ever: for the land is mine; for ye are strangers and sojourners with me" (Lev. 25:23). Hence one who sells his soil sells only the fruit thereof (*ibid.*, 16). Hence also the Psalmist sings: "The earth is the Lord's and the fulness thereof; the world, and they that dwell therein" (Ps. 24:1).

16. See Charles, *Apocrypha*, I, 191.

17. The story is well known about the calf which, when being taken to the slaughter, broke away and hid its head under Rabbi's skirts for protection, and Rabbi said to it: "Go, for this wast thou created." Thereupon, they said in heaven: "Since he has no pity, let us bring suffering upon him." See *Bereshit Rabba* 33:3; *Baba Mezi'a* 85a. See also *Bereshit Rabba* 96:9.

18. See also Deut. 24:6-7. In general, it seems that the Bible looks askance at the taking of a pledge as well as to the taking of interest. See Ezek. 18:16; Amos 2:8; Job 22:6; 24:9.

19. It is true that the passion of revenge also breaks forth occasionally. See Jer. 18:23; Ps. 28:4; 41:11; 69; 109. And there were situations in history when to forgive seemed above the power of man. Suffice it that biblical law demanded man to try to rise and exerted an upward pull. See also the splendid passage in *The Testament of Gad* 6, 3-7, demanding forgiveness for the enemy. "And if he be shameless and persist in his wrong-doing, even so forgive him from the heart, and leave to God the avenging."

20. See Plato, *Cratylus*, 420a.

21. A parallel is found in the *Zohar* III, 110-11, where we read about R. Hiyya and R. José who, while walking in the wilderness, came to a mountain and saw two men accosted by a third, who asked for bread and water. They saw one of the two men surrendering to him all the provision he had taken along. Said R. Hiyya: "God did not desire that this good deed should be done by us." Thus R. Hiyya apparently thought like Ben Patura and not like R. Akiba.

22. The love of man for God we find in Deut. 5:10; 6:5; 7:9; 10:12; 11:1, 13, 22; 13:4; 16:20; 19:9; 30:6. The love of God for man occurs in Deut. 7:8, 13; 10:15; 23:6. According to this list of references, we may say that the Old Testament emphasizes more the love of man for God, while the New Testament emphasizes the love of God for man (I John 4:10). Judaism is thus more concentrated in the ethical element, in human conduct, and Christianity—in the theological element.

23. See, e.g., Jer. 31:13; 33:18, 22, 24-26; Ezek. 44:15 (though both of these prophets were also priests), and the next note.

24. See also Lev. 10:11; Deut. 33:10; Ezek. 7:26; 22:26; 44:23; Hos. 4:6; Mic. 3:11; Zeph. 3:4; Hag. 2:11.

25. For various expressions of joy during the offering—the term "rejoicing" itself is characteristic of Deuteronomy—see Lev. 23:40; Num. 10:10; Deut. 12:7, 12, 18; 14:26; 16:11, 15; 26:11; Isa. 9:2; 30:29; Ps. 4:8; 42:5; 43:4; 58:15; 68:25-26; 100:2; 134; 137:3; 149:3; 150:3-6; II Chron. 5:12. See furthermore Exod. 32:6; II Sam. 6:13-15. As to talmudic sources, see *Sukkah* 51a; *Sheqalim* V, 1; *Shevuot* 15b.

26. Exod. 15:6. See also Lev. 21:8, and particularly Num. 16:3, 5, 7.

27. *Emunot we-De'ot*, IX, end chap. 1.

CHAPTER 9

1. See above chap. 1.

2. Therefore, one should not dismiss too lightly the version in Maimonides' *Moreh Nebukim* I, 58: "He has no essence beyond existence," in spite of the Manuscripts and the Arabic original, because this reading seems more acceptable according to the context. We have already seen that Yehudah ha-Levi also took this view. This is indeed how Maimonides is understood by Joseph ibn Kaspi in his *Ammudei Kesef, ad loc.*, and by Crescas, *ad loc.* Among Arabian thinkers, this view is held by Algazali, according to Crescas, *loc. cit.*, (and see Algazali, *Maqasid al-Falasifah* (Cairo, n.d.), pt. 2, chap. 3, p. 139; but Averroes, as quoted by Shem Tob ibn Palqera in his *Moreh ha-Moreh* (Pressburg, 1837), pt. 1, chap. 57, p. 28, is reluctant to part with the idea of divine essence and makes it identical with divine existence. See also Harry A. Wolfson, "Crescas on the Problem of Divine Attributes," *JQR*, VII, 190, n. 85.

3. It is interesting that already Lactantius in his *Divinarum Institutionum*, observed: *Deus ipse se fecit.* See *Lucii Caecilii Firmiani Lactantii Opera Omnia* (Paris, 1844), Book 1, chap. 7, p. 153.

4. See above chap. 1.

5. Aristotle, *Politics* I, 1, 1253a, 25.

6. See above chap. 1.

7. Aristotle, *Politics* I, 1, 1253a, 3.

8. Plato, *Republic* 519 ff.

9. Aristotle, *Politics* I, 1252b, 27 ff.; 1253a, 20.

10. Gen. 6:5-6. See also Gen. 8:21: "For the imagination of man's heart is evil from his youth." Comp. also Deut. 31:21; Eccles. 9:3. The idea of universal sinfulness begins to develop particularly at the end of the First Commonwealth. "For there is no man that sinneth not" (1 Kings 8:46). "For there is not a just man upon earth that doeth good, and sinneth not" (Eccles. 7:20). See also Jer. 17:9; Ps. 130:3; 143:2; Prov. 20:9; Job 4:18-19; 15:14; 25:4; Eccles. 9:3.

11. *Phaedo* 66. But comp. A. E. Taylor, *Plato* (New York: Meridian Books, 1960), 492.

12. See above chap. 4.

13. See Simone Weil, *La Pesanteur et la Grâce* (Paris, 1948), 48.

14. See *Midrash Tanhuma* (Vilna, 1833; not found in Buber's edition) on Exod. 7:9, and Rashi on Exod. 7:13. Comp. *Shemot Rabba* 11:7; 13:5. Nahmanides too commented in this spirit on Exod. 7:4.

15. See Josephus, *Jewish Antiquities*, Book XIII, 5, 9.

16. This is the opinion of R. Hanina in *Berakot* 33b; *Megillah* 25a; *Niddah* 16b. He himself stated in *Hullin* 7b: "No man bruises his finger here on earth unless it was so decreed against him in heaven, for it is written, 'It is of the Lord that a man's goings are established' (Ps. 37:23), 'How then can man look to his way'" (Prov. 20:24). We may, therefore, say that the deterministic verses were not meant to invade the territory of "fear of heaven" or ethics. If so, there is no decisive proof that Ecclesiastes too is deterministic in spite of verses like 3:14; 6:10; 9:1. Comp. also the following deterministic verses: Isa. 63:17; Jer. 10:23; 17:9; Prov. 16:4, 9, 33.

17. See Hermann Diels, *Die Fragmente der Vorsokratiker* (Berlin: Weidemann, 1903), Fr. 119.

18. Compare the dictum of Hillel: "If I am here, everyone is here" (*Sukkah* 53a)—I referring to God, according to Rashi. See also *Tosafot* (*ibid.*). On the festival of Sukkot, while going around the altar, they prayed, according to R. Judah, "I Waho, save now" (*Sukkah* 45a). The *Jer. Sukkah* 54c reads *ani we-hu* —"I and He." As to the meaning of *Waho*, see Rashi, *ad loc.*

19. See above, chap. 1.

20. See Maimonides, *Moreh Nebukim* I, 60.

21. *Kiddushin* 32b.

22. Simone Weil, *op. cit.*, p. 46.

23. The Talmud too pondered over the enigma of regret in its retroactive power. "They asked wisdom: A sinner—how shall he be penalized? Said she to them: 'Evil pursueth sinners' (Prov. 13:21). They asked prophecy: A sinner—how shall he be penalized? Said she to them: 'The soul that sinneth it shall die' (Ezek. 18:4). They asked the Law: A sinner—how shall he be penalized? Said she to them: 'He shall bring a guilt-offering and it shall be atoned for him.' They asked the Holy One, blessed be He: A sinner—how shall he be penalized? Said He to them: 'Let him repent and it shall be atoned for him'" (*Yalqut Shimeoni*, Ps. 702; comp. *Jer. Makkot* 31a). In other words, the power of repentance is charismatic.

24. Thus Abraham ibn Ezra on Exod. 34:6: "For He alone is the knower, the knowledge, and the known." Similarly, Maimonides in *Mishne Torah*, "Yesodei ha-Torah" 2:6: "The Creator, blessed be He, is the knower, the known, and the knowledge itself," or, as in his *Moreh Nebukim* I, 68: "God is *the intellectus, the ens intelligeus,* and the *ens intelligibile."*

25. "If they are meritorious, he will come 'with the clouds of heaven' (meaning 'swiftly,' according to Rashi), if not—lowly and riding upon an ass"—R. Joshua ben Levi in *Sanhedrin* 98a. This may be an attempt to remove the supernatural suggestiveness from these Messianic verses.

26. See above chap. 1.

27. Thus Rashbam and ibn Ezra explained the verse "Hear, O Israel, the Lord our God, the Lord is one"—alone. See above chap. 1.

28. See the discussion on the nature of the infinite in Efros, *The Problem of Space in Medieval Jewish Philosophy* (N. Y.: Columbia University Press, 1917), 88-109.

29. The term "the world to come" (*'olam ha-ba*) occurs for the first time in Jewish literature in *En.* 71:15, i.e., in the first century B.C. See Charles, *op. cit.,* II, 237.

30. See *Kol Kitebei Ahad ha-Am* (Tel-Aviv, 1956), pp. 12, 350.

31. Thus Messiah answered R. Joshua ben Levi, to his question as to the time of his coming: Today. When R. Joshua complained to Elijah: "He spoke falsely to me, stating that he would come today, but he has not," Elijah replied: "Today, if ye will hear his voice" (Ps. 95:7). See *Sanhedrin* 98a.

32. See above chap. 2.

33. Plato, *Laws* I, 644d; VII, 803c.

CHAPTER 10

1. *Ta'anit* 89b; *Yoma* 69a. Comp. Josephus, *Jewish Antiquities,* Book II, 8, 4-6.

2. See Plato, *Crito* 49.

3. See, e.g., Lev. 19:18; Ps. 7:5-6; Prov. 20:22.

4. See Aristotle, *Nicomachean Ethics,* VII, 3.

5. Aristotle, *op. cit.,* II, 6, 1106a, 30.

6. See Xenophon, *Memorobilia* III, 8, 6.

7. An intellectualistic approach like this is, however, at the basis of the opinion of Resh Lakish: "A person does not commit a transgression unless a spirit of folly enters into him" (*Sotah* 3a). Compare the more extended form of this opinion in *Debarim Rabba* 9:3.

8. See Isa. 53:11: "By *his knowledge* shall my righteous servant justify many." By "knowledge" (*da'at*) is meant ethical living, as in Mal. 2:7, *et al.*

9. Comp. also *Abot* 3:9: R. Hanina ben Dosa said: "Anyone whose fear of sin precedes his wisdom, his wisdom is enduring; but anyone whose wisdom precedes his fear of sin, his wisdom is not enduring." See the comment of Charles Taylor in his *Sayings of the Jewish Fathers* (Cambridge, 1897), *ad loc.*

10. See Maimonides, *Moreh Nebukim* III, 54.

11. Heraclitus attributed an order of righteousness also to the processes of nature: "The sun never trespasses its measure, else the Erinyes, the maids of justice, will find her out." See Hermann Diels, *Die Fragmente der Vorsokratiker* I, 96, Fr. 94.

12. Plato. *Symposium* 211. See also Plato, *Republic* VI, 19, 508b, 9, where the highest Form is called the good, but the good and the beautiful in Plato are one.

13. See A. E. Taylor, *Plato* (Meridian Books Inc., New York), p. 37.

14. Plato, *Symposium*, 204e.

15. Aristotle, *Politics* VII, 1, 1323b, 25. It should be noted, however, that in the Greek tragedy and in some Orphic-Pythagorean passages in Plato we have a different strain of the Hellenic spirit. We deal here with the self-conscious philosophical articulation of Greece.

16. *Baba Mezi'a* 62a, and with variations in *Sifra* on Lev. 25:36.

17. Thomas Carlyle, *Heroes and Hero Worship*, Lect. III.

18. Hermann Cohen, *Jüdische Schriften* I, pp. 314, 321.

19. See Plato, *Phaedo* 62; Aristotle, *Nicomachean Ethics* VII, 1138a, 11.

20. *Mekilta* on Exod. 17:16; and see above, chap. 3.

21. In *Abot de-Rabbi Natan* 31, 2, the text is: "one soul" without the addition of the words "of Israel."

22. See above chap. 2, at the end of the discussion of justice, and chap. 3, in the discussion of the "Social I."

CHAPTER 11

1. In talmudic-midrashic literature there are various references to the relation and interdependence of ethics and religion. In the introduction to *Eikah Rabbati* 2 we read: "Would that they had forsaken Me and kept My law . . . the light that is in it would have led them back to the right way" (comp. the text in *Jer. Hagigah* 76c), from which it seems that faith is, nevertheless, primary, and deeds are a bridge and a means. Also in the *Mishnah Berakot* 13a: "R. Joshua ben Korhah said, Why was the section of 'Hear' ['Hear O Israel'] placed before that of 'And it shall come to pass'? So that one should first accept upon himself the yoke of the kingdom of heaven and then take upon himself the yoke of the commandments" (See variants in *Sifrei* on Num. 15:39); faith is conceived as the foundation for deeds. It should be noted that the verse, "But the just shall live by his faith" (Hab. 2:4), has no connection with this question, for the meaning here of "faith" is trust or confidence, perhaps an allusion to a passive policy in international politics, as in Isa. 7:9: "If ye will not believe, surely ye shall not be established." Yet the Talmud (*Makkot* 24a) infers from this verse of Habakkuk that this prophet reduced all commandments to one faith. See also above chap. 4, n. 9.

2. Sartre quotes this statement in approval and as a starting point for existentialism in his book *L'Etre et le néant* (Paris: Gallinard, 1943), p. 321.

3. Cf. the interesting passage, indicating grades in the relations to the spiritual, in *Pesahim* 88a: "Not like Abraham, in connection with whom 'mountain' is written ['the mountain of the Lord'] . . . nor like Isaac, in connection with whom 'field' is written . . . but like Jacob, who called it 'home.'" The relation points both ways. The feeling of at-homeness is woven out of metaphysical experiences, out of spiritual relations and contacts.

GLOSSARY

A. Hebrew and Syriac Terms

אור עולמים 47
אחד 8, 136
אין 165
אנשי דעות 169n9
ארץ 163
גבורה 30
גורל 39, 169n12
דעים 169n9
חיים 164n5, 172n31
טוב 163
ידעים 42, 47, 169n9
(כבד) יתכבד 168n70
כבוד 27, 35, 47, 121, 170n25, 170n31
בגדי הכבוד 35
כליל הכבוד 47
מקדש הכבוד 35
עטרות הכבוד 35
שמן הכבוד 35
כבודים 11, 168n37
כבוד אל 41
הכבוד הגדול 35
כל 164
מדרש 41
מדרש תורה 42
מדת הדר 47
מופלא 27
מורה צדק 41
מים במים 171n8

מים עליונים 52, 53, 58, 60, 64, 171n8, 173
מכובדים 168n37
מלכות 10
מקווה 47, 168n33
מרכבה 31, 33
נגלה 42
נחרצה 39
נכבדים 168n37
נמצא 42
סוד 168n33, 169n14
סוד עולם, סוד עולמים 47, 168n33
סברא דלעלם 168
סברא דעלמא 168
עולם הבא 28, 47
עם 166
עתיד 168
פלא 27, 166, 169n11
פלאות 168n33
צדק 164
רז, רזים 43, 44, 169n14
רזיא 169n14
רזי פלאים 43
רידיא 64
רצון 40
(שבח) משבח 168; נשתבח 168
שכל 42
תשבוחתא 168
תשבחתא דעתיד 168

B. Greek and Latin Terms

δόξα 35
δύναμις 30
ἐλπίς 168n33
gloria 35

glorificeris 168
μεγάλη δόξα 30, 168n39
μὴ ὄν 165n3
nihil 165
πνεῦμα 53
spes mundi 168n33
spem aeternam 168n33
perennis spes 168n33

INDEX

Abba bar Kahana, 69, 70
Abbahu, 63, 66, 67, 71, 174, 175; on
concept of man-God, 76; and Greek
learning, 176 n32
Abbin, 70, 72
Abbayye, 75
'Abodah Zarah, 74, 168
Abot, 67, 115, 116, 122, 131, 144,
162, 163, 174, 175, 177, 182
Abot de Rabbi Nathan, 172, 173, 175,
182
Abrabanel, 102
Abraham ibn Ezra. See Ibn Ezra
Adam and Eve, 164
Adonizedek, 82
Aggadah. See Halakah
Dic Agada der Tannaiten, 164, 171
Aggadat Bereshit, 175, 176
Against Heresies, 163
Agathos, 67, 83; compared with ethical
infinite of Bible, 137
Air: second, 10
Aha, 68, 76, 175, 176
Ahab, 21
Ahad ha-Am, 105; interpretation of
Judaism, 110; insistence on exact-
ness of "as thyself," 110; interpreta-
tion "And thou shalt love" nega-
tively, 111-112; collectivistic view of
Judaism, 128-129; absence of con-
cept of Hereafter in Bible, 137
Aher, 37, 56, 59
Akiba, 53, 66, 67, 70, 93, 97, 104,
105, 155, 171 n5, 172, 176, 177,
179; follower of Glory, 53; justice
and mercy, 60; theory of free-will,
110; "two traveling on a journey,"
110; ethical approach, 110-111;
fatherhood of God, 175
Al-Ash'ari, 156
Alexander of Macedonia, 141
Alexander (Rabbi), 176
Algazali, 180
Allegro J. M., 169
"Al Shetei ha-Seippim," 110

'Am: mankind, 166
Amenhotep IV, 82
Ammudei Kesef, 180
Ammi, 66
Amos, 17, 99, 105, 125, 148, 167, 178
Amos and Hosea: school of Holiness
and Glory, 12; views of angels, universalism vs. "covenant," justice vs.
mercy, 12; alignments of succeeding
prophets, 17
Amos and Hosea, 165, 167
Amoraic thought: speculative philosophy and interest in law, 63; negations of attributes, intermediaries,
and man-God, 65, 76; angelology
and anti-gnosticism, 72; apocalyptic
ideas of ascension, 76; medieval Jewish philosophy returning to Holiness,
76
Angels: 11, 29, 32; Amos and Hosea
on existence of, 11, 12; Seraphim,
11; Holiness and Glory on, 11, 20;
in Zechariah, 20, 30; in Wisdom-
literature, 32; apocalyptic literature
and Holiness, 32; and Wisdom, 32;
direction of, changes, 32, 73; humanization of, 32; when created, 167
n26, 32, 33, 72; no angelology in
Dead Sea Scrolls, 41; mediating
purposes in apocrypha, 40, 41;
kebodim, Glories, 168 n37; in Amoraic period, 73; one-third of world,
and mortal, 73; attitude toward
angel-cult, 73. See also Logos
Anaxogaras, 52, 171
Anoki. See I-Anoki
Annihilation: fear of, 161
Antigone, 139
Antigonos of Soko, 177
Anaximenes, 53, 171
Apocalypse: why pseudonymous, 29,
31; different from prophecy, 30;
angels and Hereafter, 31; moral
causality and direct revelation, 34;
creates historiosophy, 34

185